TO GALLIPOLI AND THE SOMME

TO GALLIPOLI AND THE SOMME

F. S KELLY;
WAR HERO, OLYMPIC CHAMPION AND PIANIST COMPOSER

THÉRÈSE RADIC *and* MARTIN CROSS

Pen & Sword
MILITARY
AN IMPRINT OF PEN & SWORD BOOKS LTD.
YORKSHIRE – PHILADELPHIA

First published in Great Britain in 2026 by
PEN AND SWORD MILITARY
An imprint of
Pen & Sword Books Limited
Yorkshire – Philadelphia

HB ISBN 978 1 03619 035 4
PB ISBN 978 1 03619 036 1
ePUB ISBN 978 1 03619 037 8
ePDF ISBN 978 1 03619 039 2

A CIP catalogue record for this book is available from the British Library.

Typeset in 10/13 Times New Roman by
SJmagic DESIGN SERVICES, India.
Printed and bound in the UK by CPI Group (UK) Ltd.

The Publisher's authorised representative in the EU for product safety is Authorised Rep Compliance Ltd., Ground Floor, 71 Lower Baggot Street, Dublin D02 P593, Ireland.
www.arccompliance.com

For a complete list of Pen & Sword titles please contact
PEN & SWORD BOOKS LIMITED
George House, Units 12 & 13, Beevor Street, Off Pontefract Road,
Barnsley, South Yorkshire, S71 1HN, England
E-mail: enquiries@pen-and-sword.co.uk
Website: www.pen-and-sword.co.uk

or

PEN AND SWORD BOOKS
1950 Lawrence Rd, Havertown, PA 19083, USA
E-mail: uspen-and-sword@casematepublishers.com
Website: www.penandswordbooks.com

FSC
www.fsc.org
MIX
Paper | Supporting responsible forestry
FSC® C013604

CONTENTS

PREFACE

The Somme, France, September 1916: In a clearing in Noulette Wood, the men of a regimental brass band walk into position, raise their instruments, adjust their music, draw breath and, at their conductor's sharp down beat, plunge into the chutzpah of the 1812 Overture – a fitting if startling choice for the occasion if ever there was one – the score's canon supplied by the nearby guns of their own battery, 'firing like hell' at the enemy[1]. The conductor was F.S. Kelly. Four weeks later a single shot to the head took him out.

Frederick Septimus Kelly (1881–1916) was thirty-five when he was killed in action at Beaucourt-sur-l'Ancre, France on 13 November 1916. By then he had won gold for Britain as a rower, for all that he was an Australian of Irish extraction, sacrificing his international reputation as a sculler to take a failing eight to Olympic victory. His background was Australian money, Eton, Balliol, London high society and the intense world of the concert pianist. Against opposition from the critics, who thought athleticism and real musicianship could never be successfully combined, he made his mark in London as a pianist-composer at a challenging time. As president of London's prestigious Classic Concert Society he acted as Maurice Ravel's patron. As an officer in the Royal Navy Volunteer Reserves bound for the Dardenelles, he formed a friendship with the poet Rupert Brooke whose shipboard death he memorialised in his best known composition. His 'conspicuous gallantry' during the evacuation of the Gallipoli Peninsula saw him awarded the Distinguished Service Cross but his extraordinary life was to end abruptly in a violent death for King and country – a country not even his own.

INTRODUCTION

This biography is based on the diaries of Australian composer-pianist, soldier, Olympian and London based Edwardian man-about-town, Frederick Septimus Kelly. Acquired in 1979 from the antiquarian book-dealing firm of Henry Bristow Ltd of Dorset, England, these are held by the National Library of Australia, Canberra, as MS 6050, and consist of eight elegant quarto size volumes bound in half red morocco with gilt lettering housing 2600 hand written pages. They open at 1 October 1907, when Kelly was a music student in Frankfurt and end with him aboard H.M.T. *Grantully Castle* off Cape Helles on 29 April 1915 as the Gallipoli campaign begins. It seems likely that there was at least one earlier diary detailing a round-the-world tour. The final wartime diaries exist as a typescript edited and annotated by Arthur Melland Asquith, Kelly's friend and fellow officer and the son of the British Prime Minister, Herbert Henry Asquith and is now held by his great-grandson, John Rous. The NLA copy was provided by Christopher Page, author of *Command in the Royal Naval Division : A Military Biography of Brigadier General A. M. Asquith D.S.O.* (Staplehurst: Spellmount 1999). This runs from 16 September 1914 to 11 November 1916. Kelly was killed on the Somme two days after that final date. His effects were sent to his sister in England. According to Asquith, Maisie Kelly placed one thick leather bound volume, (probably volume eight of the NLA collection), and seven half-quarto pocket sketch books containing further diary entries at his disposal with a view to publication. This did not eventuate and the sketch books disappeared. In 2014, ninety eight years after they were written, one of the sketch books miraculously resurfaced and was bought by the NLA from the broker Larry Hutchinson of Dunfermline, UK. Today this is kept by the library as MS Acc 13.201. It tallies with the typescript, authenticating it.

Thérèse Radic was commissioned by the National Library of Australia to edit and introduce a selection from these diaries which it published in 2004 as *Race Against Time.* The later wartime diaries appeared in 2015 edited by Jon Cooksy and Graham McKechnie as *Kelly's War: the Great War Diary of Frederick Septimus*

Kelly 1914–1916 (UK: Blink Publishing), later reissued as *The Lost Olympian of the Somme.*

The National Library of Australia also holds published and unpublished original Kelly scores and sketches as MS 3095, donated in 1974 by Beatrice Jane McPhillamy, Kelly's niece.

The biography has two authors: Thérèse Radic (music and society, Chapters 1–4,6–11, 14)) and Martin Cross (rowing and war, Chapters 5, 12 and 13, with additions to Thérèse Radic's chapters 2–4).

Appendices, including Kelly's concert programmes at Eton, Oxford, Frankfurt and for the Classical Concert Society, can be found at https://www.pen-and-sword.co.uk/To-Gallipoli-and-the-Somme-Hardback/p/62270

CHAPTER ONE

SYDNEY 1881–1893

In Sydney in the mid-1880s a half-decker, the *Thisbe*, 'about the most active in the Harbour', could be seen any weekend, year round, sailing between Double Bay and Manly, captained by mining magnate Tom Kelly. He was a quiet man, popular and sociable. He was also politically conservative, competitive, lavish with his money and passionate about yachts. William Stannard, his yarn-spinning friend, would be lending a hand.[1] Stannard was an ex-Royal Naval seaman who said he had fought hand-to-hand in the China war, sailed the world's roughest seas in cargo clippers and braved the Australian gold fields at their rambunctious height. Listening avidly was Kelly's youngest son. Their mooring was off Double Bay, looking up the slope to the family mansion, 'Glenyarrah'.

Frederick Septimus Kelly, 'Sep', was the seventh and last of Tom Kelly's children. He began life on 29 May 1881 at 47 Phillip Street Sydney, part of a terrace built on the grounds of the first Government House. His mother was Australian-born Mary Anne Dick, who married his Irish father in Sydney on 5 September 1864 'by Presbyterian rites'.[2] Some eighteen months before her birth, her father, Zachariah Dick, then a convict, was granted a ticket of leave. His offence was 'Grievous Assault' for which he was sentenced to seven years transportation. He served five.[3] Today Australians take great pride in their convict heritage. In Sep's day it was kept sotto voce.

Of his six siblings, two, Violet and Florence, died in infancy. Carleton, the eldest boy, succumbed to tuberculosis when he was 27. The two remaining brothers, Thomas Herbert (Bertie) and William Henry (Willie) were respectively six and four years older than Sep. He remained on good terms with Bertie but not with Willie. Bertie would take over the family business. Willie became a state politician. Sep's surviving sister, Mary Australie (Maisie), two years his senior, was to have him join her household in England. During the First World War she married John Kelly, an unrelated family friend and later an Admiral of the Fleet. She became Lady Kelly when her husband was knighted shortly before the Second World War.

The patriarch of this Austral-Irish family, Thomas Hussey Kelly, was born in Athlone, County Westmeath, Ireland, and was baptised at the Catholic parish church of Saint Peter on 4 May 1830. At 33 he took ship out of Liverpool in the *Arabia*, arriving at Melbourne on 24 October 1860. The manifest lists him as a labourer. He found work with the Sydney-based firm of Gilchrist, Watt and Co., first as a clerk, then as a wool-buyer. In his forties, he turned wool-and-produce broker with considerable success. In time he became a director of the Union Bank of Australia, South British Insurance, the Perpetual Trustees, and Australian Kerosene Oil and Minerals, and was a large shareholder in the companies of Burns-Philp, Tooth, Colonial Sugar Refining and Aarons' Exchange Hotel. His real interest, however, lay in the development of Australian mining, which earned him the nickname 'Copper' Kelly.[4] By the turn of the century he was a large shareholder in no fewer than twenty gold and copper mining companies though he was best known as the managing director of the Sydney Smelting Co. The list is impressive; so was the fortune it produced.

In 1885 the Kelly family shifted from the central city to Glenyarrah, a large Victorian Gothic seafront mansion at Double Bay that began life in the sixties as Seaford House, built on three acres of the highly desirable Point Piper estate. It boasted stone walls and stained glass, imposing staircases, high ceilings, multiple bedrooms, a large dining room, a ballroom and servant's quarters. For eight years this was Sep's home, house and harbour, only discarded for holidays in the Blue Mountains at Katoomba, where tramping about bush tracks in the cool clear air was seen as an antidote to the mugginess of the semi-tropical city in summer.

It was said that as a child the youngest Kelly showed precocious musical talent, playing Mozart and early Beethoven piano sonatas before he could stretch the octave. Bertie wrote of his little brother that he did not remember him playing scales or finger exercises or, indeed, being taught at all and that he played by instinct, taking nothing seriously, not even music. He did recall Sep's facility bringing him to much attention among the city's musicians and that at 8 his rapidly memorised repertoire included not only those Mozart and Beethoven sonatas, but Schubert Impromptus, Chopin Nocturnes, Polonaises and Ballads. Bertie believed Sep instantly grasped the spirit of these works in spite of his finding reading music irksome.[5] They would have been well beyond his emotional grasp.

Bertie and Maisie were also musical. Bertie studied with the legendary Joseph Joachim in England and would later play with several Sydney chamber groups. He was also among the first violins in Roberto Hazon's Sydney Amateur Orchestral Society. Maisie was a singer. Sep wrote many of his songs for her but failed to persuade her to turn professional. Their father became Grand Minstrel Primo at Balmain's Royal Albert Lodge.

The Sydney of Kelly's schooldays had a population of just over 221,000. It had long since shed its convict origins, but could not yet rival Melbourne, its southern gold rush city sister. What Sydney had was a solid, if somewhat stolid, provincial society and a spectacular harbour. A lively concert, opera, theatre and art scene had developed, with elaborate trade exhibitions, a state art gallery, museums and libraries housed after the British model. Kelly spent a privileged childhood watching a city literally rising from the ground. In 1893, when Sep left for Britain, an economic depression was devastating the country. Kelly senior's interests miraculously weathered this storm and prospered.

After a long and heated struggle, Federation was accomplished in 1901. The colonies ceased to be. States emerged. The ties to Britain began to unravel. Given the conservative political stance of his father on the issue, there is reason to suspect his youngest son's boyhood was shaped by pro-Empire attitudes that emphasised Australia's origins as the new Britannia rather than as a new nation with a separate destiny. Certainly when it came to education, the Kellys followed the tradition of their class and took their brood 'home'.

In October 1891 in preparation for this, 10-year-old Sep was enrolled at Sydney Grammar School in Darlinghurst, 8 kilometres from home. He was not the first Kelly there. Carleton, Bertie and Willie all preceded him. Willie, who had developed asthma, was sent to take in the clearer air of All Saints Anglican boarding school, a Spartan institution some 125 miles away at Bathurst, before his enrolment at Grammar. Sep, though also asthmatic, was less affected than his brother and was spared the Bathurst solution.

'Grammar' is one of the oldest schools in Australia still in use. A non-denominational independent private school, it was founded by Act of Parliament in 1854 as a feeder for the University of Sydney and was obliged by the Act to offer 'all classes and denominations of Her Majesty's subjects resident in the Colony of New South Wales without any distinction whatsoever, the advantages of a regular and liberal course of education'.[6] It was an obvious choice for the younger boy, a preparatory exercise in how to survive English public-school life for all that he was at Grammar for barely fourteen months. Nonetheless, the Kelly family's ambitions seem to have been advanced through the school's reputation and connections.

At Grammar his two strengths, music and rowing, were at the fledgling stage. A Musical Society was established in 1883 with the enthusiastic support of Albert Bythesea Weigall, the tone-deaf headmaster during Kelly's time. He saw 'the value of music as an instrument of intellectual culture', and that 'its affects in refining the taste and in extending the range of human sympathies' gave it a place in the education of boys seen as destined for leadership. Weigall saw the Society as conducive of esprit de corps, and the means of providing an annual concert that would act as a school reunion. He regretted that at first the Society would be unable to supply the individual teaching needed 'to train scientific musicians'. but hoped it might 'impart a general facility in reading music and in picking up tunes'.[7] It was only in April 1892 that 'scientific' music teaching was introduced – and then as an extra, taught out of school hours by Frederick Morley, the organist of St John's Church Darlinghurst. Given Sep's musical precociousness, Weigall's elementary musical appreciation and Morley's late appearance in Sep's period at Grammar, it seems unlikely that the school had much to do with his development as a musician. His music teacher and main influence at this early stage remains hidden from view. We know the name of the head gardener at Glenyarrah: a Mr Stevens in 1881, and a Mr Howlison in 1888, and that a Miss Kate Mannering acted as a governess, but not the name of the teacher who sat with the youngest son at the piano and taught him his Mozart. It has to be said that violinist Bertie was gilding Sep's pianistic lily; the boy was taught, and taught well. The then resident Polish-French composer Henri Kowalski is the most likely candidate. He was the best on offer and Tom Kelly bought only the best.

Attempts to maintain a rowing club before Sep's day failed, though a few boys managed to represent the school through membership of the Sydney Rowing Club. In 1892 the Grammar Rowing Club was revived and may have caught Sep's attention but as a junior he was unlikely to have been permitted to join.

His academic career also got off to a slow start. The list of Junior school subjects examined in 1892 included English, English History, Geography, French, Latin, German, Arithmetic, Algebra, Geology, Geometry, Inorganic Chemistry and Physics. Sep's results were anything but outstanding: a modest string of Bs in English, French, Latin, Arithmetic and Geometry.

Perhaps of more importance was Weigall's insistence that he be allowed to recruit English-educated teachers as staff. This included Morley and a number of other imports from the elite English educational institutions. Grammar and its inter-colonial peers were at the core of this import-export trade, teaching along English lines, certainly preparing boys for the University of Sydney but also for English schools and universities, with the expectation that they would return to Australia as future leaders. Faith in the system was indelible. It was made public and underscored through the medium of the school magazine, *The Sydneian*.

The year before Sep was enrolled, it ran an article lauding an address, 'Eton and the Empire' delivered to his old school's Literary Society by Geoffrey Drage, an influential English political writer, sometime novelist and, later, a Conservative Party politician. He visited Australia in 1890 ostensibly to observe educational systems in the colonies. His 1889 novel *Cyril* was still being favourably reviewed locally. Weigell almost certainly had a hand in shaping the *Sydneian*'s anonymous opinion of Drage's piece, an opinion that conveniently underscored his own:

> We read it with so much pleasure … its general tone is very refreshing, its morality high and yet practical. […] With him the ideas of loyalty and affection for one's school, of schoolboy responsibility towards the young, of esprit de corps and the like are no half-accepted

> articles of an old-world creed, but living principles of vital action – the foundation indeed of all true school life. Throughout his travels Mr Drage has maintained very fully his faith in the English public school system as the best discipline for an earnest and fruitful life. […] Here there is true liberty to those who can use it, true equality to those who deserve it, and true fraternity to those who are congenial. Neither birth, nor wealth, nor favour, can raise one boy above another in the eyes of the school, but merit and merit alone, at play or work.[8]

It was Weigall's proxy manifesto. Drage's propaganda piece went on to claim that there was 'no part of the vast empire on which some Eton boy has not left his mark for good, no part where some Eton boy has not cheerfully laid down his life for his country and his Queen'.[9]

Sep Kelly absorbed this call to arms, with its uncomplicated boyish ethics, secular orientation and simple decency, at a highly impressionable age. He was at home in this artificial but consoling world. In some sense he never left it. The darker aspects of school life were, in his case, to remain hidden, if they were there for him at all. Eton and the call to do or die had found its mark.

His mother, Mary Anne Kelly, remains an enigmatic figure though she was equally central to his education. Her name surfaces only on rare occasions – in the social columns of the local newspapers. She appears, for example, at Lady Jersey's farewell reception for ladies at Government House in February 1893, and again with her husband at the Countess' garden party in March at a time when T.H. Kelly was being pushed to enter politics because of his opposition to the introduction of personal income tax.

On 4 March 1893, five of the Kellys – Bertie, Willie, Sep, Maisie and their mother – embarked in the very new and very fashionable P&O liner, *Himalaya*, bound for London. Kelly senior stayed behind, immersed in business and still courting public attention with a political future in mind. Something of this can be gauged from the reports of his social life he made sure found their way into the Sydney press. Early in June he gave a queen's birthday dinner at Glenyarrah for 'a number of Austrian officers'. His wife's role as hostess was taken by her sister, Dr Frances Dick, the first woman to practise medicine in New South Wales.[10] In true loyalist style T.H. 'would not permit the day to pass without a special toast to the "Queen of England and Empress of India, the best woman and best sovereign who had filled the throne" and the guests joined right heartily in his sentiments.'[11] No doubt Kelly senior meant it, but this over-emphasis may in part have been due to the fact that the Irish in Australia, as in England, were viewed with suspicion, particularly since Henry O'Farrell's attempted assassination of Prince Alfred in Sydney in 1868. Kelly needed to be seen as loyal in order to do business in a British colony. He became a Mason. Catholic born, he was buried as an Anglican.

Among the officers who entertained after dinner was a Lieutenant Remenyi, pianist nephew of the celebrated violinist Eduard Remenyi who toured Australia in 1884. It was a typical Kelly event, lavish, cultured, flaunting its connections and, above all, in support of traditional British values.

Sep Kelly saw none of his father's exercises in self promotion. He was 12 when he left Sydney. He was to return briefly at 18 in 1899 at the end of his Eton years and again in 1901 when his father died. In 1911, when he was 30, he came home to make his professional debut as a pianist, only to leave for England yet again, this time for good. Fading memories of homeland and family travelled with him. More importantly, so did the ethics instilled by a quasi-English education and the bequest of a mysterious music teacher.

CHAPTER TWO

ETON 1893–1899

It may not have been an easy decision for the Kellys to send Sep and his brothers some 12,000 miles from home to be schooled at Eton, but Australia had nothing comparable to offer. Kelly senior dealt with this problem by resolutely staying at home while generously financing his wife's unremitting international travel, ostensibly undertaken to complete the education of their children.

Bertie had been at Eton since 1890 and was already well into the five years he was to spend there when Sep and Willie joined him in April 1893. He was to lead the school's orchestra, row in the same house as Sep and rise to a coveted membership of 'Pop', the Prefect's club, and of the Literary and Scientific Society. Willie left in 1896, Sep in 1899. For three years the boys were together in the one place but their age differences placed them at separate points in the student hierarchy. Sep was to remain at the school for the next six years, from April 1893 to July 1899. His housemaster was the Rev. Henry Daman, an old Etonian described as an 'amusing pedant'.[1] His tutor was Richard Stephen Kindersley. Both men were Oxford graduates, as was the headmaster.

The physicist Henry Moseley, an OE of Kelly's vintage, recalled that juniors began with Greek, Latin, mathematics, natural history, and French, 'taught by classical masters who pronounced it like English'. They went on to a choice between Greek and modern history, German and science. At about 16 they would specialise in either modern languages, classics, history, mathematics or science.[2]

Kelly minor rapidly found his feet in his new environment, mainly because of his brilliant if wayward pianism, even being allowed a piano in his room. The practising was relentless. On holiday he and Bertie would escape their mother's sightseeing by hiring a practice cell or commandeering their hotel's piano, in spite of this attracting a sometimes too enthusiastic audience. His older brother remembered him as 'an unaffected child bubbling over with genial good humour', who 'loved to carry on animated friendly discussion on any sort of topic … so animated and so well in accord that he was apt to quite forget his surroundings.

He would recall some humorous incident and burst into a boisterous fit of laughter to the astonishment of any passerby.'[3] The laugh was later interpreted as uncouth, an embarrassing residue from his Australian days. He was to test everyone he met with his argumentativeness, another supposedly Australian characteristic. This liking for a verbal stoush found its outlet in his election, first to the house and school debating societies and eventually to the exclusive social and sporting Eton Society known as 'Pop'.

Both Bertie and Sep achieved membership without apparent effort. For sons of the colonial nouveau riche this was social climbing at its best. Meanwhile, Sep's mother and sister had been presented at court, the mother by the Marchioness of Ripon, then Maisie by her mother, as was the custom. Lady de Grey was a patron of the arts, involved in the restoration of Covent Garden. She numbered the Australian diva Nellie Melba among her friends. So did Bertie at a later date. One suspects that Kelly senior, by promoting his family in this way, was positioning himself for a knighthood.

At 15, Sep Kelly morphed into 'Cleg', a nickname derived from Samuel Rutherford Crockett's 1896 novel *Cleg Kelly: Arab of the City.* Its protagonist is a feisty Edinburgh waif, fundamentally rebellious, a defiant underdog boy-hero caught up in a series of improbable adventures. 'Arab' at the time implied a street urchin or larrikin. A 'Cleg' was a gadfly, someone who annoyed or criticised others in order to sting them into action. His peers had caught his character dead to rights.

When the Kellys arrived Eton had long been an elite institution to which the aspiring colonial nouveau riche looked for validation. Its traditions were ancient, its acreage and buildings impressive, its reputation harsh, its premier position as England's top school seemingly unassailable.

Edmund Warre, in Cleg's day its headmaster, had a reputation as a first-class rower, an expert in ancient Greek naval history and as a much-opposed but relentless improver. His boys emerged with a firm belief in their own primacy, trained to leadership through decisive action and responsibility to their communities. They were also seen as sports mad, narrow-minded traditionalists, and ready-made props of Empire.[4]

Warre formalised Eton's highly competitive but brutally chaotic athletic life, and by creating a popular hierarchy where the best sportsmen were raised to leadership positions and college celebrity he created aspiration and order. Six hours of prayers of a Sunday and half an hour in chapel on weekdays with housemasters conducting evening prayers, served to promote Warre's ambition to create bonds within a community through shared beliefs.

Cleg, who was to remain close to the Warre family for the rest of his life, took on his headmaster's views, though with less fervour. It was Willie who embraced military training at college, not Cleg, for all Warre's growing eagerness to expand its influence at Eton. In 1900, when the Boer War was at its height and the Kelly boys had moved on, this culminated in his call for an Act of Parliament to make military training compulsory in schools for boys over 14.

During Warre's reign 1,424 Old Etonians volunteered for the South African War, a curtain raiser in which 129 OEs died. The main event, the Great War, saw 5,650 ex-Etonians enlist, of whom 1,157 were killed in action, roughly double the ratio of that in the British armed forces as a whole. Thirteen won the Victoria Cross. Warre and the Etonian ethos were to cast the long shadow that darkened Cleg's life and shaped his death.

The study of ancient languages, intended as a strict mental exercise, completed Warre's design for a better Eton where bullying, beatings and buggery were to be repudiated. Manliness epitomised by sporting discipline and patriotic duty would redeem it. In Cleg Kelly's case, it would kill him.

At Eton music was recognised as a further discipline to be encouraged. Kelly, already musically formed, rose rapidly to the forefront of the college's well developed concert life and immediately came under the notice of the precentor, Dr Charles Harford Lloyd, a pupil of Sir John Stainer. Lloyd was the epitome of the Victorian English organist-composer, churchy, worthy and well-connected, though considered more performer than composer. He had been organist at Oxford and Gloucester cathedrals, conductor of the Three Choirs Festival, for which he composed his major works, a teacher at the RCM, president of the RCO and, in his student days, president of the Oxford University Musical Club which he founded with Hubert Parry. Kelly was to have a long connection with this group. As a mentor, Lloyd was effective if conservative. What his students might expect was thorough training, a remarkable musical peer group and useful connections.

Two of Lloyd's pupils formed lasting associations with Kelly – Edward J. Dent, later to make his mark as a musicologist and critic, and composer George Butterworth. There was contact with Walter Parratt and Arthur Goodhart, as well as Charles Villiers Stanford and his composition student, Thomas Dunhill, then an assistant master at Eton. Dunhill was another of Butterworth's teachers, and may also have briefly taught Kelly; he remained in contact and mentions Cleg in his diaries. Roger Quilter, four years older, appeared in concerts with Bertie, with Cleg in attendance. Quilter found it impossible to fit in at Eton. He was physically frail in an environment where athleticism was paramount and where his sexual orientation was ridiculed.[5] Cleg, on the other hand, conformed to expectations and was not only accepted but lauded for his achievements, both as an athlete in his latter school years and as a musician throughout his time at the college. Both Quilter and Kelly went on to study at Frankfurt at the Hochschule, and with the same teachers, but once again the age difference was a handicap. No close contact is recorded, though Kelly was to form friendships with other members of the Frankfurt group to which Quilter belonged, Henry Balfour Gardiner and fellow Australian Percy Grainger.

What these connections indicate is that Kelly was moving at the edge of a circle of the most influential of English music's theorists, educators and composers, and this at a time when Englishness was becoming a sensitive issue for musicians long overshadowed by first Italian, then German, music – not only in England, but also in the dominions.

Connections aside, Kelly saw Lloyd primarily as his composition teacher. He was later to dismiss the works he composed at Eton, including *In May* (a piano piece from 1893 – when he was 12), an Etude in A flat major for piano, and a setting of Shelley's 'Dirge' (from 1897), a brief choral treatment of the 31st Psalm 'O Lord have mercy', and the piano works *Irish air with variations* in E flat major and 'Allegretto in F major' (from 1898).

In May was published by Palings, Sydney, in 1895 and is dedicated 'To My Mother'. Cleg wrote to Maisie: 'Ask the motherly to send me a copy of "In May" that I may see how many mistakes they have made in printing it.'[6] 'Irish air' and the 'Allegretto in F major' were not published until 2020.

Eton and Winchester: A song of the Eton & Winchester match was published in 1899 by R. Ingleton Drake at Eton town. Cleg wrote to his father:

> I am greatly excited at present about a song of the Eton and Winchester match (I sent you the words about six weeks ago from Paris) which I have written and is now in the process of publishing. [...] You'll be pleased to hear that I made £1 out of it, the first I have ever made in my life! When the song is ready it will be done in the school concert this half, and also at Winchester.[7]

News of other early works flit across the pages of these schoolboy letters. Early in 1896 Cleg informed his father that he had written 'three more pieces for piano' and was working on a sonata for violin and piano.[8] Later, he wrote from Paris that he was sending Bertie a violin and piano sonata composed for the brothers to play for Kelly senior when Cleg returned to Sydney 'in the spring', possibly the culmination of the same work. 'It's chief merit,' he wrote, 'seems to be in having a movement in 5/4 time, in which hardly a dozen pieces have yet been written. The rest, however, is written in a simple way, and is not very hard to understand.'[9]

Similarly, he wrote to their mother:

> I have written four fresh songs for Maisy [*sic*] who I hope is now all right two of them are to be sung at a concert that a master is giving next week by a small boy named Hely-Hutchinson, son of the Governor of Natal or some such place in that part of the world.[10]

At least one vocal work of his own and in which he himself sang was performed at Eton in 1898. Kelly had entered his house quartette in 1897, drawn in to compete when Lloyd put up an annual prize. He wrote to his father: 'I have written an anthem which is going to be done by the choir in the chapel in a few weeks time, so when I get up to sing my own music in chapel I shall quite realise the Proverb that says that every dog has his day!'[11] He also told his father that he was reading the first of Ebenezer Prout's books on orchestration, 'so as to be able to score my symphony'.[12] Unlike his pianistic development, Kelly's compositional life seems to have been slow and sedate, something difficult and dutifully carried out.

Hidden behind Lloyd's large presence in Kelly's musical life was his reserved German-Jewish piano teacher, the unbending Gustav Morsch whose main claim to fame seems to be that he had played viola in Bayreuth under Wagner during the premiers of several of that composer's operas. Previously at Cologne's Conservatorium, Morsch was an assistant instructor at the College from 1893 to 1909, covering Kelly's entire six years there. He retained a friendship with both Lloyd and Morsch for the rest of his life.

It was taken for granted by his teachers that Kelly would be involved in Eton's Musical Society, in his day it had a thousand members and only a hundred of the most musically talented were selected to become Performing Members. Both Cleg and Bertie were among them, occasionally appearing together in the same programme. Sir Charles Villiers Stanford conducted the Society's orchestra and chorus and mentored a select few. Bertie went on to lead the Society's orchestra and to perform not only in the College chapel but in St George's Chapel Windsor with Lloyd and Sir Walter Parrat, then Master of the Queen's Music and the Chapel's organist. For two years the older boy was secretary of the Society, a post Kelly took on temporarily in 1899, replacing Walter Edward Guiness – the young man who was about to become his nemesis. Remarkably, every concert involving Kelly – twenty-eight in all – was reported in the *Eton College Chronicle* and in the Society's minute books. These show rapid personal growth and the College's recognition of Kelly as a talent far above its norm. Every item he played was significantly more technically advanced than the last, sometimes requiring an emotional maturity that was beyond the boy's years and, one suspects, his ability. They ranged from a sprinkling of Bach preludes to Rachmaninoff's prelude in C sharp minor, from Beethoven's Rondo a Capriccio op. 129 to an unnamed extract from one of his piano concertos and from Schumann's Aufschwung from Fantasiesrucke op. 12, to Chopin's Polonaise in A flat op. 53, the Mendelssohn Capriccio Brilliant op. 22, and Liszt's Rhapsody in F sharp minor no. 8, Weber's March and Finale from *Konzertstuck* in F minor for Piano and Orchestra, op. 79, and the first movement of the Schumann Piano Concerto in A minor. His own piano work, *In May*, was performed on 1 June 1895 in the music room on Keates Lane, his *Anthem* on 3 July 1898 in Eton's chapel, and his *Eton and Winchester:*

A song of the Eton & Winchester match on 17 and 18 March 1899 in the concert series. frogpupp

Every concert programme was given twice. Morsch was working his student hard. There was also the compositional challenge set by two works extensively rehearsed and premiered by the Society during Kelly's stay: Arthur M. Goodhart's *Sir Andrew Barton, a ballad for chorus and orchestra* and Edward Dent's Overture in C minor. Kelly min. was receiving privileged and practical exposure to the craft of composition from role models drawn from Eton's own resources. At the same time he was surprising even himself with his ability to memorise, writing on holiday in Paris to his father:

> this morning I tried an experiment with a piece of Schubert 10 pages long. In my room I looked at it for about quarter of an hour, and when I came down I played if off by heart. I didn't know it before, except one or two airs from it.[13]

Shortly before his fifteenth birthday, Kelly was taken to Paris to play for Antoine-Francois Marmontel at his son's apartment. At nearly 80, Marmontel was no longer teaching at the Paris Conservatoire where he had been on staff for some fifty years. Bertie wrote to his father:

> Monsieur Kowalski gave mother a letter of introduction to Marmontel who is the best music master in France. During the last week he has heard Cleg play and is most enthusiastic about him. He at once volunteered to undertake Cleg's musical education, saying he could become a great pianist; he also says he will after grounding introduce him to Massenet and Saint Saens who are two of the best living composers, from whom he is to learn harmony and composition. I really think that this is not an offer to be thrown away … studying Music is as good an education for the brain as Latin or Greek.[14] […] The old man received us most cordially and listened with evident interest and pleasure to Cleg's playing. He sat close to the piano murmuring 'bien, bien', under his breath as his interpretation of the music proceeded to his satisfaction. Marmontel declared that Cleg had exactly the right spirit in all Chopin's works which he played to him.[15]

Cleg wrote to his eldest brother Carleton: 'Yesterday we went to the old Marmontel to hear his opinion about my being a musician and his answer was in the affirmative; the young one was delighted and kissed me twice on the forehead.'[16] Marmontel offered to teach the boy for nothing if he would devote himself to music, but his parents eventually rejected the offer because they felt it narrowed the boy's choices too early.

Nine months later an undeterred Kelly wrote to his sister: 'This half I have got to play Chopin's grand Polonaise with the octaves which just now I have been practising. It is a terrible piece to play at the concert and I am awfully afraid that I shan't be able to get through the octaves.'[17] He played this work, the Polonaise in A major Opus 53, (the *Heroic*) on 24 March the following year and for the first time met with criticism. The *Chronicle*, although tactful, thought he had bitten off more than he could chew. On 6 June 1896 though 'he brought down the house' with the Liszt Rhapsody in F sharp minor, no. 8, played with 'irreproachable technique and 'great power', his touch was deemed 'hard'.[18] It was an unsettling observation to be repeated many times during his 1912 London debut season, a judgement that came close to unseating him. For the three remaining Eton years Kelly's progress and the admiration he received as a musician spiralled upwards. From modest beginnings he moved to repertoire staples, putting in place works designed to sustain his concertising for life. It culminated in his being awarded the Nettleship Scholarship for music at Balliol in his penultimate year and it was this that finally scotched any idea of his becoming a diplomat, a suggestion he had made to his father early on. It may have been Kelly's status as the current holder of this award that led to his performing before HRH Princess Henry of Battenberg at Windsor Castle in his first year at Oxford.[19]

Glimpses of another life beyond Eton's gates occasionally surface in Kelly's schoolboy letters: Cleg and Willie riding hired bicycles, no hands, through the Bois de Boulogne, going to an early French film and enthusing to his father: 'You can actually see the smoke issuing from a pipe or cigarette';[20] meeting celebrated French-Canadian soprano Emma Albani, seeing a play in London with Mrs Gregory; canoeing with Willie and Bertie at Oxford where he stayed at the Mitre Hotel, 'which was very old fashioned'; finding the ban on smoking and matches in the Radcliffe library 'very strict';[21] and going with Bertie to hear 'the Brahms sextet which is a ripping thing'.[22] Holidays were occasionally spent at Sir Edgar Sebright's home. One of the results was that in his final year Kelly played for 'some of the ladies in waiting at the Castle with Sir Edgar, who came over from Beechwood to introduce me to them, one, a Miss Cochrane is a great friend of Lady Esher, whom I frequently see down here in a launch'.[23] This was Minna Cochrane, lady-in-waiting to Princess Henry.

The encounter with Marmontel was barely over when Bertie wrote:

> It was after I returned to Australia that his rowing career really began. His celebrity as an oarsman put many obstacles in the way of his public success as a musician. The Public would have it that he was an athlete dabbling in music. Any acquainted with him in early

> life would have realised how integral a part of his nature his music had always been.[24]

At the end of the nineteenth century, there was probably no better place to learn to row than at Eton College. Apart from being ideally placed next to the river Thames – opposite Windsor Castle, the school was fortunate in having the services of an experienced first eight coach: Reginald Samurez de Havilland. He was backed by the enthusiastic headmaster, Dr Edward Warre, who had previously done the same job. Over an extended period Warre had brought to Eton a willingness to coach senior boys to improve their rowing, together with a determination to extend the opportunities for competition outside the College's traditional race against Westminster School. It was at Warre's urging that Eton's first eight was allowed to enter the prestigious Ladies Challenge Plate at Henley, winning for the first time in 1864.

Since its inception in 1839, the regatta at Henley had grown rapidly to become the focal point of the British Rowing season. Normally held at the end of June or beginning of July, the regatta's most prestigious event was the Grand Challenge Cup, for the country's fastest eights. The Ladies' Plate had been added in 1845 to provide a competition specifically for eights from academic institutions. With the opening of the town's Station in 1857, the trains of the Great Western Railway had begun to carry tens of thousands of Londoners to the regatta. This crowd, when mixed with the locals and the thousands that travelled down from Oxford and beyond, created an atmosphere that was unique. By 1886, Henley Regatta had grown to three days of racing, gained royal patronage and become part of the London season. It was also an ideal shop window to showcase the talents of Eton's young oarsmen. And it was de Havilland's coaching expertise that would give his charges the chance to shine. Between 1893 and 1899 he coached the school's first eight to an unprecedented and unbroken series of Henley victories.

Early on, there was little indication that Kelly would shine at the sport. It was not until his final year at school that he had a chance of making the school's first eight. Even then, the initial omens for the 1899 season, were not good. In March, though Kelly was at least chosen to sit in the key stroke seat for trials, his crew lost to their opponents. Perhaps Kelly was just not up to setting a strong enough rhythm?

Walter Guinness was one of Kelly's contemporaries who would have taken note of Kelly's performance. Not only had Guinness already won the Ladies' Plate twice, in 1898 he was part of an Eton eight generally reckoned to be one of the fastest the school had ever produced.[25] Guinness' rowing career had been stellar enough to see him appointed as the School's Captain of Boats for the 1899 season. It was his responsibility to select the best eight men to represent the School at Henley – in effect to decide if Kelly made the boat or not.

By 1899 Walter Guinness was already acknowledged to be one of the School's leading lights. A man who set himself the highest standards in anything he turned his hand to. His contemporaries had recognised this, electing him to be the president of the School Prefects Pop club. For the year of 1898–99, Guinness was also chosen to be the Honourable Secretary of Eton's Music Society. Kelly, who was one of the brightest stars in Eton's musical firmament, was the Society's Assistant Secretary.

So, even outside of their association through rowing, the two men would have known each other well. And it's important to understand the lens through which Guinness viewed Kelly. Not least, because in Guinness' record of the 1899 season, written in his own hand – usually after each outing – we have the first real evaluation of Kelly as an oarsman. And according to Guinness, Kelly's rowing ability was lacking.

No doubt as Captain of Boats, Guinness, felt the burden of responsibility not only for selecting the eight, but also of ensuring that it was successful at Henley. He wanted his captaincy to be remembered as one which would see Eton's seventh successive victory in the Ladies' Plate. Despite that defeat in the March trials, Kelly was at least given more chances to try out in the stroke seat. But as far as Guinness was concerned the Eton eight with Kelly at stroke was just not good enough. When they went out in the eight, Guinness tended to row a seat or two behind Kelly. That meant the captain could spot any of the Australian's awkward movements. As far as Guinness was concerned, when Kelly didn't perform, his crew went slowly.

As other captains had done before him, Guinness recorded all his thoughts on his apparently malfunctioning crew in the Captain of Boat's diary. It is undoubtedly one of the most colourful, revealing and entertaining documents that a reader might come across in any sport – let alone rowing. The level of criticism about the attitude, technique and rhythm of individual rowers is often unforgiving. Its purpose was apparently to 'help' future captains put together a better first eight. But one can't help thinking it also served as a means of the captain expressing their own frustrations. Guinness had plenty of them during that 1899 season it seems; the criticism of both individuals and his crew in the records for that year are particularly severe.

The diary records the painful process of selecting the first eight. Kelly was given another crucial trial race in the stroke seat on 1 June. It was slightly disrupted by the Boat Club's practice for the 4 June Procession of boats and seems to have been largely inconclusive. Guinness recorded: 'We had 2 journeys in the afternoon. 1st with … FS Kelly (str). Secondly with Nelson stroke. We rowed each time for a minute and a half. Very bad.'[26]

But Guinness seemed to favour Nelson and was determined to give him every chance to shine. On 6 June Nelson got another trial at stroke in the first eight, while Kelly was relegated to the second crew. After that session, Guinness complemented Nelson. The captain wrote: 'Far more rhythm. It was possible to get a beginning without breaking one's back.'[27] Nelson of course came in for some technical criticism, but Guinness' evaluation at the end of his entry is telling: 'All the same I prefer him [Nelson] to Kelly.'[28]

Left to Guinness, it was clear that Kelly would be consigned to the second eight. But for some reason, Kelly had a champion in de Havilland. The experienced coach had clearly seen some quality in Kelly that Guinness was apparently blind to. And de Havilland must have persuaded his Captain of Boats to give Kelly another chance. On 7 June Guinness confided to his diary: 'Tried F.S. Kelly at stroke. R.S. dH likes him but I think he buckets.[29] Certainly far more comfortable behind Nelson.'[30] So that day, Guinness – maybe against his better judgement – followed de Havilland's advice and Kelly was back in the stroke seat of the first eight, with his captain now resigned to accepting the advice of Eton's experienced coach. For now, at least Kelly's place in the first eight seemed secure. But for Guinness, the problem of the crew's unreliable rhythm remained.

At least Kelly's crew had a bit of good news at the end of June. On the 23rd – the crew rowed a 'half-course' in 3.20 – a second faster than any of the five 'half-course' times that the 1898 boat had set.[31] That time must have lifted the spirits of the whole crew and made sense of the brave – or perhaps foolhardy – resolution to enter the crew in Henley's top event – The Grand Challenge Cup. Guinness' crew would have to race in two events! To be fair, the decision to enter the event for top university and elite club rowers, was not unprecedented. Eton's top crew had decided to enter in 1895 – the day after setting a new 'full-course' record of 6.58.[32] Ostensibly, the reason that Guinness gave for his decision in 1899 was that there were only expected to be three crews competing for the Ladies'. Entering the Grand would give Eton's eight a chance to have at least two races at the regatta. But it would mean Kelly and his crew would be up against both the very best Oxbridge Colleges, as well as the cream of the oarsmen from the elite Leander club. And that could also add to the pressure that the crew would feel.

Unsurprisingly, as the regatta grew closer, that pressure became more intense and with that the eight's level of performance seemed to drop. And from Guinness' perspective, Kelly was to bear the brunt of the criticism. In the afternoon of 29 June, the first eight jousted with their second crew over two 'one-minute' sprints. The outcome was less than satisfactory. And Guinness had no doubt that Kelly was to blame. Especially for what Guinness saw as Kelly's tendency to fit too many strokes into each minute, leading the crew to feel rushed. The captain's diary records: 'In the 1st minute str: was told to row 39. He apparently lost his head and rowed at 41½ Short. Bucket no time to finish.'[33] The conversation between Guinness and Kelly is not recorded – if indeed there was any. But it was on that evening that Kelly received his 'flannels': a sign that he was now, officially, a member of the Eton first eight.

Then, just two days before the regatta, after the eight's last training piece on the Eton reach, Guinness launched an astonishing attack on Kelly's stroking. On

3 July, he wrote: 'We have been trying to persuade stroke to row it out at the finish. He did it in paddling, but pulled himself up to his oar worse than ever when rowing. He frequently nearly catches a crab by feathering under water.'[34] As if that wasn't bad enough, Guinness then launched into a barely disguised personal attack on Kelly. 'Altogether sickening and apparently very pleased with himself.' Guinness then left no doubt that Kelly should not have been in the crew and added. 'Wish to the devil we'd got Benson at stroke could anyhow trust him.'[35]

The occasion of this outburst was a crab caught by Kelly during a close contest with a strong scratch crew – ironically stroked by Guinness' new favourite: Benson. Kelly's mistake caused the Eton first eight to 'fall to pieces' and to lose the contest by quarter of a length. Guinness knew that the Eton eight would face much stronger opposition at Henley and despaired. He wrote: 'Wish we'd got another fortnight, and then we might hope not to make an exhibition of ourselves as we undoubtedly shall do the day after tomorrow.'[36]

On Tuesday 4 July, Kelly's crew left Eton by the 3.31pm train from Slough. That evening, they paddled on the course and did a two-minute row with Leander Club's eight, keeping the deficit between the two crews down to just under a length.[37] Bearing in mind that the best part of the Eton crew's row was their start, that margin was probably a little too much. And according to Guinness, the evening's work was: 'Not satisfactory.' Furthermore, Kelly's rowing was: 'Short and careless.' It was not the best preparation for the following day's heat of the Grand Challenge Cup, again st Trinity College Cambridge.

However, if Guinness thought that his crew was not in the best of shape for the regatta, it was not public knowledge. On 3 July, *The Times*, noting that Eton had entered for the Grand as well as the Ladies', recorded: 'The Eton College crew is so good that it has entered for this event as well as the Ladies.'[38] Clearly, the paper's rowing correspondent had not been talking to Eton's Captain of Boats. But the subsequent burden of expectation probably – in part created by *The Time*s – led to some of the stiff criticism that Eton's 1899 crew were to face.

It was no surprise that Kelly and the '99 Eton eight lost their first race at Henley. Conditions were flat and the crew rowed significantly better in the race than they had in training. But the Cambridge crew – with six of the men who had won the Boat Race that year – were just too strong. Eton got dropped off the start. And though they stuck to Trinity until halfway, they were not able to get back on terms. Kelly was later to write to his mother: 'We were beaten in the Grand Challenge Cup by an eight which contained 6 of the Cambridge eight that beat Oxford this year, so that we could hardly hope to have beaten them.'[39] The result was no disgrace. But it seemed that some of those watching expected better things of an Eton eight and began to express their disappointment.

Those whispers would become more apparent as the Regatta unfolded. But it was hardly a helpful backdrop for the crew's 'rest' day on Thursday. Eton had been fortunate in drawing a bye to the final and could therefore watch Pembroke College Cambridge beat Radley College easily. Eton's training that day consisted of a two-minute piece off the start. Guinness recorded that even that was a little rushed and short. Moreover, the boat still must have felt heavy, with the crew's rating 'only at 38' strokes per minute.

The final of the Ladies' Plate took place on Friday afternoon and Eton took no chances. Their pace in the first minute took the wind out of Pembroke's fast start. Thereafter, the school crew drew away to win comfortably in a time of 7.20 seconds. The photo taken near the finish, which later appeared in the *Illustrated London News*,[40] shows Eton rowing long and clearly – from the looks on their faces – giving it 'their all'. The massive back of Lord Grimston at '5' seems a little hunched and there seems to be a discrepancy between the heights of the handles on stroke and bow side. This could have signalled a balance problem. But otherwise, Kelly's rowing at stroke does not stand out as either better, or worse than any of his crewmates.

Nevertheless, for Guinness, victory in his final year was not sweet. It seems that his crew's inability to beat Cambridge in the Grand had been a signal for the detractors among the 'British rowing public' to 'abuse' the 1899 crew. The sense of being unfairly wronged rings out in Guinness' words. 'Because we were beaten in the Grand we were considered far below the average of Eton crews,' wrote Guinness on 27 July 1899. And he went on to add: 'This is certainly not the case. We were undoubtedly a ponderous crew but this was not due to the material.' The captain went on to blame an: 'error of judgment' in choosing to row with a tougher gearing, which led to the crew rowing without the 'dash and lightness' that generally characterised Eton crews.[41]

Guinness concludes his analysis with an evaluation of each of his crew – as was customary for the Captain of Boats. His entry on Kelly is by far the shortest – in fact, just three words: 'Improved at Henley.'[42] The 18-year-old Kelly is damned by faint praise. Having just won his first Henley medal and received the kudos that went with it – including a raucous welcome by the whole school back at Eton – there was nothing to suggest that the Australian was anything other than a young oarsman who'd done well to get into the first eight and would probably – if his captain's opinion had anything to do with it – struggle to get into crews of higher standing later on.

As he took a year out from rowing for family business in Australia ahead of his Oxford scholarship, it seems that Kelly was certainly not the naturally talented oarsman that his later record would seem to suggest. In fact, it would take much hard work and determination for Kelly to prove to others that his was an indispensable presence in any top boat. Kelly would also have to face repeated disappointment as he failed to make the Oxford Boat Race crew both in 1901 and 1902. But his response to these apparent failures was to draw the best out of him. Music however was a different matter.

At 18 Cleg Kelly was a competent, reserved and musically sensitive composer. Though a conventional craftsman, he was worth listening to. Three songs, 'The widow bird', 'Dirge', and 'The Isle', all settings of Percy Bysshe Shelley poems, were written in the summer of 1899 and complete the Etonian opuses. It was a modest beginning.

On 20 August 1899 Cleg's eldest brother, Carleton Kelly, died at Glenyarrah after a long battle with tuberculosis. He was 27. By 22 September Cleg was in Sydney. It was the end of his schooldays and his first close encounter with death, even though it had been expected for some time. On the voyage he completed two vocal works: a setting for medium voice and piano of Tennyson's poem 'Break, Break, Break' and a Latin setting of Horace's 'Ode to Venus. The first is understandably a tribute to his brother but the second invites Venus to a celebration of youth and the Graces.

What he did in Sydney is not known in any detail. There is a reference in his diaries to first trying over Grieg's *Old Norwegian Melody with Variations* with Jessie Fraser (formerly the Leipzig-trained pianist Jessie Middleton) in Sydney in 1899, but nothing about Carleton has surfaced. Yet during his Australian visit in 1911 Kelly recorded that he had found a waltz in C minor written for banjo in one of Carleton's manuscript books and played it at Glenyarrah on 15 March when pugilist John Dalley came to dinner. He wrote wistfully at the time: 'It is rather musical and I should like to be able to make use of it in some way as a memento to him. I remember his playing the beginning of it about 1892.'[43] Nothing came of it.

Two songs completed at Glenyarrah survive: a setting of Tennyson's 'Crossing the Bar' dated 14 November 1899, and a another of Shelley's 'One Word is Too Often Profaned', dated 25 November that year. Both could be read as meditations on his relationship with his eldest brother, a conventional response to a death in the former, his remoteness from him in the latter's questioning of love. He made no comment himself. The *Sydney Morning Herald* of 1 December 1899 reported Kelly as playing at a fundraiser at his old school, Sydney Grammar. Then, on 4 December, he left for Marseille on the *India.* The Oxford years were about to begin.

CHAPTER THREE

OXFORD 1900–1903

His brother's death and a bout of chickenpox delayed Kelly's attendance at Balliol until early in 1900. He was to take out his BA (with a lowly 4th in Modern History) in October 1903 and his MA in 1912. In Kelly's day, though the central governing body of the university set examinations, conferred degrees and provided lectures by staff, daily life was focused on the self-contained colleges whose tutors guided the undergraduates though their reading, leaving them more or less to study at their own pace and their own convenience – or not at all. There was an average of 150 students to each of the twenty-five colleges, which generally had their own libraries, art collections, clubs, recreation grounds, river houseboats, grand dining halls and elaborate dress codes. College chapels conducted matins and evensong daily, with some offering a high-level musical service with a professional choir. Student debt was endemic and flouting rules (the curfew and the ban on drinking in public houses for example) was a norm. Sport was of paramount importance and emptied the colleges in the afternoons. After dinner 'revelry' ruled.[1] For Kelly, however, the real draw was the university rowing scene and the performance opportunities offered through the Balliol Sunday evening concerts, and those of the Oxford University Musical Club.

In 1900 80 per cent of Balliol undergraduates were English. One in four was an Etonian. Overseas students numbered under 10 per cent. There were cliques, notably the Etonians, that featured a cohort of Balliol men who were both exceptionally clever and remarkably unruly.[2] As a colonial, Kelly was one of a small minority and though an Etonian, he was neither academically advanced nor a rule breaker. Normally, this would have been quite enough to see him marginalised. Instead, his public profile as a pianist and as an oarsman was to draw admiration and social inclusion from the start.

Over time, three tutors were appointed to direct his Modern History studies: the distinguished historians Arthur Lionel Smith and Henry William Carless Davis, and the far less distinguished Francis Fortescue Urquhart, who spent much of his time entertaining students – among them Evelyn Waugh, who used him to create the character of Mr Samgrass in *Brideshead Revisited.* None of them seem to have impressed Kelly. That was left to his mentor, Donald Francis Tovey, holder of Balliol's first Nettleship Scholarship in Music and coach to the next three holders. He was six years older than Kelly. In spite of holding a 3rd in Greats, Tovey showed little interest in broadening any of their minds – the major stipulation of the Nettleship. Instead, he immersed Kelly, Tom Spring-Rice and Ferdinand Speyer in every possible aspect of music. At Eton Spring-Rice had been Kelly's duo-pianist friend. He was later a diplomat. They were to share programmes at Oxford and friendship with Edith Sitwell.[3] Some twelve years later Ferdinand Speyer's music-patron father, Edward Speyer, would choose Kelly to succeed him as chairman of the prestigious London-based Classical Concerts series. His ghosted memoirs, in which Ferdinand had a considerable hand, record that on first meeting Kelly, Speyer considered him blunt and ill-mannered, though the older man thought this stemmed from his great dislike of pretension. As he got to know him he found that Kelly proved to be good company, warm, genial and enthusiastic, and attributed his success as both athlete and artist to what he saw as an extraordinary degree of energy and tenacity.[4] It was an opinion widely shared.

Tovey, later Reid Professor of Music at Edinburgh, was then establishing a career as a pianist, composer and conductor. He was to develop a formidable reputation as a musicologist, much of it built on lectures, extensive programme notes and essays later collected as the music student's bible *Essays in Musical Analysis.* He met Edward Speyer in 1900, and from 1902 assisted for nine years with Speyer's concert projects and his valuable music manuscript collection. For a generation this collection at the Speyer house, Ridgehurst, at Shenley, was a magnet for prominent musicians of the day. They came to study and stayed to perform, Kelly among them.

Tovey's concert career was still in the ascendant. It was to have a tortuous progression that left little time for them to be on the same ground together, time occupied either by encounters at Oxford or at Tovey's cottage, Vanstone, near Northlands at Englefield Green in Surrey. Northlands was a school for the children of Eton masters, of which Tovey was one. Its founder, Sophie Weisse, all but adopted him, became his music teacher and, during his own years as a teacher there, his domineering patron. After his studies at Balliol, she transformed Northlands into a vibrant intellectual and artistic hub and built a concert hall for performances and lectures, showcasing his talents as a pianist and composer alongside prominent artists. Joachim and his quartet were frequent guests, and London orchestras were engaged to give Tovey conducting experience. Consequently, Northlands became a significant centre of artistic activity.[5] Weisse's concerts were said to rival similar London events in scope, though they were given in semi-private circumstances. When Kelly first encountered him, Tovey was still in the shadow of this ever more dominating figure and would remain so, to Kelly's increasing dismay. What was more, Weisse was not averse to making overtures to the younger man who was by then too frequently in her protégé's letters.[6] Kelly politely ignored her.

In Tovey's Oxford days, and beyond the reach of Miss Weisse, both men were engaged with the fashionable all-male Oxford University music clubs, Tovey with the Oxford Musical Union, and both with the Balliol Musical Society and the Oxford University Musical Club.

Tovey and Ernest Walker (later the college's music director but then merely assistant organist), had long since formed an alliance intended to raise the standards of the fortnightly college concerts. Kelly joined them as the junior member of a remarkable trio of pianists. Walker's 'great liking' for Kelly had, by then, matured into 'a strong belief in his promise for the future'.[7]

The society had the money to allow Walker a good deal of entrepreneurial freedom, with 375 composers represented in his programmes between 1900 and 1915. Walker's Balliol premiers of major repertoire are still seen as important in the development of British concert life. Stealing a march on premiers at London's Monday evening concerts gave him particular satisfaction.

His soloists included some of the most popular artists of the day: baritones Harry Plunket Greene, Davis Bispham, Campbell McInnes, the tenors Steuart Wilson and Gervase Elwes, sopranos Marie Fillunger and Dorothy Silk, the pianists Fanny Davies and Leonard Borwick as well as Donald Tovey, cellist Robert Hausmann, the violist Lionel Tertis and violinists Marie Soldat, Adila Fachiri and her sister Jelly d'Arànyi, Alfred Gibson, and Adolf Busch. All of them became part of Kelly's musical circle. Jelly d'Arànyi was to fall in love with him. Walker's aim was to use these figures to attract attention to young performers and composers from the college, providing them with an audience of aficionados. They were guaranteed exposure and notice, though not in the press, which was banned from attending. The modest fees offered were accepted as being of little consequence compared with the honour conferred by an invitation to perform with the society.

In his first year Kelly's name appears in the Balliol Sunday evening concert programmes five times: for 6 May, in a programme that featured the violinist Hans Wessely, then a professor at the Royal Academy of Music, when Kelly played his own Variations in E flat major and his Allegretto in F major and was 'warmly applauded';[8] on 10 June, in an undesignated Beethoven piano and cello sonata in G minor [probably op. 5, no. 2.] with B.P. Parker a well known British cellist; on 21 October, in the Schubert Impromptu no. 2 in E flat D899 and sharing an accompanist role with Ernest Walker in a programme featuring violinist Maud MacCarthy, who had grown up in Australia (socialist Annie Besant's companion in India and later a pioneer ethnomusicologist); on 18 November, in his own Valse in E major and Etude in A flat major in a programme that included violinist Eldina Bligh, a pupil of Joachim and Kruse, with a well established concert career in England, and the singer whom Olive Harcourt later transformed into lutenist Isabelle Eden, a lecturer on Theosophy and Spiritualism; and on 25 November, as the second accompanist in the Brahms vocal quartet and piano duet Liebeslieder Walzer (second set) [presumably op. 65] with Marie Fillunger, Evelyn Downes, Seth Hughes and baritone/bass Arthur Foxton Ferguson, folk-song collector and inventor of the Folk-Song Quartet. Ernest Walker was the first accompanist. Fillunger was the Viennese lover of Eugenie Schumann and a noted lieder singer who toured Australia in 1891. On 10 February 1901 Kelly gave three Scarlatti sonatas, designated only as in C major, C minor and A major respectively. This time he shared billing with violinist – composer Joseph Ludwig, another pupil of Joachim who had made a name for himself as leader of a string quartet 'of the highest artistic attainments'.[9] Although perhaps not with the elite of British music, he was nevertheless rubbing shoulders with some of its best, whose backgrounds and, indeed, their credentials, were far from ordinary. In a similar way, he was moving into the rowing milieu.

If Kelly had seemed to be out of favour with his Captain of Boats at Eton, at least the same did not appear to be the case at Oxford. Not only were two of Oxford's best oarsmen former Etonian rowers but they were also members of Balliol – Kelly's college. They were Felix Warre and Horace Hale. Warre later became one of Kelly's closest acquaintances. In Kelly's first year, Warre became the President of Oxford University Boat Club. In effect, it would be he who decided if Kelly was good enough to make the Oxford team for the 1901 Boat Race.

The contest for which Warre was preparing his Oxford crew was one of the oldest and most famous races in the world of rowing. The boat clubs of Oxford and Cambridge universities had started their private match racing back in 1829 at Henley. Since then, the race had moved downriver and was usually raced on the incoming tide from Putney to Mortlake – a distance of 4.2 miles. Its status had grown rapidly. Members of both selected crews were awarded prestigious 'Blues'. Winning the Boat Race mattered. Therefore, training would start much earlier in the season for potential Blues than for either school or club rowers. The prospective Blue would have been on the water as early as October, most probably racing for their college and hoping to make an impact ahead of early squad trials in November. There was more to follow in the New Year. The race itself was usually held around Easter time. When all was said and done, Warre did not have that much time to put his best crew on the water and though he was close to Kelly, the Australian could expect no favours over selection, particularly as the Dark Blues had lost the last two races to Cambridge.

Kelly also had the advantage of having already been through the Eton system, which had favoured the same Orthodox style that Warre wanted his Oxford crew to adopt. So, initially at least, Kelly looked to have ticked many of the boxes necessary to get into the Dark Blue crew. But he must have known that as a freshman, his lack of experience in university rowing combined with his relatively small frame would probably count against him. With Cambridge looking to turn in a hat-trick of victories, Warre had to find a combination powerful enough to overturn the Light Blue's dominance. And that crew would not include Kelly.

Warre got his selection absolutely right. In the 1901 Boat Race, his men had been led for most of the course but held their nerve to row through the Light Blues in the final part of the race. And in the wake of that famous victory, the glow of an Oxford Boat Race triumph would have radiated around the university, so at least Kelly could share in part of that success while rowing in a very strong Balliol college eight. That crew would undoubtedly be one of the favourites for the University Headship that would be raced in May of 1901. After that, a successful Henley campaign might well have followed, most likely with Kelly as part of a Balliol four, that would start as hot favourites for the Visitors Challenge Cup. However, fate was to intervene.

It was to be nine months before his name appeared in the rowing reports or the Balliol Sunday concerts lists again. He had been at Oxford for just over four terms when news came that his father was dying. He shipped out in mid-May and disembarked at Sydney on 14 June 1901 from the same ship which had brought him back to England after his brother's death, the P&O liner *India.*

Shortly before he left Kelly completed a setting of R.T. Walker's 'It is not dawn till you awake'. It is dated 6 April 1901 and inscribed 'Hunter's Inn Heddon's Mouth N. Devon.' A rare survivor, this is an ecstatic love song left to us without context but suggesting a great deal.

The Sydney Kelly returned to was not the one he remembered. This was a city in retreat. The six self-governing states had formed a Commonwealth and established a system of federalism. With it came a sense of nationhood. Kelly senior had long been opposed to such a move, but like the city, his powers were failing. Melbourne, and not Sydney, had become the seat of the newly independent Australia's government six months before.

Thomas Hussey Kelly, then 70, died at Glenyarrah on 25 July 1901 after a long illness and was buried in the Church of England section of Waverly Cemetery. His will was proved at £280,075, which today is the equivalent of £30,776,908 ($A52,444,540). Within a year, when he turned 21, Kelly was probably in receipt of an annual income in today's money of at least £109,888[10] (or $A229,217) derived from vested shares with full control only when he turned 30. This is unlikely to have been the full extent of his inheritance.

A single composition survives from this period, a violin and piano sonata in D minor intended to be played with Bertie and inscribed: 'Begun circa 20 June. Finished Aug. 2, 1901 Glenyarrah, Sydney', written while his father lay dying in the family home and completed there about a week after his death.

On 22 July 1901 Kelly wrote to Balfour Gardiner from Glenyarrah:

> I was delighted with your letter and have benefited by it considerably. I must let you know that your good advice of last April was not sown in barren soil, and although it may have been surrounded by tares to start with, it has since taken such a firm root that the tares have had to migrate elsewhere, to put it more concisely. I have been thinking, and have written one or two good tunes on the piling up system. That is to say, with no half closes or dominant cadences in them. About a month ago I started a violin and pfte [*sic*] sonata for my brother and me to play, and I am delighted to find that I am now in the middle of the last movement, but it has been a tremendous effort literally thinking out every bar of it, as I find my ideas are fearfully stunted, and I can no more get things to flow consecutively than fly, however I am very pleased with my first attempt at thinking, as it is far and away the best thing I have done yet, although there are one of two weak things in it. I have also set one of Shakespeare's sonnets 'Shall I compare thee to a Summer's day?' etc but it is fearfully influenced by your friend Grainger's 'Away in the Land of the Japanese'. In thinking that tune over I have been very much struck with the freedom of his harmony, and the easy way in which his melody flows, and am disappointed at not being able to take advantage of the introduction you gave me Sydney in your letter. [*sic*] I expect to be back for the October term and hope to have lots of things to shew you,
>
> Ever yrs
> F.S. Kelly.[11]

Leading musicologist Stephen Banfield considers that in his eight published songs Kelly,

> shows a fertile delight in technical invention. In the *Two Songs, op. 1* – 'Shall I compare thee' 1901 and *Aghadoe* 1903 – this is coupled with a well-controlled sense of craftsmanship in a manner no less accomplished than that of the early Frank Bridge. We have here an Edwardian style perfectly preserved, unravaged by any forebodings of linguistic crisis.

Aghadoe he considered a technical tour de force.[12]

Gardiner was at New College when Kelly's friendship with the composer began, moving on to music studies in Frankfurt where Kelly followed him. Gardiner was one of the 'Frankfurt Group', of which Grainger was a member. Balfour Gardiner, Roger Quilter, Percy Grainger, Cyril Scott, Norman O'Neill and Kelly were to share the same composition teacher at the Hoch Conservatory, Iwan Knorr, though several years apart. Balfour Gardiner was hardly the man for a struggling composer to consult. He, too, had inherited wealth and found it weakened the drive to compose, possibly because, like Kelly, his life did not depend on the outcome. He was also a perfectionist, destroying the works with which he was not satisfied so that little now remains.[13] He was, for his fledgling acolyte, a dangerous man.

After a four-month absence, Kelly was back in Oxford in late September. Eight months after his father's death his mother suffered a stroke. She died two days later on 18 February 1902. This time Kelly did not return home.

'Anon' of Balliol's war memorial book (probably Kelly's close friend, the pianist Leonard Borwick), later claimed that after the Sydney visit his uncertainty about his career distracted him but that in his last Oxford days he was coming to grips with his work: 'he saw clearly, judged soundly and forgot nothing, though he had not yet learned to write easily'.[14]

Though he may have been treading water as an undergraduate, Kelly's musical commitment to the Society and the OUMC continued unabated. Gardiner's biographer, Stephen Lloyd, who claims Kelly rose to be President of the OUMC, saw him as no distracted musician, but one who exerted a strong influence on musical life at Oxford.

As 'F.S. Kelly' Cleg took part in another ten concerts for the Balliol Musical Society while he was still an undergraduate, and a further four after he left Oxford. Two given in 1902 included works of his own: the Sonata for violin and piano in A flat, written at Glenyarrah, was given on 9 February, two of his own Intermezzi on 23 November. The fourth post-Oxford concert of 3 May 1908 included his Impromptus in C major and in C minor, and on 23 May 1914, on the eve of war, he gave the premiers of his four studies from op. 9 (1913): no. 1 in F major; no. 5 in B minor (trills); no. 10 in E major; and No 12 in D minor.

Between these college concerts but well beyond them lay the much more sophisticated recital milieu of the OUMC. Most importantly for Kelly, member's compositions were aired.[15] This grouping together to form and direct experience and to fuel careers was part of a much larger movement in British music that had its origins deep in the previous century. By 1900, when Kelly first appeared at Oxford, music was finally being recognised as an intellectual discipline within the universities, though even today the issue of its status there goes unresolved.

As far as musicians were concerned it was essential that music should be identified as a profession, as respectable as any other. It was a position from which to trade, for all the pious mouthing of arguments over the moral good of high art music that went the rounds of the cloisters. With universities considered national institutions and music being linked with national identity, what better way to lift the prestige of musicians than to sail their craft in the wake of flag-ship academe? Many attempts were made to do just this, including the offering of scholarships of the order of the Nettleship, intended to mould the musician into an academic by adding other disciplines within the arts to modify his artisan status. Music degrees were modernised, but their rethinking kept to the established academic models. The result was a constrained conservatism that permeated music on campus, both within the courses on offer and in the rapidly increasing practice of music by members of the universities as well as the undergraduate bodies. Though he was not enrolled as a music student, Kelly was at the centre of this movement, unexpectedly riding the crest of this very particular wave, one that would support him in his ambitions even as it sucked him into conformity.

He was to appear twelve times with the OUMC: three in 1900, five in 1901 when he was librarian of the club, two in both 1902 and 1903, and three beyond graduation in 1906.[16] As was customary, his own works were not performed. In Kelly's day Ferdinand Speyer was the secretary, the president was George Butterworth and the list of performers included Ernest Walker, Donald Francis Tovey, H.H. Joachim, B.P. Parker, Thomas F. Dunhill, Leonard Borwick, Johann Kruse and his quartet, and students from the Royal College of Music.

On the afternoon of 3 February 1910 Kelly appeared in the nineteenth season of the OUMC, not at a club meeting, but at its Public Classical Concerts series given at the Oxford Town Hall with Dr H.P. Allen's Orchestra and wind players from the London Symphony and the Queen's Hall orchestras in the Beethoven Concerto for pianoforte and orchestra no. 5 in E flat major op. 73. It was a significant step up. In his final OUMC concert given on 29 January 1913, Allen conducted Kelly's Suite in E flat major, breaking with tradition. Kelly's own notes in the programme date it as completed in autumn 1906. The concert ended with another Australian's orchestral work, Percy Grainger's 'Mock Morris'.

In all this concertising Kelly the athlete was invisible to his audiences, though his life as a rower and as a musician were making constant and parallel demands on his time and attention. No one saw anything questionable about this duality. It was only when he turned professional that reviewers began to find the mix counter-productive. In the meantime he was arriving at his peak as a rower and about to become something of a celebrity, his achievements reported extensively as far away as America, Canada, and, of course, Australia.

Despite Kelly's absence, on his return, he would have been given every chance to make the 1902 Oxford crew, especially with Hale as Oxford's new president. And as the Dark Blues began their process of selection in the autumn of 1901, Hale – like Warre before him – chose to give Kelly a run in the stroke seat for the Oxford trial eights. But once more Kelly's performance was not convincing enough. Again he was not selected. Instead, he became the 'spare man' for the Blue boat: subbing in for unwell rowers, jumping into some of the 'scratch' crews who paced both Blue boats nearer to the Boat Race itself, and of course keeping himself fit by training in a single scull.

Perhaps some oarsmen might have called it a day after the disappointment of missing selection yet again. There can't have been many of Kelly's contemporaries in either the Dark or Light Blue boat clubs, who needed to spend so many extra hours – in addition to their studies – conscientiously working on piano practice. Kelly might well have considered he had more than enough reason to spend future summers without the distraction of rowing to take him away from his music. But Kelly's self-belief, especially now, as it related to his ability to succeed in what was – for him – the relatively untested skill of elite single sculling remained strong.[17] Whatever the case, Kelly seemed to have used his failure to make the 1902 Oxford Boat Race crew as a springboard for bigger and better things. Just over three months after the Dark Blues were comprehensively defeated, the 21-year-old was to stun the rowing world with his speed in a single scull at the world's most demanding regatta. The event he was to enter was the Diamond Sculls, one of Henley's elite contests.

Since his time at Eton, Kelly had been a competitive sculler. But being '9th' man for two years running meant that to keep fit, Kelly had to train in a single scull. Those close to him would have also noticed something different about the Australian – he was coaching himself. Unlike almost all his opponents, Kelly did not engage the services of a professional sculler to help him train. Professional watermen were not allowed to race at Henley – partly because it was considered that as they rowed all year round, it would not be a 'fair' contest. Most of the amateur scullers generally started training in a boat two or three months before Henley. Some of them, like the prolific Henley champion Guy Nickalls, did keep themselves 'in shape' during the winter by 'running with the beagles', or other outdoor activities. But come the early summer, they would all engage the services of a professional to give them advice on both technique and training. Kelly's determination to coach himself thus stood out. Before the Diamond Sculls of 1902 started, some may have considered it foolhardy, even perhaps conceited.

There may have been a touch of arrogance in Kelly's decision. But his willingness to combine an arduous series of racing in the single scull at Henley, together with representing his college in the Visitors Challenge Cup race for fours, shows that Kelly had a strong sense of duty too.

By Henley, which started on 8 July, there was no doubt Kelly was in good shape, but nobody thought much of his chances before the regatta started. All the talk was that a foreign sculler would win the Diamonds: the most likely being the hot favourite from the USA, Constance Titus. And if the American did not prevail, then it was reckoned the Canadian, Lou Scholes, would triumph. In fact, the draw pitted Titus and Scholes together on the first day. Kelly received a bye and had the chance to watch the two favourites serve up a fantastic contest during that morning's racing. The American sculler had to row down his opponent to win by just over a length in the fast time of 8.33.

The American was using a much more upright style, marked by a ferocious leg-drive. It was the technique favoured by the professional scullers and contrasted completely with that used by Kelly, who used less leg-drive but more body swing. The *Guardian*'s correspondent eulogized over Titus' 'amazing neatness'. He concluded by saying that: 'The man part of a centaur can have scarcely been more essentially part of his horse than Mr Titus seems to be part of his boat'.[18]

Kelly progressed easily through his heat on Tuesday when his opponent hit a wooden pile. But a much tougher test was to come on semi-finals day, when Kelly had been drawn against the flying American, Titus. And with expectation and excitement high throughout the crowds that lined the course, Kelly was to seize his chance. His fluid body-swing and easy drive saw him off to a good start. At the end of the island – less than a minute in – both men were level.[19] They sculled this way, on: 'perfectly smooth water' for the next two minutes, when Kelly began to open out a slight lead, just by the Remenham Rectory. By the halfway mark, the Australian was edging clear. Titus, who had expected to move thorough at any moment was now anxious and, according to the *Times*' account: 'frequently looked over his shoulder'. Kelly continued to draw away though and won by seven lengths in a time of 8.39.[20]

Undoubtedly, Kelly had the more advantageous Bucks station. But this was not enough to explain the margin of victory. Even today, reading through the race accounts, it would be hard to miss the delight among the British supporters at Kelly's victory. Not only had the red-hot favourite been beaten by a sculler using the English Orthodox style. But a new talent had been uncovered. It sent the *Guardian*'s rowing correspondent into rhapsodic eulogies about Kelly's 'Swing, perfect unison and cleanliness'. He added of Kelly's victory that it: 'showed us what we did not know before that in Mr Kelly we have one of the greatest scullers seen at Henley'.

Kelly's rival in Thursday's final would be Etherington-Smith, known to his friends as 'Fluffy'. But the Cambridge man's sculling was anything but that. Coached by a professional sculler, Etherington-Smith used a far more aggressive 'catch' than Kelly, who preferred to place his blades more gently into the water, relying on his body swing to accelerate the drive. But Etherington-Smith had proved time and time again that he was a 'stayer'. What's more, he was drawn on the 'Bucks' station and though he would be disadvantaged by a slight stagger on the start to compensate for two small bends on the course, there was a 'bushes wind' expected. That gave significant shelter to the Bucks station.[21] Kelly, out on the Berkshire Station, would be up against it.

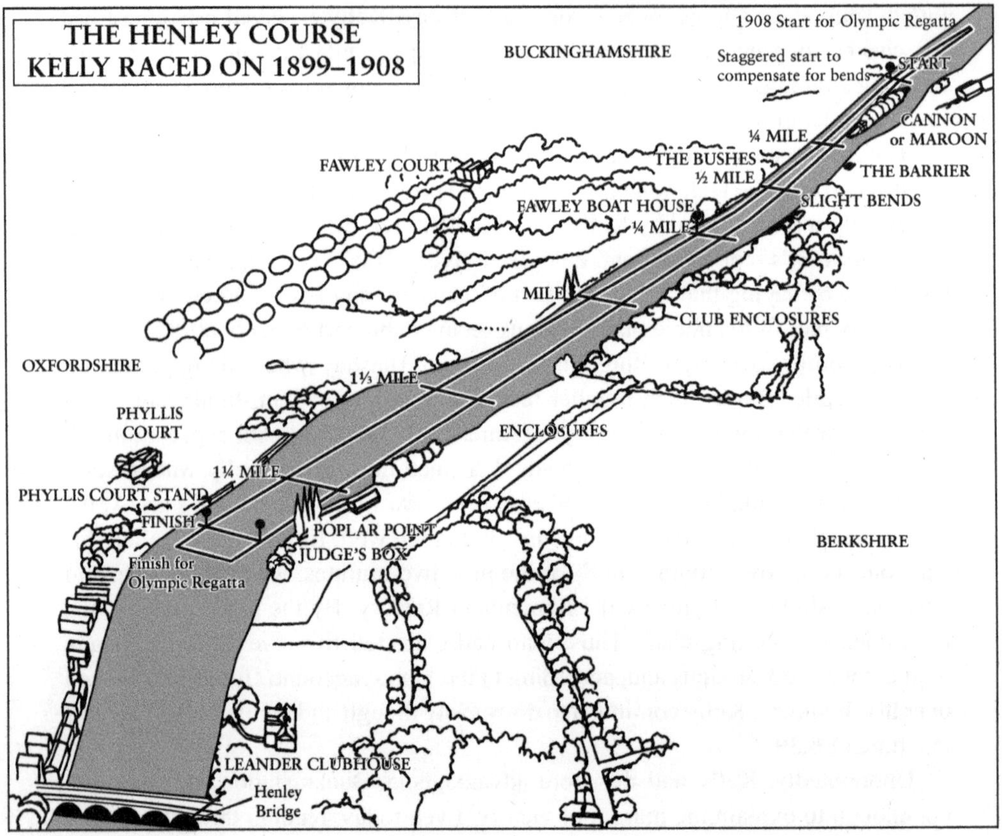

Just before one o'clock on the afternoon of Thursday, 11 July 1902, the full fury of a brief summer storm swept over the start of the Henley Regatta course. The so called 'bushes wind' was an unseasonably cool south-westerly, which swayed the treetops, ruffled the tall, distinctive bushes lining the Buckinghamshire bank and agitated the waters of the normally smooth River Thames. It was accompanied by both rain and hail, which was, to say the least, an inconvenience for the tens of thousands of spectators, many of whom were out on the river in their rented skiffs, punts, or wherries.

That afternoon as the 1pm start time approached, both Kelly and Etherington-Smith sat alert and ready. The big names from the USA and Canada had been knocked out. Now, whatever the result, a new name would be added to the winners of the Diamonds. One of these two men would be catapulted into the ranks of 'rowing greats'. Fame – of a sort – awaited the winner. But it was fame that had to be bought at a price. Both competitors believed they were the better man. They would put bodies and minds on the line to get to the finish line first. Those watching were not to be disappointed. As the correspondents were later to recognise, the final of the Diamonds was to be remembered as the: 'Grandest struggle of the Regatta'.[22]

In the moments before the signal to start was given, both men had probably blocked out any noise from the spectators – their minds set on the task ahead. They were undoubtedly experienced enough to keep their fragile wooden craft straight – even though the storm, as it passed, must have thrown itself against their blades, boats and bodies. But there was too much at stake for the uncomfortable conditions to be more than just a fleeting distraction. The intensity of the struggle ahead, let alone what was at stake, demanded the scullers' complete focus.

Despite Kelly's high initial rate of striking – 39 strokes per minute to Etherington-Smith's 35 – the Australian could not keep up with the Light Blue's early pace. At the quarter mile, Etherington-Smith had overcome the stagger on the start and his lead was half a length. By the end of the second minute, it had grown to three-quarters of a length. Slowly but surely, by the half-mile mark, Etherington-Smith had edged his boat into a clear water lead. It was a desperate situation for Kelly, who had to throw in a dramatic spurt just to stay in the contest. In the short term it was effective, bringing the Oxford sculler nearly level by the halfway mark. But Etherington-Smith, using the advantage of the slight bend on the course, showed he too could use the same tactic and drew away again. Once more, Kelly had to use another spurt. With just over a quarter of a mile left, Kelly drew nearly level again. Now the verdict of the race hung in the balance. Both scullers seemed to have little left to give and so the two men sculled stroke for stroke. It would be too risky to chance another spurt until the finish drew closer.

It was Etherington-Smith who struck first. He edged his bows into a quarter of a length lead. But by the Leander enclosure the Cambridge man was tiring. Kelly once more drew level. This was the Australian's time, his moment. Sensing it, Kelly threw in his last and most effective spurt. With just over a hundred yards or so left, Kelly edged out to a length's lead. Etherington-Smith was utterly exhausted and virtually stopped sculling. Kelly won the race by a margin of 2½ lengths. The relatively slow time of 8.59 indicates the presence of a strong crosshead breeze; something which made Kelly's victory – from the unfavoured 'Berks' station – even more noteworthy.

Even if an exhausted Kelly could not help his crew prevail in the Visitors' Cup later that day, nothing could dent the impact of his Diamonds win. In effect, his life had been changed. He was now a champion sculler. He was the first Australian to win the prestigious title. The *Guardian*, under a headline: 'THE NEW SCULLER', wound up its plaudits even more. 'He might have fallen from Olympia', it proclaimed on the Friday morning. Kelly's style was even compared with the grace of the legendary Canadian professional World Champion sculler, Ned Hanlan.[23] Since Kelly had started rowing back in 1893, he had always found himself in the shadow of better oarsmen and scullers. When that Friday morning dawned, he must have realised that he had finally burst into the light. Whatever direction his musical career might take in the future, in rowing, his name would now be one of the first on the crew-list. Kelly had arrived.

On his return to Oxford towards the end of 1902, Kelly seems to have been treated differently. His seat in the 1903 Oxford Boat Race crew now seemed assured. He would sit in the middle of the boat in the '4' seat. The expectation was that it would be a close race.

The 1903 Boat Race did achieve some notoriety – but not for the closeness of the race. Still less, for Kelly achieving his belated Blue. Instead, it's remembered for the complete 'cock-up' that the first-time Umpire Freddie Pitman – a distinguished oarsman – made of the start. The unfortunate official couldn't fire the starting pistol properly. And it was Cambridge who took advantage of this error, starting their race around 2 seconds ahead of their opponents.[24] The Light Blues were nearly clear by Craven Cottage and went on to win by 6 lengths.[25] The short-term impact on Kelly is not known. Should Walter Guinness, Kelly's old captain at Eton, have been watching, he would probably have noted that Cambridge were stroked to victory by Roland Nelson: one of the men who Guinness had wanted to stroke the Eton eight instead of Kelly back in 1899.

Nevertheless, in the long-term, the result did Kelly no harm. That summer, he would not only win a second Diamonds title at Henley – beating all of Britain's top amateur scullers – but would also win his first Grand Challenge Cup medal, rowing in the '4' seat of the elite Leander Club eight. The final at 1pm was the first race of the day. And Leander were up against a very strong First and Third Trinity crew. It was a thrilling contest – the race of the regatta some thought, one of the finest ever seen at Henley.[26] There was never more than a few feet between the crews. Though Kelly's eight had led through the middle of the course, it was the First and Third men whose bows were in front approaching the big grandstand by the finishing post. Somehow though, Leander found a last-gasp spring and took the cup by just 6 feet in the final few strokes. Kelly and his crewmates must have been absolutely spent. But the 22-year-old then underlined his outstanding fitness. With less than four hours' rest, he was back in his single, beating Julius Berresford comfortably in the final of the Diamonds. By any standards, it was a stellar summer's performance. If Kelly needed it, he could point to that win in the Grand as evidence that he was now one of the best oarsmen in Britain. But the next season would bring a different set of challenges as he tried to adapt to the life of an oarsman and sculler outside the 'protective womb' of the University Boat Club.

On 24 October 1903 Kelly graduated from Oxford. Frankfurt and four years of intermittent study as a pianist and composer at the Hoch Conservatory lay ahead. As a pianist he was nearing formation. As a composer he was far from it. Only two compositions from this period have survived: the violin sonata in D minor (1901) and *Aghadoe* for voice and piano (1903). The latter was published by Schott in 1912 after a number of performances by Maisie Kelly. It is dedicated to the contralto Muriel Foster. In 1914 Kelly made an orchestral arrangement of *Agahdoe* in anticipation of a June 1915 performance by Dame Clara Butt and the Queen's Hall orchestra. The singer had requested the transition, but war intervened and the work remained in manuscript for nearly a century. Kelly may have seen himself as a still unformed musician, but as an athlete he was mature, already a public figure and about to reach his apogee.

CHAPTER FOUR

FRANKFURT 1904–1908

Late in 1904 Kelly took rooms in Frankfurt close to Das Hoch'sche Konservatorium where he was to study for the next four years. Breaks were spent with friends in London or at Bisham Grange, the Thames-side Gothic revival house near Marlow leased by his sister. He could row from its mooring and drive the short distance to Henley and the Leander Club, of which he was a member. He came to regard this house as home. At 23 he could afford to train anywhere but he chose this German banking town's established school rather than the uncertainty of one of the newer British institutions. Tovey's Schumann-Brahms loyalties may also have played a part.

There were other attractions. The school was popular. Clara Schumann's name as a founding staff member was drawing international students and her former pupil, Ernst Engesser, was available as a piano teacher. Leonard Borwick, her favourite pupil, would become Kelly's closest friend. Bernhard Scholtz, loyal to the conservative Brahms-Schumann tradition, was its director and as a consequence the Hoch was openly hostile to the experiments in new forms advocated by the rival Liszt-Wagner factions in other institutions. For Kelly it promised technical and emotional security. Its long list of distinguished students included Cyril Scott, H. Balfour Gardiner, Percy Grainger, Roger Quilter and Norman O'Neill, together known as the Frankfurt Group. All of them were to have dealings with Kelly.

Iwan Knorr from the Kharkiv Conservatory, a Ukrainian branch of the Russian Imperial Music Society, taught him composition. Knorr liked to boast of his friendship with Tchaikovsky and that Brahms had recommended him for his post at the Hoch. Grainger, too, was a Knorr pupil, He was to become an important influence in Kelly's musical development and not only because they were fellow Australians. Grainger found Knorr witty, charming and cultured, but felt humiliated by his practical jokes and thought he went too far in trying to impose his personal tastes on his pupils. In contrast, Kelly's response was formal but affectionate.

Kelly's name appears in the school's records until 1908 as Engesser's pupil, though not as Knorr's. Quite possibly he was taking lessons with both men privately. Between 7 October 1904 and 31 May 1908 his name appears nineteen times in the list of student recitals, with one major gap. By then disillusioned with the Hoch, Kelly disengaged to travel for some months, from late 1906 to at least July 1907, sailing to Singapore, India, Burma, Malaya, China, Japan, Hawaii, the USA and Canada.[1]

What ensued was the building of a standard piano repertoire of Bach, Mozart, Beethoven, Mendelssohn, Weber, Brahms and Chopin and a creative output that included the Quartet for horn, violin, viola and pianoforte, completed on 18 November 1904 at Im Sachsenlager 5, his lodgings in Frankfurt, the Intermezzo in C minor for Orchestra completed on 3 April 1906, presumably in Frankfurt, the 1906 Orchestral Suite in E flat major (of which the Intermezzo may be part), the 1907 *Theme, Variations and Fugue* op. 5 for two pianos dedicated to Knorr and Engesser (Kelly's graduation piece, probably written to impress Knorr, the counterpoint expert), the 1908 Allegro de Concert op. 3 for piano, *A Cycle of Lyrics* op. 4: 6 pieces for piano, and 'It was a lover and his lass', a six part round for voices.[2]

Pianistically it was a step back from Kelly's Oxford concertising and even from the programmes of his Eton days. His own works seem to have been found wanting. Knorr constantly demanded corrections. The Hoch was stifling him. It took a slow awakening, a year's travel and the Olympics to pry him loose, though he was to express gratitude to his teachers years later. It left its mark. Bertie wrote in his memoir of his younger brother:

> After several years of hard work and study in Frankfort Sep's character underwent a change. He became very self-critical and imbued with a conscious desire to increase his knowledge of many things which as a boy he had laughingly disregarded because they did not interest him. He showed the restraining effects of the straight waistcoat of rigid mental training. But he did not feel at ease, for his natural honesty of character would never be content to rest in a mould of accepted opinion. He was never one to follow a hue and cry. Long before it was the correct thing to do he had been an admirer and player of the works of modern musicians such as Debussy, Ravel, and Scriabin, but he would never join the crowd who in copying their mannerisms imagined they were explorers of new musical continents. Each age has their great ones and their sycophants.[3]

In some ways it was Donald Tovey who rescued Kelly from this rigidity, though he was to present him with difficulties of a different order. Tovey, still acting as mentor, visited him in Frankfurt early in 1904 and wrote to Sophie Weisse:

> Kelly is very comic; hugely nice and horribly afraid of my disgracing myself before his spiritual pastors and masters. He looks after my diet (which he has found out) – and, as to music he is, apart from Knorr's really splendid teaching and example, inspired by a proselytising hatred of all the things I ever told him not to do – such as heavy basses, – and is shocked at my laxity about such matters in my songs. I fear he is sometimes pained at the difficulty he finds in taking the conceit out of me.
>
> But it's really most remarkable what a difference Oxford and Eton makes. After even the very nice younger generation one finds in certain places in Berlin, Kelly produces an effect not so much of a return to one's native land as a coming into a larger world. His interest in his newspaper, and in people, and in whatever musical technicality or artistic impression comes his way; – all these things have a certain unprovincial quality added to them and a kind of coordination which makes it impossible for him to say anything superficial, however much he may give himself away. Knorr says he has never seen anyone grasp the technique of contrapuntal writing so quickly; but he doesn't know for certain whether Kelly has a real talent for composition 'as we have just begun'.
>
> I believe Kelly will feel miserably void of ideas for the next two years or so, and I spend half the time here ramming into him that he must never get into the blues about that but plod along without ideas, even if Knorr himself loses interest. I'm afraid Kelly must think me awfully patronising; but he has his revenge in trying to cure me of my slowness and hesitancy of speech and my arrogant dogmatism … If only he tides over the next two years he will become a real composer, and he is pretty certain to be a great player.'[4]

To this end Tovey initiated 'a kind of musical correspondence' in which they exchanged 'canons (to be solved by the recipient), and waltzes for pianoforte duet. The plan was to compile a set of waltzes, each composer contributing one alternately.'[5] Towards the end of this exchange an excited Kelly began tracking its progress in his diaries, related musical sketches skittering across the pages. In September 1904 he wrote to Tovey:

> The first vivid effect your waltzes made on me has not abated and I don't know to which I give the palm … I have done my E minor and D minor. The latter is obstinate and keeps harping back on to one phrase. Your A major is quite a masterpiece for its range … The F minor is a splendid penultimate and I am rather up a tree to give you

> all the splendours it promises, – it was rather a mean trick of you to play […] Knorr is delighted with the lot, and says my contributions have quite set his doubts at rest as to my imagination-but I only hope it will last.[6]

Tovey again confided to Weisse: 'Our Waltzes are most successful … I shall join mine on to the old ones and send them to Schott. I feel as if it would be purely ridiculous ever to give Kelly advice again.'[7] Tovey's *Balliol Dances* op. 17 (sixteen pieces for four hands), were published by Schott in 1907 with a dedication to Ernest Walker and F.S. Kelly.[8] Six years later Schott published Kelly's *Waltz Pageant* op. 2a (18 for four hands) and 2b (nine for two hands), both dedicated to Tovey.[9]

About this time Tovey's feelings for Maisie took an amorous turn – unappreciated by her brother, who now saw him as a predator; Maisie had her own considerable fortune. A proposed Italian holiday with Tovey was cancelled. Donald wrote to Miss Weisse: 'I have only begun to realise that his wealth is a difficult thing to get over. He *is* very sensitive and will be awfully distressed if he finds any difficulty in understanding my attitude towards him on that score.'[10]

Boiling point was reached during a weekend at the Grange when there was an angry exchange over some songs by Cyril Scott. Kelly, irritated by Tovey's long-winded pontifications, told his mentor a few home truths, the gist of which was that he was wasting his time with teaching and concertising at Northlands. Tovey was shaken and appealed to Miss Weiss to intervene. 'Whatever happens,' he wrote, 'Kelly must not be allowed to lose sight of us. And that's where your diplomacy – i.e. your perfectly natural grip of the situation, comes in. I can do no more, but you can get hold of his sister.'[11] Miss Weiss was only too willing. By this time Kelly was in real fear that Tovey would come to dominate him as he himself was dominated and that the move on his sister was effectively a move on him.

On the surface at least, Kelly might have imagined that his time on the water during these years would afford him less problems. He was the defending Diamonds champion and his stock with the world's best rowers was high. But the 1904 racing season for Kelly was to deliver one of the Australian's most traumatic experiences. It would impact him in the short term physically, but in the longer term it would leave emotional scars. But as ever, in 1905 and in the following year, Kelly would recover enough to come out fighting.

Part of the reason for Kelly's traumatic year in 1904 was that he had not trained enough. If the official account of racing for the 1904 Henley Regatta is to be believed, then he did not get into his sculling boat until mid-June.[12] This meant his fitness at the regatta would not be as strong as it should be, but the entries for the Diamond Sculls probably didn't unduly alarm him. Lou Scholes from Canada looked to be the main threat. As 1903 ended, Scholes was seen as the fastest sculler in North America.[13] The 23-year-old would have arrived in Henley early enough for the cognoscenti to be reminded that his sculling style was completely different to Kelly's. In short, Scholes sculled like a professional; he compressed his legs more than Kelly and relied on a dynamic leg-drive, rather than Kelly's natural body swing, to propel him.

It was on semi-finals day that Kelly came up against Scholes. And the Australian's tactics were clear from the first stroke. The former Balliol man exploded off the start. His rating hit 40 strokes per minute, some 3 beats higher than his opponent. Kelly cleared the end of Temple Island – in just 48 seconds.[14] It was a pace that Scholes could not live with. And over the next couple of minutes, though Scholes did not allow Kelly to move away as quickly, the Australian added another length to his lead. It was enough to allow him to move his boat over towards his left so that he was now sculling directly in front of his opponent. This was a tactic that any professional would have been proud of: to use the wake of the boat and the swirls caused by the blades to unsettle the balance and flow of an opponent – which was fine if it worked. The problem came if the trailing sculler responded with a spurt to lessen the deficit and reclaim his water. That would force the leading man to adjust his course, a manoeuvre that could cost any valuable distance gained.

That was exactly what Scholes did. With half of the race still to go, Scholes did just enough to force Kelly to move back on to the Berkshire station. That manoeuvre cost him at least half a length. Kelly still had a clear water lead over the Canadian, but the Henley champion now knew he was in a race.

The crowds along the banks were massed over ten deep in their punts. Those in the craft that lined the entire course would have revelled in this contest. The noise for both scullers must have seemed deafening. Perhaps Kelly, sensing home advantage, drew some comfort from this because by the mile, although Scholes had closed to within a length, the holder still had a lead. But for the Canadian, with less than 500 yards to go, the race was just beginning. Sensing that the Australian was fading, Scholes threw in a burst and began to edge his bows back on Kelly's boat. With just 20 strokes to go, the scullers were level. Kelly was broken. So much so that Scholes moved out to a two-length lead in a matter of yards. Right in front of the finish grandstand, just yards from the finishing post, Kelly stopped. It wasn't just that he was beaten, he was in so much pain that all he could do was slump over his sculls.

The victory went to Scholes. Verdict: not rowed out. Kelly couldn't even make it to the finish line. Noticing his obvious distress, a Thames Conservancy Launch drew up next to Kelly's boat and the men who were there to guard the course from any wayward craft, lifted his inert body into their launch.

To say that this race must have had an effect on Kelly would almost certainly be an understatement. He would never make the mistake of going into Henley with so little training again. More than that, like a champion boxer who had been ahead on points before a last round knockout, he would yearn for another crack at the man who put him on the canvas. In the future, that desire, mixed no doubt with trepidation and fear, would even tempt Kelly out of retirement when he heard that the Canadian too, was going to race at the 1908 Olympic Regatta.

For the next few hours though, Kelly's priority was recovery. And it seems that in this at least, he was more successful. The next day he raced in the Leander eight, picking up his second consecutive Grand Challenge Cup medal. Just thirty minutes later – Kelly must have watched the conclusion of the race – and in record-breaking conditions, Scholes came down the course in the final of the Diamonds against Arthur Cloutte. It was yet another titanic contest, which the Canadian took by just over a length in a new record of 8.23. It was the first time a Canadian had won the Diamonds and the impact was apparent from the crowd of over 70,000 that greeted Scholes on his return to Toronto.[15]

Any unease felt among the British rowing community was almost certainly due to the fact that Kelly's beautifully orthodox 'English' style had been beaten by a technique that was becoming increasingly used by Continental Europeans and seemed to be de rigueur among North Americans. For better or worse, the Australian had now become – for some – almost a standard bearer of a way of life that the upper classes had come to view as part of their 'English' birthright. For others, there may have been some resentment that such an apparently talented sculler chose to spend most of his life away from the river training up his musical, rather than aquatic abilities. In his autobiography published in 1932, Vivian Nickalls – brother of Guy and multiple Henley winner – wrote: 'Kelly hated training and spent his whole time playing the violin.'[16] Nickalls did not know Kelly well enough to realise that though he composed for violin, he spent most of his time playing the piano. Whatever the reason, the 1905 rowing season would see no let up in Kelly's relentless drive to improve his musical skills. So, the question for the rowing community was: could the 'Colonial' still deliver on the water?

Kelly clearly thought so. He determined to enter both Diamonds and the Grand as part of the Leander eight in 1905. The best guess as to when Kelly returned to Britain to start training was in the last week of May, or even early June 1905. And the towpath cognoscenti were already formulating their own evaluation of the musician's race-fitness. Opinions varied.

A few days before the regatta opened, Kelly had done a full course trial. Conditions were 'favourable' and Kelly had recorded a faster time than the record set by Scholes the previous year. But despite this, on 3 July, *The Guardian* seemed ready to place the Australian into the ranks of the: 'has-been'. Their correspondent wrote: 'Kelly does not seem to be sculling up to his old form, and if towpath opinion goes for anything there will be no great surprise if he does not win.'[17]

But Kelly's crewmates in the Leander eight were determined to see him triumph in the Diamonds. Nowhere was this more the case than with Guy Nickalls. The veteran oarsman was both very experienced and extremely opinionated. He had seen how the Australian had lost the Diamonds in 1904 and was determined that Kelly should not make the same mistake again. In effect, Nickalls thought that Kelly could not afford to start as quickly as he had against Scholes. Instead, the Australian should pace himself, and use the efficiency of his technique to ensure that he won the race in the second half. Nickalls wrote: 'I impressed on him every day and even before the start of the final that he was only to do a strong paddle to Fawley.'[18]

In addition to Nickalls' advice, Kelly also had the support of the Leander eight. Richard Burnell, son of Charles Burnell, who raced with Kelly in 1908, recorded his father's reminisces of Kelly and not all were complementary. According to Burnell, Kelly was: 'a bad trainer and a dirty eater!'[19] And Richard Burnell, himself a 1948 Olympic rowing champion, added that the Australian was: 'also reputed to be a poor judge of pace, apt to run out of steam before the end of a race'.[20] Whatever the truth of that remark, in the 1905 regatta, Kelly's Leander crewmates were determined to do all they could to see him win back the Diamonds title. For the final, they agreed to walk down the bank towards the first half of the course where, according to Charles Burnell, they would be: 'positioned at strategic points along the bank to exhort [Kelly] to ease up'.[21]

But what is really touching about the older Burnell's comments is that Kelly's crew not only cared enough about the performance of their '2' man, but also believed in his potential to deliver a top-quality performance. Perhaps they knew how important it was for English rowing that Kelly sculled at his best.

For both Kelly and the Leander eight, the toughest races begun on Wednesday – semi-finals day. At 12.30pm, the Leander eight was drawn to face the Americans. Then at 6pm Kelly would line up against A.A. Stuart in the Diamonds.

The relatively early start time for what was billed as the race of the regatta so far, meant that despite the warmth of a beautiful and still July day and what was at stake in the world of rowing, the Thames was still not yet packed full of craft as it would be later in the afternoon. But those who were there, got to cheer on a brilliant display of orthodox rowing from the Leander men. *The Times* gratefully noted: 'Once more the long stroke and body swing of the English style proved superior.'[22] In fact, despite a close race till the halfway mark, the British were never led and won by a length. Buoyed by that victory, Kelly went out and won his Diamonds semi in confident manner.

With Kelly doubling up, the stewards would have been careful to place the finals of the Grand and Diamonds as far apart as possible, so that the Australian would have time enough to recover. So once again, the regatta's premier event – the Grand – was given the first slot of finals day. Kelly, like the rest of his crew, would have been on-edge, especially as their opponents, the Belgians, were drawn on the Bucks station which would shelter them from a 'bushes' wind.[23]

But if the Leander men suffered from nervousness, the same would also have been true for their opposition from Sport Nautique de Gand, perhaps even more so because by the start, the wind had dropped. This had the effect of nullifying the advantage to the Belgians' station. The tension before the race was high enough anyway, so it was imperative that the oarsmen remained focused as they set off at a furious pace from the start. This would mean keeping both their minds and eyes in their own boat. But unfortunately, for the Gand crew, their stroke man, Ernest Tralbaut, chose only the fifth stroke of the race to glance to his right, presumably to see how well his British opposition had started. Looking out of the boat can be risky at the best of times, but so early in the race, with his crew nearing their maximum speed and effort, it was foolhardy and Traulbaut paid the consequences. He lost control of his oar and stopped rowing for a couple of strokes.[24] Without their stroke man rowing, the Belgians lost significant momentum and Kelly's crew immediately profited and took a half-length advantage. It was all the experienced Leander men needed to be able to take full control of the race. They effectively neutralised the Belgians' repeated spurts and drew away down the course to win against a demoralised opposition by two and a quarter lengths in the fast time of 6.58.[25]

So, as he recovered in the early afternoon, Kelly must have been delighted. Not only had the 'honour' of English rowing been restored, but the relatively comfortable victory would have given the Australian plenty of opportunity to recover properly in time for the Diamonds final at 6pm. It was suggested that Kelly had felt so confident after his victory in the Grand, that he announced he would go out to break the record for the Diamonds. While impossible to verify, it's the sort of confident statement that does fit with Kelly's psyche and perhaps contains something of the self-belief – or possibly over-confidence – that had once so frustrated Guinness at Eton. But for the last race of the day, Kelly knew he would have the members of his Leander crew at strategic points along the bank. With support like that he might have wondered how he could possibly fail.

However, his opponent in the final, the 36-year-old Henry Blackstaffe, was both fast and vastly experienced. In fact, the Vesta man had already made the final of the Diamonds on three previous occasions, only losing each time to a fast American sculler. But when 6pm arrived on that Thursday evening both scullers would have felt the north-westerly breeze pick up, as it presaged potentially record-breaking conditions for the final. The Australian was drawn on the Bucks – slightly less advantageous for the wind conditions. But he would at least have a good line to steer for the first minute of the race. Kelly went off the start determined to heed Nickalls' advice. In the first minute of the race, Kelly under-rated his opponent by two strokes a minute, taking only 35 strokes to Blackstaffe's 37. And the Australian's efficiency and skill saw him move into a narrow half-length lead by the end of the island. He maintained that to the quarter-mile mark. Not long after that though, Blackstaffe sensed he had a chance to beat Kelly and threw in a spectacular burst, catching Kelly unawares.

Gradually, the Vesta man's bows edged through Kelly's boat and out into nearly a length's lead. The scullers passed the halfway mark with all to play for. Moreover, Blackstaffe had set a scorching pace. The mark of 3.55 was five seconds quicker than Scholes had gone through the same point in the previous year. Crucially, though, Blackstaffe's move had not caused Kelly to panic. And as he went away from Fawley, Kelly 'turned on the afterburners'. Its impact on the contest was sensational. In a short time, the Australian took almost four lengths out of his opponent. With the enclosures fast approaching Kelly could have afforded to switch into cruise-pace. In fact – clearly mindful of the record-breaking pace – he did the opposite. He kept his rating up at 32 strokes per minute the whole way down the course and inched away from Blackstaffe with each of those strokes. At the finish Kelly was over fifteen seconds ahead.

After some delay, Kelly's winning time was announced. It was 8.10 seconds. By any standards, it was a stunning mark. It stood for thirty-eight years. The regatta records also noted that it was 'five seconds quicker than the record for the Goblets'.[26] Normally pairs should have been some 25 seconds quicker than a single. Under any circumstances – even with the sublime efficiency of Kelly's technique – this was an outstanding performance that could only have been made by a fully fit athlete. Writing in 1989, Richard Burnell judged Kelly's time to be the 'most remarkable' of all the Henley records.[27] More than that, with Kelly's stunning victory, combined with Leander's win over Belgium in the Grand, English rowing seemed back on top of the world.

But the following year on the water would see all that change. The Henley Regattas of 1906 and 1907 would find British rowing rocked to its very foundations. Belgian eights, based partly around the men that Kelly's crew had beaten in 1905, would beat all comers – including Leander – in the world's most prestigious eight's race, the Grand. In 1905, as part of the winning Leander crew, Kelly might have helped British rowing to feel confident about its status. A year later, with Kelly and Nickalls worried about the lack of British talent to produce an eight. They made the controversial decision to enter a four instead – leaving the way clear for the Belgians. In addition, rather than race his single, the Australian decided upon a speculative entry in a pair with his fellow crewmate from the four, Archie Graham. The result was not a good omen for the Leander four. Kelly and Graham were beaten by two powerful Cambridge oarsmen from First and Third Trinity. The two victorious Light Blue oarsmen, Banner Johnstone and 'Ronnie' Powell, were also in the four that were to race Kelly's crew in the final of the Stewards Challenge Cup. To those in the know, it seemed that the First and Third four were the 'better' crew and potentially significantly 'faster'.[28] Kelly and his crew were up against it.

The fours final was held early in the final's day programme, to afford the First and Third men a chance to recover for their pairs final. So, at noon, under a cloudless sky with barely a breath of wind stirring the mirror-like waters of the Thames, the two fours: Leander and First and Third, were started. Quickly, the favourites moved out to a lead of just under a length. But along the course, instead of using their power to move away from Leander, the Light Blue oarsmen were clearly trying conserve energy for their races later that day. That allowed Leander to somehow drew level. With just twenty strokes, to go, the rating of Nickalls – who was stroking the Leander boat – went up to 40 strokes per minute. At that point, the *Guardian* correspondent had both crews: 'dead level'. Nickalls, who almost certainly would have had a better sense of who was in front, recalled that First and Third led by a: 'foot or two'. Though the Light Blue Powell, had miscalculated, his crew might still win. The boats could hardly be separated and as they raced together in front of the packed enclosures and grandstands. The noise must have been absolutely deafening. With less than five strokes left, from somewhere, the 'old man' Nickalls produced: 'three or four gigantic strokes'. They were enough to push Leander across the line first. The margin: just two feet. It was Kelly's final race at the Henley Regatta. But the day after, *The Times* seemed far more concerned with the affront to British rowing, leading with the fact that a Belgian crew had carried off the Grand Challenge Cup by comfortably beating Trinity Hall Cambridge and that Leander should never have been in a four.[29]

We don't know what Kelly thought of the *Times* piece. But two years later, the presence of a Belgian eight on the Thames at Henley, would once more play a key role in the Australian's life. For now, though, Kelly was done with competitive rowing and a world tour beckoned.

After eleven months of travel, probably recorded in the lost first Kelly diary, Frankfurt reclaimed him in September 1907. He set up at Im Trutz Frankfurt 29, installed an Ibach piano, fetched his music from his old digs at Im Sachsenlager 5 and opened the Brahms Piano Concerto in B flat, op. 83, a work that was to bedevil him.

He resumed his daily routine: three hours' practice spaced across the day, a dumbbell workout, a vigorous walk, and the timed running of very cold water over his forearms to correct a weakness that was beginning to alarm him. He was frequently to be found in local cafes taking coffee, cigarette in hand, reading the English newspapers, studying scores and mentally composing what he would later notate in his rooms. He cultivated the men who mattered, dining domestically with the Hoch staff, but more formally with the town's wealthiest – among them the von Grunelius family of bankers and the brothers Carl and Arthur von Weinberg, arts patrons and heirs to an industrialist's fortune. He took it for granted, for example, that he would be invited mid-February to join the hundred guests at *Walfried* to celebrate the Jewish Weinbergs' elevation to the Prussian nobility. Dinner and seven *tableaux vivant* accompanied by an ensemble of name players with dance transitions devised by Madame Zacchero was on offer. Kelly played

St Francis showing the stigmata in Giorgione's *Castlefranco Madonna.* The diaries laconically record that: 'The whole entertainment was done regardless of expense and went very well.'[30]

He crammed in concerts and the opera – *Norma, Carmen, Hansel and Gretel, Salome, Aida* and *Rigoletto* among others, critiquing them in his diary at the end of the day. He was 'intensely disgusted with the action' of *Salome* and found it 'ugly'.[31] He almost missed Caruso in *Aida*; 27,000 people who had applied for tickets were refused, Kelly among them. One of the von Grunelius wives came to his rescue, offering him her Loge. Delighted, but impatient, he wrote that 'Caruso only sang up in one place – in the duet with Aida and then he brought the house down.'[32]

On 27 October he found his name being touted for the Olympic team:

> I went to the Cafe Bauer and read the *Frankfurter Zeitung* and *Sportsman.* There is a correspondence going on in the latter about 'the ideal crew' for the Olympic Games in 1908 and in most of the crews suggested my name appears as a stroke for the crew. To be bracketed, however, with oarsmen like Beresford (Thames R.C.) and Cloutte (London R.C.) is a doubtful honour.

Nonetheless, it remained a grain of sand, rubbing away at something more than the back of his mind.

The lessons with both Knorr and Engesser, with their continual nitpicking over his compositions (the elegant but brutal Variation and Fugue for two pianos in particular) and with his pianism (the confinement to the Brahms B flat Concerto and over-studying of small pieces) left him respectful but seething with frustration. Engesser's insistence that Kelly was heavy-handed in the Chopin op. 25 No 7 had him confide resentfully to his diary 'so I am really going to try to get this "ungebewere leichtigkeit" without the affectation which most of his pupils display'.[33]

That December he borrowed philosopher William James' *Talks on Psychology and Life's Ideals* from Frau von Grunelius and later wrote earnestly:

> I was particularly struck with a paragraph in the Chapter XII on 'Memory', in which the words occur 'If you only care enough for a result, you will almost certainly attain it .... Only you must *really* wish these things, and not wish at the same time a hundred other incompatible things just as strongly.' I thereupon decided to be a great player and a great composer.[34]

Naïve as this seems, Kelly meant it.

The short winter break saw him at the Grange and in London with excursions to Windsor to ask for Parratt's opinion of his Fugue and Variations and the Bisham Waltzes. Parratt passed on the fugue but urged Kelly to publish the waltzes without changes. At Easter he returned to play his 'impromptu cycle'. Parratt was impressed, saying it should be played by some great pianist, and offered to speak to Leonard Borwick about performing it.

In London he renewed his club life, taking architect Edmond Warre and a party to Bernard Shaw's *Anthony and Cleopatra*, then on to the Savoy. His brother Willie was in town. They spent Christmas with the Grimstons at Gorhambury where the entertainments on offer included bridge, chess, word games, squash, hockey, golf in the snow played with red balls, the hunt, shooting, dancing and invitations to neighbouring grand houses. Kelly played his own compositions for the company and, unusually, sang popular songs to his own accompaniment.

By this time William Kelly was the Liberal member for Wentworth and newly opposition whip in the New South Wales House of Representatives, known for his levity, his Etonian drawl (for which he was mocked), his exuberance, his practical jokes, and his debating skills. Willie wanted an Imperial, not an Australian naval response to the threat posed to Australia by German naval expansion in the region. London was interested in him. What he wanted of Kelly was help in drafting a letter to *The Times* on 'the Oriental question in the west of Canada'.[35] There was no mention of Willie's fiancée, actress Olive Morell, reportedly a great beauty, whom he had met the year before when she was touring with the J.C. Williamson company. Kelly was puzzled. A month later Willie announced that he and Olive would marry in Paris: 'I had made up my mind when in England,' Cleg confided to his diary, 'that this was all off, but one must never be surprised at the unexpected.'[36] Neither Maisie nor Cleg were invited to the wedding but a Paris meeting with the newlyweds was scheduled for three days after. Cleg had an asthma attack and opted out. Until then he had been in two minds about going, though he knew it was the last chance for a meeting before the couple left for Sydney the following week. He wrote: 'W.H.K. has been very mysterious about the whole affair and neither M.A.K. nor I knew whether the wedding had already taken place, and I still don't know even yet.'[37] This indecisiveness and sudden onset of an illness was to occur whenever Willie reappeared. By 7 January 1908 Kelly was on the train to Frankfurt and remarking that the thaw had set in.

His own thaw was in the making. He began to be irritated by everything to do with music. He tried working on an orchestral suite in G minor, begun some fifteen months before. A piano quartet began to emerge. It was stale bread. To his distress, the revised Variation and Fugue was picked to pieces again by his teachers. He was sceptical of Cyril Scott's new found enthusiasm for Yoga – 'he hopes later to see and hear glorious things in trances' – and uneasy about the quality of the string quartet Scott played for him – 'unrestful and a terrible monotony harmonically'.[38]

He was disconcerted when Fritz Bassermann interrupted his own Conservatory rehearsal of Kelly's orchestral suite in E flat to hand the baton to the composer for the first time. Kelly had never conducted before. Not a good start for what was to be a very brief conducting career. The monotony of copying his own orchestral parts 'depressed' him.[39] He found Mischa Elman's violin tone forced, and condemned him for replacing the composer's cadenzas with his own. Not long afterwards he was doing exactly that himself. Irritation rippled through him, swelling under everything he did and over everything he encountered.

Engesser saw something was amiss and offered Kelly a two piano version of the Brahms B flat Concerto for a Vortrag's Abend. He grasped at the opportunity, seeing it as a way to shed the Brahms at last and a way to be allowed to begin work on the challenging Beethoven op. 106. The Conservatory performance on 18 January 1908 began badly. Both Kelly and Engesser were very nervous in the first movement but managed to pick up thereafter, though Engesser was unsure of the reduced orchestral score and kept increasing the tempo until Kelly had,

> an awful job getting in all there is to play and pushed himself so hard that in the last movement he felt the 'old electric shock once more in my left hand, which I have not felt really since I was treated by Krentzberger in September last. My playing, however, had a success with the audience (a rather sparse one) and I received a great many congratulations afterwards.'[40]

In spite of this Engesser announced that the orchestral performance of the Brahms was to be postponed until the end of May without specifying a date, a crucial omission as it turned out.

By mid-February his new orchestral work had matured into what he began to refer to as the Symphony in G minor, but he found the orchestra and sonata form 'a tough job though I mean to plod my way steadily through the whole of this symphony'.[41] This he may have done, but although he records starting to commit it to paper on 1 March 1908, no such work has been found. He was to make references to thinking out the score to the end of his life.

Six days before the Variations and Fugue was due to be performed, Knorr arrived late to hear Kelly and Franzen play it, stopped them short, criticised the work and asked for changes that Kelly found impossible to make in time. On 3 March, still without the amendments, it was given at the Conservatorium. Kelly thought it went rather well. So did the audience. Scholz and Knorr were still not satisfied. In spite of this rebuff, Kelly went off to dinner with Scholz and the Engessers at the Golden's where he was presented with a rowing automaton and basked in the kind of comfortable domesticity that he always found so attractive:

> As soon as dinner began Lulu Engesser brought in an absurd little wooden boat with a wooden figure in it which rowed when wound up by clockwork and placed it in front of me in full rowing action. The effect was instantaneous and we all laughed ourselves silly. On the boat were three inscriptions in pencil 'Herrn Kelly, zum ewigen Andenken' 'Mod. Von Professor Hilderbrand, Florence' and 'Wer Tönen u Wellen gebieten Kann, Der ist fur wahr ein grosser Mann'[42] In rough translation these read 'Mr Kelly in eternal memory.' 'Model by Professor Hildebrand, Florence' and 'Whoever commands [both] sound and waves is certainly a great man.

Some few weeks later when he played his newest works to Engesser he got a mixed response. The old trouble with his hands returned. Not even a first hearing of *Madame Butterfly,* which reduced him to tears, could appease him. Then Engesser announced a rehearsal of the Brahms before the Easter break. He had insisted that Kelly learn a number of Chopin pieces in addition to the Beethoven 106, and perfecting the Brahms, crowding out Kelly's schedule. Out of temper, he could see no way to finish work on the Beethoven 106 as required before leaving for England. His hands had now become so unreliable that cancelling the May concert seemed the only way out: 'anything is better than the possibility of a fiasco,' he wrote.[43] He took to concentration exercises for his hands, convinced mind could conquer matter. He read St John's Gospel, preoccupied with the thought of whether riches were compatible with Christian principles: 'I feel sure that if I only apply it [mental discipline] to other difficulties in the same way a Christian life will cease to seem unpractical. But one must be humble "as a little child"'.[44] Fortunately this phase was short-lived. He lost confidence in the treatment.

At Easter he was in Paris with his sister and May Long-Innes, listening to the Mignon reproducing piano in a shop, renting a practice room for them to play and sing, and discussing 'social questions in rather a Tolstoi spirit which made us all feel uncomfortable' over dinner.[45] Kelly first heard the Mignon on 17 February at 'Andre's shop' and after a half hour of Paderewski, Busoni and d'Albert, he concluded that 'It is a most marvellous invention and I came away bursting with ambition to become a great player and have my playing recorded.'[46] In spite of this, no Kelly recordings, whether from the Welte Mignon or on any other recording medium, have surfaced.

In early May he performed at Balliol's 500th concert celebration. At the OUMC beforehand Tovey sight-read Kelly's Variations and Fugue. He was not enthusiastic. Kelly took over and played him his Allegro de Concert and 'Never love unless you can'. The response was tepid. Disconcerted, Kelly took to his room to be alone. At 7.30pm he went to dinner in hall, sitting between the president of the Olympics, Lord Desborough, and Ernest Walker, the formality of the night temporally displacing his unease. At 9.30 the concert began. It did not go well: 'M.A.K. told me afterwards my tone sounded extremely thin.' In fact he came to see his performance as a disaster, both in the Chopin Impromptu in F sharp op. 36 and his own Impromptus in C major and C minor. At the after-party he found Tovey holding forth on opera and though he found him as engaging as ever, Kelly remained overly alert to the danger of his presence in his life.[47]

As we shall see, Kelly was worried about whether his concert would come too late for him to train properly for the Olympic regatta. On 14 May he went to see Direktor Scholz, but still there was no certainty about the date of his concert. He spent the day in indecision 'actually writing a letter to Tarka Gold to say I would scull but I didn't post it'. At a quarter to midnight he finally took his courage in both hands and slid it into history. It would seem that at this moment he jettisoned thoughts of his concert and decided to celebrate his decision by walking up the Feldberg in the Black Forest, the highest peak in Germany outside the Alps. Spectacular views and mountain air revitalised him and his sense of humour returned.

On the 19th he announced to Engesser that he would not be returning to Frankfurt the following year and asked his advice as to what to do. He was disgusted by the answer: 'He did not say anything definite about going to someone like Letchetissky,[48] but insisted that the most important thing, wherever I went, was to practise all 24 Chopin Etudes, Liszt's Campanella and Feux Follets and a number of small pieces to perfection.' Instead, Kelly began to train for the Olympics, walking, running and 'some exercises by way of preparing my stomach muscles for rowing'.[49]

A week later there was an orchestral recital of the Brahms concerto, followed by Kelly's Suite. His hands were cold and stiff in the concerto but the suite:

> sounds very well, especially the introduction to the fugue, but the 1st movement is very weak musically and some passages give me an uncomfortable feeling of shame. The fugue would sound excellent if played well, but in addition to its being very difficult for the strings the fact of its being in manuscript makes progress slower than it otherwise would be.

At Andre's music shop, nervous and still unsure of his performance, he tried out a Steinway that he hoped might be an improvement on the one he used at the Conservatory but found it no better. At Thomas Cook's he inquired about travel via Ostend to England. At the Goldens' he found Mrs Golden reading Mrs Eddy's *Science and Health* while her husband was reading Mark Twain's *Christian*

Science. Kelly's interest was aroused. For some time after this he read around the subject and discussed it with anyone willing to hear him out. Two days later there was another rehearsal, this time marred by an argument with Bassermann over tempo in the Suite.

At last, his moment came. On 31 May, he went out running at 8am, bathed, put on his dress clothes, tried through parts of the Brahms B flat major Concerto and spent twenty minutes 'in concentration over my hands and arms'. At a quarter to eleven he walked to what was to be his last concert in Frankfurt at the Conservatory, talked with friends and at 11am, as he later wrote:

> I sat by myself while my suite [the orchestral Suite in E flat major] was being played and was much gratified by its going about twice as well as it ever did in the rehearsals [...] I had a much greater success than I anticipated and I had to bow twice afterwards.[50]

He slipped out to Engesser's rooms upstairs during the following item for a ten minute run at the Brahms, then walked on stage, ready at last:

> By virtue of all the concentration I had done the night before I was not the least nervous and in consequence my hands and arms felt perfectly well all the way through to an extent that surprised me and seemed too good to be true. The whole work went better than it had done in any of the rehearsals and all the difficult passages came off with the exception of the octave passage in the Scherzo which did not go so well as it has done sometimes. Feeling confident of my hands I thoroughly enjoyed playing it and played with more ease and freedom than has generally been the case when I have played in concerts. There was a good deal of applause after each movement and at the end I was recalled twice. Engesser was delighted with the way it had gone and a good many people congratulated me afterwards.[51]

Yet it was only in 1913 that his name began to appear among the former Hoch students mentioned appreciatively in the annual reports, and then as a composer, not as a pianist.[52]

There was a celebratory lunch with the Engessers and friends, 'a dreary 1¾ hours packing',[53] a farewell round of visits to his teachers and a dinner with the von Grunelius family and Frau von der Marwitz. At 12.45am he climbed aboard the Ostend express with a friend. In his solo sleeper he spent twenty minutes concentrating on his hands and arms before turning out the light and with it the Frankfurt years.

He was leaving because he finally saw that his personal concerns were not being heeded. He had outgrown Frankfurt. Because he was a private student there was only the final concert standing between him and the pursuit of final solo dedication. He had to step out from being the eternal student. He had been hiding behind other people's verdicts. This is the moment when he becomes his own man. The catalyst was the Olympics.

CHAPTER FIVE

THE OLYMPICS 1908

In the run up to the 1908 Olympics, Kelly would have understood that the standing of English rowing was threatened. That threat had been created by unexpected Belgian victories in the Grand Challenge Cup both in 1906 and 1907. Their upright style, with shorter strokes, together with their higher rate of striking was very different to the English Orthodox style. And the impact of their victory naturally made coaches at both Oxford and Cambridge question whether they should now copy a perhaps superior Continental style. The fear was that maybe the traditional body swing used by a generation of English crews might now be redundant.

What had really hit home was the Leander eight's defeat in 1907. After Belgium's second straight victory, the fall-out filled plenty of column inches in the press. There were those that saw the Belgian victory as a sign that the current crop of top English oarsmen just wasn't as good as their illustrious forebears. Others sought desperately to proclaim that the Orthodox style – properly executed – still had life in it.[1]

The debate was to go on. But underneath the arguments, there lay a sense of urgency. The following year London would host the Olympic Games. More importantly, the rowing events would be held on the Thames at Henley – over the same course that the Belgian eight had proved to be invincible, both in 1906 and in 1907. Naturally, the Belgian eight were sure to start as favourites to take gold, in the blue-riband event of the regatta. That gave British rowers – Kelly included – less than twelve months to redeem the honour of their sport.

The Olympic rowing events would take place some three weeks after Henley Regatta proper had concluded, and would start on Tuesday 28 July. That timing couldn't have been more fortuitous for Kelly. Had the Olympic Regatta been any earlier in the month, it is possible that because of his commitments in Frankfurt, he might not have raced.

However, given that he had not raced since the summer of 1906, it would have been unwise to make a comeback in an event as important as the Olympics, with any less than seven, or even eight weeks of full training under his belt. In 1907 the Australian had made clear his advice to scullers seeking to regain their: 'old form'. For this he had recommended a period of training of around 'two and a half months'.[2] Kelly's diary entry for 10 May 1908, written while he was still uncertain about the date of his concert in Frankfurt – at which he was expected to both play and conduct – reveals his thinking. 'If [the concert] is on 31 May I shall just have time to get into trim for the 28th July, but if later, I shall have to give up all thought of [competing in the Olympics].'[3]

It is worth looking even more closely into Kelly's state of mind on 10 May, when he found out that Scholes might be competing in the Olympics. It was while perusing *The Times* that afternoon in his usual haunt at the Café Bauer, that he read a piece of rowing news that stopped him in his tracks. His reaction to it, over the next couple of days, was to send him into a paroxysm of indecision. What Kelly had read was a short piece entitled 'Olympic Regatta Preparations'. It started by outlining the oarsmen who were currently trying out for the British eight and went on to reveal some details of entries from other countries, including the names of those who might row for Canada. Kelly would have enjoyed reading this, but it was the article's final sentence that caught him in the gut: 'The representative sculler is to be Louis F. Scholes, who won the Diamond Sculls in 1904 and is the only sculler who can claim to have beaten F.S. Kelly in that race.'[4]

Scholes' potential presence in the Olympics at once catapulted the question of Kelly's participation in the regatta to the front of his mind. How else does one explain the strength of his reaction over the next couple of days? His emotions ranged from determination, through indecision, to downright angst. Initially, he wrote that the news, 'roused my fighting spirit so much, that I went off to ask Director Scholz about the date of the Concert at which I am to play.'[5] Kelly was undoubtedly seeking redemption for 1904. He wanted to be able to: 'scull and have my revenge'.[6]

On Wednesday 13 May, he still had not got an answer on the date of his concert. To make matters worse, the day before, Kelly had received a letter from Tarka Gold, one of the Olympic selectors. It asked the Australian whether he intended to scull in the Olympic Regatta. Not only did Kelly have to consider what he'd do about Scholes' participation, he now also had to reply to that official letter. And time was not on Kelly's side. That night, the Australian began to draft what he called: 'a tentative refusal'.[7]

Thursday brought no relief. He remained utterly conflicted. Nevertheless, the balance in Kelly's mind seemed to have tipped into thinking he would scull. Even so, on that day, Kelly composed two letters to Gold: one saying he would scull and the other refusing to compete. His obvious indecision made him fret and pace up and down his room: what should he do? Finally, Kelly's competitive instincts prevailed. He was to become an Olympian.

At least there was some relief for the Australian when he found out that the date of his final concert in Frankfurt was to be on 31 May, giving him enough time to return to the Britain and complete eight weeks of training. Almost immediately, Kelly started morning walks and runs. Later in the day, he would complete a kind of body weight circuit, by way of: 'preparing my stomach muscles for rowing'.[8] The physical road to Olympic preparation was to be a long one. And other fast British scullers would try to get selected ahead of Kelly.

Meanwhile, in March, the grizzled old veteran Guy Nickalls had been commissioned by the Olympic selectors to put together a British eight. As Nickalls later wrote: 'we were known to one and all as the old crocks'. Evening rowing began in earnest on the Saturday, 21 March – some two weeks before the Boat Race. By early May, a relatively settled eight was going out five times a week, from Putney to Kew, some twelve miles.

Kelly left Germany for England and his Bisham home on 1 June. One would expect that the time he could now spend at Bisham would allow him plenty of opportunity to begin the long, low-rating paddles in his single scull that would begin to build up his fitness: first, for selection at Henley – now less than four weeks away – and then for the potential match-up against Scholes in the Olympics at the end of July. Remarkably though, he does not mention anything in his diaries about either sculling or the Olympics until Tuesday, 16 June.

However, Kelly's inaction had probably set the tongues wagging on rowing's grapevine – especially those men currently training to row in the British Olympic eight designate. They knew that Kelly had indicated that he wished to scull in the games. Now the Australian was home, the eight must have asked themselves: why was he not yet in training? Had he had changed his mind about competing in the single after all? The eight put together by Nickalls was currently training at Henley under the watchful eye of their coaches, Fletcher and Gold. With the final make-up of the eight still to be decided, Kelly's intentions assumed a greater importance. The challenge of taking on the Belgians was a daunting one. Naturally, all concerned wanted the best nine men for the job. As a three-times Grand winner, Kelly's name must have cropped up as someone who might just add to the speed of the boat. If he wasn't going to scull, then his rowing skills made him too valuable a man to leave on the bank. Either Fletcher or key members of the crew began to wonder if Kelly might be tempted to throw his lot in with the eight.

That much became clear when, on Thursday, 18 June, Kelly received a telegram from the crew's captain, Etherington-Smith, asking if he would row in an eight going out at Henley that afternoon. Instead of pondering whether there was more to Etherington-Smith's note than might have initially met the eye, Kelly chose to assume that someone from the eight was unwell and therefore the crew needed his services as a 'sub' for the day. He telegraphed Leander to let them know he would indeed row with them that afternoon. The Leander eight wanted to use Kelly for far more than just that afternoon. Possibly, Etherington-Smith assumed he'd made that apparent in his telegram. But Kelly's quick reply must have made it clear to the Olympic crew's captain, that he would only help them out that day. So just after 10am that same morning, Etherington-Smith visited Kelly to make it clear that he wanted nothing less than the three-times Diamonds champion to step into Britain's Olympic eight as a permanent fixture and thus put his chances of winning the Olympic singles title on the line.

Of course, one can only speculate as to the likely conversation between the two men. But going into Bisham Grange that morning, Etherington-Smith must have remembered Kelly's helpful response to his appeal before the Henley Regatta in 1906. Then, Leander had been short of quality oarsmen for their crews and the Australian had agreed to make himself available to row – at the expense of an entry in the Diamonds. Now, two years later, the cause was even more compelling. The honour of British rowing was at stake in what was likely to be one of the most prestigious rowing contests ever held. Kelly might have desperately wanted to race Scholes one more time, but the necessity of a finding a British eight that was good enough to defeat Belgium's all-conquering crew was apparent to anybody involved in British rowing. What's more, his former crewmate could argue strongly that the Olympic eight designate were 'in a hole'. Kelly's credentials – when fit – in a flat-out race against the Belgians would have been significantly stronger than any of the three men that were currently trying out for a place in the bows of the eight at Henley.[9]

Still, a full-time commitment to the eight was not what Kelly had in mind and initially he told his visitor that he was conflicted. 'I told him I did not want to as I had a great deal to do.' Wrote Kelly that evening.[10] No doubt he understood the greater flexibility of training just as a single sculler, would give him more time to fulfil what was an undoubtedly hectic musical and social schedule.

But the call to duty was one that the Australian understood perfectly well and he was clearly influenced by what Etherington-Smith had said because he then suggested that he would help them if needed. As it turned out, with that admission Kelly was clearly prepared to put the interests of the eight above those of his single.

In fact, that afternoon, he must have been made aware by the coaches of the eight that he was not just contending for a seat in the eight – he was also in line for a seat in Britain's Olympic four. Since they had got together for the Olympics, the men from the Leander eight – especially Guy Nickalls, winner of twenty-two events at Henley Regatta, had expected to 'double-up' in the Olympics and compete in the fours event as well. Nickalls had fond memories of winning a close contest in the Stewards Challenge Cup of 1906 with Kelly on board. The kudos the Australian had gained from that result probably still resonated with the Leander rowers. Moreover, Kelly had also doubled up at Henley successfully in 1905, winning both the Grand and Diamonds. So, unsurprisingly, he was seen as the ideal rower to sit in the bows of a fast four. That day, Kelly went out for two paddles; the first as part of a four and the second in an eight.

Just a few days later, the Australian was given a real shock as to the relatively poor state of his racing fitness. Early on a Monday evening, the eight had gone out for a tough session. Their intention was to row as hard as they could over the Henley Regatta course. And though the crew planned to row the piece at the relatively low rate of striking of 30 strokes a minute, it was to be the most demanding row that Kelly had yet experienced. Mid-way through the piece he began to run into trouble. Almost certainly, he'd gone off too hard for the first minute – probably swinging in with the rhythm of the crew. But though that pace and pressure may have sustainable for men who had been training since Easter, it was most definitely not for a man who only had four days of serious rowing under his belt. During the piece, Kelly was suffering so much that he came close to stopping – an action that would have been especially detrimental to his standing in the crew. Fortunately, he kept going. But the crew's time of 7.37 in reasonable conditions was not impressive.

This would be the first of many physical and mental challenges that Kelly would face on the road to fitness and a starting berth in the Olympic Regatta. That Monday evening it had been determination that had kept him going. But that incident had at least laid bare to the Australian just how much work he had to do to regain his fitness. Later that evening – after his four's outing – Kelly started to fit in the extra work he would need and set off on a run down the towpath to Fawley and back 'by way of getting fit'.[11]

But his determination to fit in extra running on top of the two, or sometimes three sessions of rowing that he was doing did not come without cost to his personal routine. He was soon reporting in his diary that he was too tired to devote significant time to the concentration sessions that he'd begun on 14 March and had proved so important to help him cope with the 'nervousness … and … anxiety' that had marred his piano playing. The Olympic Regatta was now less than five weeks away.

As the first day of Henley Regatta drew closer, more and more crews turned up at Henley to train on the famous course. Kelly began to gain fitness. That led to him considering a speculative entry into the Olympic singles trials to be held after the regatta. But if Kelly and his crewmates were happy to consider racing in more than one event at the Olympic regatta, the same was certainly not true of the selectors. There was no question that in their minds, having their top men doubling up would make the task of defeating the Belgian eight more difficult. The applause round the enclosures for the winning crews at Henley Regatta had hardly died out when the committee acted. Their first step was to bar those in the eight from rowing in the four. This decision caused a major upset within the crew. The reaction of the Nicholls was to refuse to row in the eight. Kelly noted that his crewmate was 'very severely lectured by the committee and finally gave in'.[12]

At the same time, Albert Gladstone won his selection race for the eight. With Gladstone's place secure in the bow seat, the crew was now settled.[13] From then on, the focus on the eight would be relentless. Moreover, the intensity of the work the crew would undertake significantly increased. With Kelly still not yet at race fitness, it was not surprising that he felt the pressure.

On Saturday, 11 July, he hardly slept. He wrote that he'd spent the much of the night 'reading Alice in Wonderland'. The following day, Sunday, he wrote that he was, 'silent and very unhappy all day'. His mood must have been noticeable to those around him, not least a houseguest, one Frau von Grunelius. She insisted that Kelly take two of her sleeping tablets. At least that gave him a good night's sleep. It may well have been that the level of training that he and his crew were undertaking was making the 27-year-old particularly tired. Throughout that week, Kelly had religiously recorded the times his crew had done for flat-out rows over parts of the Henley course. Nickalls' reminisces support this view. He wrote: 'On 6 July … we did our first splitter over the course, and in the afternoon another full course. We did I believe another full course every day that week.' Tellingly, the veteran admitted that this schedule was beginning to take its toll on him. By Saturday night – the same night that Kelly couldn't sleep – he wrote: 'I had rowed myself weak and felt more like sitting down and having a good cry than anything else.'[14]

Two weeks before the Olympic Regatta proper was to begin, Kelly moved out of Bisham Grange and into the crew's Henley lodgings at Countess Gardens. That gave him a chance to spend a bit more time bonding with his crewmates and seek advice about his level of tiredness. Before an outing on 14 July, he sought out the counsel of 'Ethel', who examined his heart in one of the Leander bedrooms. But Etherington-Smith could find nothing wrong with it.[15] However, the surgeon did have a very definite idea as to how tiredness in a crew, or oarsman, might be remedied. Apart from time-off, or varying the monotony of a training regime, Ethel recommended judicious use of champagne. In a chapter on training he'd written for the soon-to-be-published book *The Complete Oarsman*, he wrote: 'when a man begins to show signs of overwork a bottle of champagne for dinner … is enough to bring him round.' Thus, Kelly recorded a couple of days later, that the crew had a 'fizz-night and I broke my teetotalling principles and had two and a half glasses'.[16]

If any relief came, it was only temporary. On Saturday, 18 July, while the eight was trying to decide if they should use a boat manufactured by the Rough or Sims boat builders,[17] Kelly was still tired, and his normally reliable technique seemed to be letting him down. That evening, during a 'firm' piece in the Rough boat, Kelly nearly caught a crab. This caused his crew to stop. It seems he took it hard. 'After dinner,' he wrote, 'I walked down to Hambleden and back by myself in the depths of depression.'[18] That Sunday, just ten days before the opening heat, Kelly wrote again about his state of mind saying it 'varied throughout the day – at times I was terribly depressed'. The only temporary relief seemed to come from music. It's hard to avoid the conclusion that his depression was led by tiredness. Most of the crew had been in serious training for several weeks before him, so it's likely he would have felt the pressure of the heavy workload more than his crewmates. At times like this, his tendency to self-criticise had stopped being useful and worked against him. Just three days later, after his crew had completed a flat-out five-minute row on the course, he wrote: 'My arms and legs were desperately tired in the last minute and I didn't expect to get home.'[19] Kelly then ramped up his personal 'worry-dial' and began to speculate that something might be the matter with his mind. He wondered if these symptoms were more mental than physical, writing: 'What worries me in the middle of a row now is whether my legs are really tired or whether I only think they are. We had another fizz-night again.'[20]

Due to the demands of training twice a day at Henley, Kelly and his crew had not taken part in the Olympics opening ceremony, held at the new White City Stadium on 13 July. But on Friday 24th, he and three of his crew had driven out to Iver Heath to watch the remainder of the fifty-five Marathon runners who had started, pass along the Slough-Uxbridge Road on their way from Windsor to the Stadium.[21] That afternoon, Henley put on a reception for the crews competing in the Olympics. By then, the Belgians were in town – including Scholes. Henley was decked out with national flags and bunting. Spectators had begun to gather in the hotels. Very soon, the crews would be doing their final pieces before the opening heats. Kelly would not have long to wait.

And if Kelly and his crew were worried by omens, then their last big piece before they raced contained plenty. The British eight had just dialled the pressure gauge up to maximum in the middle of a race against a scratch crew of professional scullers. When, out of the blue, Etherington-Smith's aluminium oar snapped. Kelly's blade had already cracked a couple of weeks before. Equipment breakages were not that common, but they were to ruin the chances of at least one of the crews in the 1908 Olympic Regatta. Additionally, Kelly's mood seemed to be affected by the pace of the Belgian crew. After the Grand champion's final piece, Kelly noted: 'The Belgians did the Olympic course in 8.4 … it was a fast night, still the time is enough to make one feel uncomfortable.'[22] At 3.20pm on Wednesday, 29 July, those doubts would be answered when the British eight went head-to-head their first opposition from Hungary.

Anticipation was high for the opening heat, which took place in glorious summer weather and fast conditions. Some had thought the Hungarians the neatest of the foreign crews in the competition and the fastest. Despite the promise of the Leander crew, there was still a legitimate question mark over whether the veteran crew could deliver. After a minute of the race, the question mark was erased. Kelly's crew had cleared their opposition within the first 45 seconds. By the end of the island, the British were out of sight and already thinking of easing down.

The next day, Kelly's crew faced the Canadians in the semi-final. According to the *Times* correspondent, the British eight 'easily' defeated the Canadians by rowing initially with 'great power' and then coming down the latter part of the course 'well within themselves'.[23] Kelly painted a somewhat different picture. In his diary, he reflected that his crew had not rowed together: 'having rowed individually instead of collectively'.[24] The implication was that this might not be good enough to defeat the Belgians. Others in Kelly's crew were also surprised by the apparent ease with which the Belgians defeated their opponents from Cambridge University, in the day's second semi-final.[25]

With the final awaiting them, the intense pressure that the Leander crew faced would layer an extra degree of difficulty onto their attempts to stay positive. Kelly – in common with most of his crew, 'hardly slept a wink the whole night in anticipation of having to race the Belgians'. And, if he'd read *The Times* on Friday, 31 July, on the morning of the race – perhaps before his crew's warm-up run and paddle down the course – his nerves might have been even more on edge. 'It is not too much to say that this is the most critical moment in the history of English oarsmanship,' the paper thundered. The correspondent went on to outline genuine doubts over whether the English Orthodox style – used by Kelly's crew – had been the 'correct' way to row. He left readers in no doubt what was at stake: 'The question at issue is not merely whether we are wrong now in our method but whether we have been wrong for the best part of a hundred years.'[26] If Kelly had seen that article, it was likely that the British crew's 10.30am paddle over the course would have done something to alleviate his nerves. Moreover, there was no lack of positive affirmation from those that surrounded the crew. Kelly recorded: 'None of our supporters had any doubt of us winning.'[27]

But if any relief did come it was only temporary. Soon after that warm-up outing, Kelly described how 'we all hung about the club in misery'. After an early lunch at 12 noon he added: 'I attempted to make up for the restlessness of the night by trying to snatch two hours' sleep, but it was no use.'[28] The honour of British rowing could only be saved by a comprehensive victory over the Belgians. The fact that many English supporters were telling the crew that they were 'perhaps the best eight seen at Henley' would only serve to enhance the value of any Belgian victory. And though Kelly must have believed his crew would win, there was also the strong possibility that the Belgians were good enough to gain a victory – especially if the veteran Leander eight did not row to their potential. As that hot summer afternoon wore on, the moment of truth – scheduled for 3.15pm – drew ever closer.

Leander's race plan was threefold. First, the nine men were to move, think and race as one – not like they had raced against the Canadians. Second, perfect oarsmanship was essential, so mistakes like the crab that Kelly had caught two weeks earlier could be avoided. Lastly, the crew would commit to only one ten-stroke spurt at some point in the race. When this came, the veterans were to completely 'let themselves go'.[29] The British eight's ability to change speed quickly to blunt any Belgian attack would be decisive. They all knew it could be their 'joker-card'. But it could only be played once, and endurance over the significantly longer course could be crucial in any sprint for the line.[30] As if to underline the significance of the contest that was about to take place, the umpire's launch following the race contained a stellar cast of Olympic legends, including Baron Pierre de Coubertin, the man who founded the Olympics.

With a gentle tail breeze helping them, both crews started exceptionally well. The Belgians showed perfect cohesion and pace as they swept down Temple Island, and to some observers it looked as though their bows were briefly ahead. But it was Leander who took a lead of 'a few inches'. Kelly reckoned that 'after ten strokes we were travelling faster than we have ever done'.[31] Along the island, his crew, were up at 42 strokes per minute and moving as one,[32] but the Belgians were 'flying' too. Their shorter stroke, cohesion and higher stroke-rate, seemed to lend itself to a pattern of surges, designed to wear down their opposition. Kelly recorded that the Belgians were confident enough to throw in the first of these: 'Grande Attaques', just as they cleared the island. This burst meant that as the crews passed through the first signal, some two minutes into the race, Leander's lead was less than a third of a length. Both crews probably sensed that what happened in the next few hundred yards of the Thames, in the stretch that led up to Remenham Farm, could prove to crucial to the outcome of the race. It was there – about half a mile from the start – as Leander's lead continued to inch out, that the Belgians made their strongest move yet. Spurting dramatically, their bows leapt forward and began to edge slowly back on their veteran British opponents.

But the confidence of the Leander eight was high. Both they and their cox, 'Cockie' Maclagan, knew that their boat was moving faster than it ever had. At this time Kelly recalled that his crew were still rating around 40 strokes a minute. Nickalls then had them a touch lower at '37'. Nickalls commented that soon after the start of the race he had 'never felt the like of it and never in my life had I felt like galloping at full tilt down the whole distance'.[33] What was beyond doubt though was that in the best traditions of the Orthodox style, the crew were swinging as one and rowing long. This indeed was a crew rowing at its very best.

In that context, 'Cockie' knew well that he could afford to wait until the Belgian surge had subsided. Then his voice rang out calling for that dramatic ten-stroke burst. 'Now then Leander, we'll have our ten strokes and let them know it! One….'[34] At that point in the race – despite the excellence of the rowing – both crews would have been hurting. And the tactic of dramatically raising the crew's pressure would have increased that pain even more. But the nine Leander men knew that their moment of truth had now arrived. In response to the call, the British eight's Portuguese-born stroke man Henry Bucknall raised the crew's rating even higher and his boat 'fairly leapt out of the water', as the eight oarsmen put everything they had into that burst.

The impact was immediate and according to Kelly, the British extended their lead to 'a little over half a length'.[35] Some observers thought the impact of the burst had been even greater.[36] Moreover, even though after the burst the British had lowered their rating to around 37 strokes per minute, the pace generated by the extra power saw the leaders continue to gradually edge out. They hit the halfway mark in 3.45, some six seconds faster than any previous time they'd recorded.[37] Soon after – around the Fawley marker – the Belgians must have realised they had to find something extra. Their stroke man, Rodolphe Poma, led his crew in yet another 'attaque'. They began to close but Maclagan must have sensed this burst had taken too much out of his opponents. The Belgians began to lose cohesion and 'rolled badly'.[38] At this point Maclagan showed his experience. Despite what he'd apparently said before the race, the 28-year-old realised that another ten-stroke burst by his crew could have a race-winning impact. If successful it would mean that the Leander eight would surge ahead and break contact with the Belgian boat through establishing a psychological advantage of over a length's lead. This would put clear water between their stern and the bows of the Belgian boat. It was a crucial moment. As the boats came into the race's final 1,000 yards, the British had established a lead of a length-and-a-half. That allowed them to lower their rating to 35 strokes per minute from the frenetic pace in the first part of the contest. At that stage, it looked like all the British had to do was hang on to secure their triumph.

But remarkably – according to the official report – the Belgians were not yet done. With just over 600 yards left to race 'they rushed their stroke rate to over 40 with one of those electrical spurts for which they had long been famous'.[39] It was a desperate effort to get back on terms and 'every Englishman's heart was in his mouth'.[40] The Belgians began to close, but according to both Nickalls and Kelly the British eight were far less bothered about their opponent's speed than the crowd. Though Kelly noted that the British crew had another ten-stroke burst as they approached the final 200 yards, he tellingly remarked that there was not really any need for them as it was evident after Fawley that 'every stroke (very) gradually increased our lead'.[41]

But as the race played out to its inevitable conclusion, there was of course another question at stake. For Kelly and his crew the chance to decisively 'settle the question over the comparative merits of the styles' now presented itself. Before the race they'd decided to 'go as hard as we could the whole way'. Normally, if the race verdict seemed to be clear the leading crew tended to coast in. Not now. Every stroke counted and Leander ground out the distance, until Mr Fenner's finishing flag fell. According to *The Observer*: 'both crews were "baked" at the finish'. The time of the British, 7.52, was probably the fastest ever recorded by an eight racing at Henley.[42] Kelly had no doubt that 'it was by far the fastest' eight he'd ever rowed in.[43]

Unsurprisingly, bearing in mind what was at stake, the crowds greeted the verdict with 'wild enthusiasm'. Kelly noted that the noise had been almost deafening during the second half of the course, and the normally understated Australian admitted in his diary that 'our win was a very popular one and vindicated the supremacy of the English Orthodox style'.

At the start of the twenty-first century it might seem ironic that it was an Aussie who had played a crucial role in 'saving' British rowing. With the British eight's victory, Kelly became the first Australian to win an Olympic gold medal in rowing. The second, Collier Cudmore, won his medal rowing in the British four some thirty minutes later. Cudmore, like Kelly, was born in New South Wales and had gone to Oxford to continue his education. Yet back then, neither man saw any conflict in being an Australian citizen yet representing Britain. In 1907, Edmund Barton, a former Australian Prime Minister, underlined the synergy between the two nations when he told the Federal Parliament that 'the bond of Empire is not only one of mere patriotism but also one of self-interest'.[44]

So, by racing for Britain, Aussies like Kelly would be fulfilling both their duty to Australia and to the Empire that bound them together. Moreover, it was only in 1907 that Australasia (which included both Australia and New Zealand) was given Olympic recognition for the first time. However, the IOC also allowed individuals to compete for the country in which they lived. So, the thirty-two strong British Rowing team at the Games, included no less than four native-born Aussies. And it was not that Kelly lacked any zeal and fervour for the land of his birth. Just four years after helping a Leander eight to defeat a Belgian crew in the Olympics, Kelly could also express pleasure at seeing the Sydney Rowing Club eight defeat his own club, Leander, in the final of the Grand.

Kelly's legacy to the sport was also significantly enhanced by his influential contribution to Rudolf Lehman's 1908 book *The Complete Oarsman.*[45] As the acknowledged expert on the art of sculling, Kelly was asked to write a chapter entitled 'Sculling'. Written in 1907, it was the champion sculler's attempt to distil all that he'd learnt from his time in a single to a wider audience. Over a hundred years later – when arguably technique, training and equipment had radically changed, Andrew Randell, the Australian coach of another British crew to win Olympic gold – this time the women's quadruple scull in Paris 2024 said:

> First impressions are just how similar my views on 'good' technique are to that of Kelly's. It seems very little has changed in the past 110 years when it comes to sculling … He, as do I, places importance on grip and early preparation being necessary to execute an effective catch – arguably the toughest skill in sculling and rowing to get correct.[46]

Kelly saw sculling as a beautifully fluid motion, which the body could effectively sustain by remaining relaxed and loose. The phasing of the programme Kelly recommends – long outings building up gradually to shorter sprint work – would be familiar to many contemporary coaches and athletes. And Kelly missed nothing when he wrote on the mental approach necessary to sustain a sculler. Mindful of the pressure in the middle of a race, Kelly wrote that every single stroke in training must b: 'of the highest quality possible'. The racing mindset, he wrote, must be built on a thorough knowledge of a sculler's likely pace over the whole Henley course – learnt by 'sculling the whole course at full pressure at least three times before the race'.

So, on the evening of his Olympic success, Kelly could at last relax, knowing he had secured a place among the greats of world rowing.

CHAPTER SIX

TOWN AND COUNTRY 1908–1910

With the Olympics behind him, Kelly traded the athlete's podium for the musician's platform and for the next two-and-a-half years intensified his concertising in London and at country houses, networking with music influencers and publishing his compositions. His ultimate goal was a try-out season in Sydney before a London debut.

Henley had been abuzz with pre-race excitement but the post-race celebrations were modest: speeches from the Olympic committee, prize-giving with national anthems, an outdoor banquet and a town hall dance. Kelly was in his element. One event in particular had repercussions; hearing the band of the 87th Royal Irish Fusiliers performing the Tchaikovsky *1812 Overture* on the riverside lawn of the Red Lion tavern. On the Somme in 1916 he would conduct his own regimental band in this piece of bombast to the accompaniment of real cannon firing at a real enemy.

The problem with his hands resurfaced. Blisters from intense rowing festered. The old weakness returned. Instead of seeking medical attention, he renewed his interest in Christian Science and the theory that sickness was an illusion curable through prayer. When this failed, he settled instead for treatments by Dr Milne Bramwell, a fashionable hypnotist.[1]

At the Grange he played for a stream of influential visitors,[2] including society hostess Violet Hammersley, who arrived in her electric launch with Percy Grainger on board.[3] Grainger had his six-hand version of Kipling's 'The Widow's Party' with him. Host and guests played it through twice on Kelly's two Steinways. Grainger then tried out Kelly's two-piano variations twice and seemed to like them. Kelly thought his playing very neat and brilliant, though occasionally loud and brutal. The Grainger work was disparaged as a cake walk.[4] Months later there was a repeat visit, a four-hour exchange of compositions and more after dinner. Kelly later wrote:

> How the listeners held out till 1am I can't imagine. Miss Bacon consumed cigarette after cigarette and I caught upon Mr Hammersley, who is unmusical, yawning. I think it was Mrs Hammersley who was responsible for the length of the evening. I felt for the audience but without being directly rude I couldn't suggest stopping. P.G. is such an original musician but does not seem to me to really care for the greater things in music. Perhaps it is the influence of H.B. Gardiner and Cyril Scott.[5]

Kelly's interest in Grainger seems to have been one-sided, however. Though both were Australian pianist-composers of the same age, both highly athletic, outgoing and competitive, and though they shared the same teacher and musical environment at the Hoch Conservatory, Kelly's position precluded any close relationship. Grainger was an outsider who had never had a day's formal general education. His views, musical and social, were eccentric, his opinions erratic, his income dependent on professional music-making. Kelly's conservative stance, musical and social, was the outcome of wealth. Grainger identified as an Australian. 'Home' for him was not England. When war broke out Kelly did not hesitate to volunteer and to seek active service as a duty. He died for his beliefs. Grainger, for whom such ties were decidedly loosened, fled to America and survived.

Tovey was back at the Grange late in the Olympic year of 1908. Kelly asked for advice on turning professional. He was told not to use an agent, but to employ a private secretary as he did himself. Kelly fumed.[6]

Other country houses were on offer: Sutton Courtney Manor, where he took tea with the socialite garden designer Nora Lindsay and met Sir Ian Hamilton, later his commanding officer during the Gallipoli campaign; The Hut, music patron Leo Schuster's riverside house at Bray, where he was introduced to the theatre critic Max Beerbohm and found Sir Edward Elgar in almost permanent residence; and Court Place, the Iffley home of prominent Quaker evangelist Hannah Whitall Smith, where he renewed a friendship with her son, Logan Pearsall Smith, whom he had known at Oxford. Two years earlier, Maisie, Kelly and Logan had confessed their personal faults to one another. At Iffley there was a reassessment. Kelly was brought up short when Logan accused him of riding rough-shod over other people's opinions.[7] Kelly was also on good terms with the Bertrand Russells, visiting them at their house at Bagley Woods near Oxford (Logan's sister Alys was married to the philosopher). Over lunch there he met Bertrand's older brother Frank, known as 'The Wicked Earl', a convicted bigamist and accused of marital sodomy, he campaigned for change to the divorce laws and, not long before meeting Kelly, stood for parliament at a by-election on behalf of votes for women. Kelly noted wryly that 'the conversation veered about between Women's Suffrage, Christian Science, Crystal gazing and ghost stories'.[8]

At Ridgehurst Edward Speyer invited Kelly to serve on the Classical Concert Society's committee, a position for which he had been angling for some time. At an early meeting in Sir Frederick Pollock's Temple chambers he tried to veto employing the Klinger quartet. It had failed to attract audiences. Speyer became heated and insisted the group remain. Kelly left in the middle of this gathering, made uncomfortably aware the CCS was, in effect, a Speyer fiefdom.[9]

Shortly afterwards Kelly met Leonard Borwick at a Ridgehurst house party. Borwick had been Clara Schumann's favourite pupil and had since built an international reputation. He played for the company and Kelly was uncharacteristically star-stuck. His impulse was to show Borwick his Impromptu-Cycle but he found himself in awe and incapable of making an approach. The next morning he confided in Mrs Speyer, who took matters in hand and spoke up for him. Borwick agreed to hear the work, following the music with some interest. Kelly plucked up the courage to show him the Allegro de Concert, but played 'very badly from the music'.[10] Though critical, Borwick offered what Kelly thought sound advice. A close friendship, if not something more, began. Borwick was on the way to replacing Tovey.

Completed on the eve of war though begun much earlier, Kelly's twelve studies for pianoforte op. 9 are dedicated to Borwick.

An invitation to perform in the inaugural concert by independent artists at the opening of Eton's new College Library and Hall on 22 November 1908 was accepted as recognition of his growing reputation. These were to be dedicated to the 129 Etonians who died in the South African War (1899–1902)[11] The king had delivered a widely reported opening speech on the 18th, urging the audience to emulate their fallen heroes.[12] Behind it lay a perceived need to reinforce loyalty and leadership amid fears of a European war and Imperial decline. Kelly listened dutifully, but was more interested in the subsequent concert by the Eton Musical Society and composers he knew personally: Elgar, Goodhart, Parry, Lloyd and Brewer.[13]

His own concert four days later got off to a bad start. He had to drive 'Clara' through 'a veritable hurricane' that blew fallen leaves in his face. At Headlam's house Dr Lloyd and other masters were 'in a great state of fuss' over the non-appearance of the piano from Steinway. Maisie, who was to sing, arrived late and the hall keeper had gone for his tea, leaving them without light. They had to rehearse using a single portable electric lamp. All this confusion unnerved Kelly. His arms suddenly weakened and he asked for a room alone to try self suggestion. Half an hour later he was on stage.[14] The concert (Mozart, Dominico Scarlatti, Arne, Chopin. St Saens, Wagner, Brahms and one Kelly song, 'Shall I compare thee') was given before an audience of some 800, mostly boys and 'went without a hitch'.[15]

Back in London, Kelly and Trevelyan met up with Laurence Binyon at the British Museum[16] to be shown a 6-yard long landscape by Cho-sa-go. It made a lasting impression on Kelly, who much admired its balance and suggestive qualities.[17] While art initially puzzled him, he took his lack of understanding seriously, seeking advice not only from Binyon and, indeed, Borwick, but from an elite group of experts that included Bernard Berenson and Roger Fry.

In December he took a serviced flat at 256 St James' Court, Westminster, now part of the Taj hotel complex and described even then as 'ostentatious'.[18] In a month filled with concerts, two at Queen's Hall stand out: Elgar's long-anticipated First Symphony in A flat op. 55, which had premiered the week before in Manchester 'with a tremendous flourish of trumpets and a speech by Hans Richter'[19] on the honour of being entrusted with this first performance. As a consequence the hall was packed. Kelly followed from a hastily bought score. He was not uncritical but thought it had 'a certain majesty'.[20] Repeated at the second concert, it was to be performed a hundred times in its first year and was programmed with the op. 39 'Pomp and Circumstance' no. 4 under Henry Wood. Kelly was roused to enthusiasm and called it 'a splendid march, genuine, popular music without being vulgar'. He was less enamoured of the repeated symphony: 'There was very faint applause after the first movement which is decidedly dull. The public warmed up after the slow movement and gave him a great reception at the end.'[21] For Kelly, the novelty had worn off.

If it was an event being talked about, like the Elgar, or the recently premiered *Rhinegold* in English at Covent Garden,[22] Kelly was there. Early in 1909 he was at the Alhambra music hall for Bizet's L'Arlesienne Suite no. 1, played with Cinematograph scenes filmed in Arles and wrote: 'the reality of seeing the trees rustling in the wind, the real bull fight and reapers in the field added considerably to one's enjoyment. The music was well played and I was quite carried away with it and the pictures.'[23] These were probably from the Pathe Freres Paris film of Alphonse Daudet's play *L'Arlesienne*, first seen at the Alhambra only weeks before. The two Bizet suites were written as incidental music for the play.[24] This foray into film scoring challenged the dominant pure music theories of the day, though Kelly seems to have been unaware of this.

He lunched with the actress Viola Tree[25] and her family, accompanied her singing and reported having 'a very jolly time'.[26] The friendship blossomed. Kelly drove her about, taking her to Adelina Patti's musical advisor Albert Visetti, who was Tree's singing master at the Royal College of Music, supplying her with his own songs and accompanying her singing. Visetti was described by his stepdaughter, the novelist Radclyffe Hall, as 'my disgusting old stepfather', and by Una Troubridge as 'that dreadful, cretinous, lecherous old man'.[27] In spite of Visetti taking a 'tremendous fancy' to his early songs,[28] Kelly disliked him too and was not impressed by his frequent references to his friendships with Wagner and Liszt.

By this time Kelly was a member of the Union Club in Trafalgar Square, a club catering to professional men, merchants and 'gentlemen at large'. The Duke of Wellington, Cecil Rhodes and Charles Dickens were once members. The rooms were spacious, the location highly convenient, the views unparalleled, and it ran a particularly good dining room. More social than political, it was not one of the elite clubs. For Kelly it offered useful contacts, proximity to everything he was interested in and a way to return hospitality.

Ernest Thesiger, then a painter but later an actor noted for his drag roles, dined there with Kelly, taking him afterwards to see George Bernard Shaw's muse, Mrs Patrick Campbell, in *Olive Latimer's Husband.* Like Shaw, Kelly was enchanted:

> I found myself fascinated by her every movement and in some of the more moving parts I was very nearly carried away. Nothing about her was conventional and she has a wonderful way of gazing into the middle of the audience and yet focusing nothing with her eyes. Thesiger took me in to be introduced to her afterwards and I found her to be more beautiful off the stage than on it. As I had been very much impressed by her acting I saw no harm in letting her know it and at the same time rather enjoyed playing up to her vanity.[29]

With his usual insistence, Kelly inveigled Thesiger to take him to see 'Mrs Pat' at her house, 33 Kensington Square, where he learned that she had a fondness for Bach and so played, among much else, the A minor organ fugue for her. He was invited to return in the evening to accompany the American comic opera star Adele Ritchie and to provide more Bach for twenty guests. Around this time Thesiger attempted a portrait of Kelly, but his subject decided it made him look sea-sick. Painter and subject agreed to stop.[30]

On 22 February 1909 Kelly and Thesiger dined at the Union Club and set off to see the newest theatrical sensation at Wyndham's Theatre, Guy du Maurier's patriotic play *An Englishman's Home*, a propaganda piece then only a month into its highly successful run. The plot sees England attacked by an unnamed enemy, presumed to be Germany. A middle-class home is invaded. The father of the resident family shoots an enemy officer and is executed for it. What gripped the public was its stark portrayal of the nation's unpreparedness for war, a concern that lingered after the Boer War fiasco. Kelly reported that 'the sight of invaders in the country moves the audience to such an extent that fourteen men went one night after the 2nd act to enlist in the Territorial army at an office which has been conveniently set up within a few yards of the theatre'. Adding that he 'carried away a little book entitled *The Briton's first duty* which was distributed gratis', and that he 'read some of it before going to bed'.[31] The full title of this controversial little book was *The Briton's first duty: The case for Conscription*[32] by George Shee, the first secretary of the National Service League, an Imperialist group founded in 1902.

The League wanted conscription in order to raise an army capable of defending Britain should the professional army be overseas, as it was during the Boer War. It warned that should Germany engage the British on the Continent, the Boers would almost certainly renew hostilities in South Africa, drawing off essential defence manpower. It quickened Kelly's perceptions.

Scattered across his diaries are records of encounters with a number of rival pianists. Jealousy was mounting. James Friskin was poetic but had no strength.[33] Raoul Pugno, a brilliant performer and Mozart interpreter who was introducing new French works, was dismissed as 'hard toned' and 'breathless'.[34] He took a violent dislike to Richard Buhlig after he was asked to play second piano for Buhlig's Brahms' Concerto in B flat at Ridgehurst. Buhlig was on the rise as a Brahms interpreter and as a champion of the new.[35] He heard conductor-pianist Adriano Ariani and *Societe moderne des instruments a vent et L'Auteur* and a version of Reynaldo Hahn's *La Bal de Beatrice d'Este* at a party given by Singer Sargent and society hostess Lady Elizabeth Lewis,[36] whose events were noted for mixing the establishment and Bohemia.[37] The group, with its nationalist agenda and its still novel combinations, was an expensive rarity. Kelly was unimpressed, distracted by Viola Tree introducing him to Ellen Terry, and by Lady Desborough and Lady Helen Vincent talking on through the music, 'while Mrs Patrick Campbell, judging from the sounds that proceeded from the passage, must have been playing chasings with someone'. He found Ariani's playing of the Bach and Schumann items 'showed a thorough ignorance of both authors', his Chopin was 'stupidly played' and brushed off the Hahn 'thing' as merely pretty.[38] He heard Ricardo Viñes y Roda and others in an all-Debussy concert given by the *Societe des Concerts Francais* at Bechstein Hall. Viñes was noted for his premiering of works by moderns, including Maurice Ravel, Claude Debussy, Eric Satie, Manuel de Falla, Enrique Granados, Isaac Albéniz and Déodat de Séverac, most of them personal friends. Kelly thought the pianist unsympathetic and the ideas expressed 'a limited art'.[39] Hearing minimalist Leopold Godowsky in a Chopin recital was quite another matter. Kelly was astonished at his flawless technique and by his feeling for tone colour, given without the exaggerations of the day.[40] He was to take Godowsky as a model, though for all his concert-going he was still resisting composers or performers who might genuinely challenge him.

On 12 March Kelly took up the baton for the first time, conducting a weekly amateur choral group at 18 Mansfield Street, at the Stanley's town house. Stanford and Brahms part songs prevailed. Kelly thought 'The voices are not bad and the people seem keen'. That evening he was at 30 Old Burlington Street for 'Sargent's and Mrs Charles Hunter's party to hear Clara Sansoni, an Albeniz pupil, play his *Iberia*'.[41] He was introduced to Ethel Smyth – suffragist, composer and sister of Mary Hunter; Kelly found Smyth 'delightful'.[42]

More importantly, he was becoming uneasy at having publicly allied himself with a conservative elite – Tovey and the CCS. *Vanity Fair* had already published an anonymous attack. Headed 'The Most Holy Kingdom of Tovey', it included this:

> Mr Donald Tovey, notwithstanding his comparative youth, is undoubtedly one of the most learned musicians in Europe. But to the writer he is interesting primarily as a symbol: for there have gathered around him a band of the elect, few in number, but not devoid of social importance, who have formed a sort of monastic order, holding themselves haughtily aloof from the rest of the musical world, despising their enemies and praying for them with about equal earnestness. These reactionary purists have enthroned Mr Tovey as their King, and their Pope. His authority remains unquestioned. His infallibility is established by divine right of the Joachim succession. Now the Capital of this State is, of course, at Oxford, where else possible? – but from time to time we heretical barbarians in London receive missions to convince us by personal example of the hopeless levity of our ways. At the present time, there is a nunciature extraordinary established at the Chelsea Town Hall, where every Wednesday, the Great Man himself instructs us how to play Beethoven, Brahms and Mozart. After all, London might reform Oxford, Oxford has reformed us so often![43]

Kelly's response was to gradually press for change. As a prelude, he invited Tovey to lunch at the Union Club on 17 March, drove about to get concert tickets, and settled down to compare their recent compositions, ending in a tête-à-tête which saw Kelly pushing Tovey to leave Northland and to set up in London.[44] Tovey was offended by this, and the implication that it was time to shed Miss Weisse. At a lunch with Tovey and the Warres at 256 St James' Court the next day Kelly's irritation became palpable: 'and it was one of those occasions when his [Tovey's] conversations or rather his monopoly of the talk became bewildering. He was giving us an account of Mallock's New Republic and we none of us could discover much sequence in what he was trying to say.' Later, back in Kelly's flat, Tovey played Schumann's Carnaval 'in a not very inspiring way and then we played my Bisham waltzes. […] I tried to induce DFT to give himself more of a chance as a pianist by devoting more time to the things he plays in public and to trying to cultivate a more delicate tone.'[45] Nothing worked.

Shortly afterwards Kelly and Tovey were guests of music patron Frances Dakyns at Higher Combe. Their hostess introduced Kelly to Tovey's Hungarian protégés, the three d'Arànyi sisters, violinists Adila (Fachiri) and Jelly, and pianist

Hortense, grand-nieces of Joseph Joachim.[46] Kelly was to play the Kreutzer Sonata with Adila at Haslemere's School Hall concert. A debut under Frances Dakyns' patronage at Haslemere was a respectable introduction to English musical society at a time when provincial festivals were a norm. Jelly recalled that not long after they arrived, 'an unusual noise outside the house announced the arrival in one of the early motorcars of another pianist, Frederick Septimus Kelly'. Rehearsals did not go well. Kelly distracted the girls with parlour games. Laughter and friendly high spirits eased the tension of their debut before an English audience the next day. Jelly, then 16, was enchanted. Joseph Macleod, the family's biographer observed: 'She fell deeply in love with this handsome young man, his piercing blue eyes, his keen face; but saw no signs that her passion was returned.'[47] Jelly was to keep Kelly's framed photograph on the Bechstein grand at Bellosguardo, her Italian home, until the end of her life.[48] He wrote: 'The d'Arànyis playing was unrestful and all their tempi too fast, but there was a good deal of fire about it.' The Haslemere interlude did not end there. After a morning spent composing 'Weep no more',[49] Kelly swept up Tovey, the d'Arànyi mother and daughters, and Frances Dakyns, to drive to Hangerfield for tea with Geissler Schubert and yet another country house party including Dorothy (Dolly) Joachim, a niece of Joseph Joachim. Kelly, Tovey and the d'Arànyis played on into the evening and resumed back at Higher Coombe. Though Jelly's feelings were not returned, Kelly went on to compose for her even at the front.

In the spring of 1909 Kelly and six friends, including Tovey in a back seat, raced their cars from Calais to Marseilles, averaging a reckless 50 miles an hour. The hazardous drive, featuring shredded tyres, broken chains, spun-off wheels and scarce garages, was the first holiday of the year. Brownsea Island with minor royals and a pilgrimage to Bayreuth followed. The rest of Kelly's crowded year included music at Northlands, Haslemere, Eton, and Ridgehurst. The gathering-up of contacts became relentless.

He was at Marya Freund's lieder debut on 2 June, when she was accompanied by her uncle, George Henschel, well known as a baritone and pianist but also as a composer and conductor. Freund became one of the first singers of twelve tone works, creating the part of the Wood Dove in Schoenberg's Gurrelieder. Kelly pressed Edward Speyer to engage her for the CCS, but she was not his real target; he was aiming for her uncle. Henschel, alert to the chase, declined to showcase the Australian's songs and merely offered advice.[50]

He tried again with baritone James Campbell McInnes, a member of his amateur choir. McInnes, at one time a folk song collector, appeared frequently in the homes of society families, trading on his association with the fashionable folklorists Lucy Broadwood and Cecil Sharp. Kelly approached him, but was blown off course when he was seated between Blanche Stanley and the PM's daughter, Violet Asquith. 'The latter,' he wrote, 'is still in the youthfully clever stage, which is perhaps natural at 22, but there is a tinge of affectation which probably will disappear.'[51] It didn't. Though Violet Asquith and Venetia Stanley were friends and her presence in the Stanley family setting was a given, this was Kelly's first encounter with her. It was to be far from the last. Violet, who was seen as too close to her father and to Venetia, and who regarded herself as Winston Churchill's de facto fiancée, was still under a cloud after a hushed-up suicide attempt brought on by Winston's announcement that he was to marry Clementine Hozier. Most of that evening's guests attended Kelly's 1911 London debut, their gossip about him a drawcard he encouraged.

Later that month he was a guest of Henry Dakyns at Higher Coombe. He induced Tovey to arrange a visit with Dorothy (Dolly) Joachim, and called on Leonard Borwick at Cooke's House, West Burton, his modest Elizabethan house in West Sussex. Kelly was genuinely enthralled by its simplicity and good taste but, uneasily aware of the need to win Borwick's approval, he backed off promoting himself. When Dakyns later sent him songs by two Australian women he was coolly dismissive, offending his host who had expected his recommendation to count. One of the women was Ivy Brookes, wealthy daughter of Alfred Deakin, the Australian Prime Minister. She took Kelly's judgement of her as a composer to heart, substituting musical patronage for composition. The other woman was Jessie Masson, who had a distinguished career as a pianist. Neither was given the chance to carry Kelly's work.

Late in June there was an Oxford gaudy (reunion) for the undergraduates of 1897–1900. Around a hundred men attended 'an impressive service' in chapel and a dinner in hall, after which the space was turned into a smoking room where Kelly and others performed. He was in his element.[52] He was also a little drunk when he offered a lift to Robert Bridges, soon to be poet laureate. There was a heated discussion of the limitations of regular rhythm. If Kelly was angling for permission to set words by Bridges, this clash put an end to it.

Immediately after this, in spite of a hangover and too much dinner (now not unusual), Kelly plunged into a house party he had arranged at Bisham. Lieder singer Eva-Katharina Lissmann and the d'Arànyi sisters had been engaged to show what he could do for the CCS.[53] The Bedford estates agent, Rowland Prothero, arrived at the same time as the delivery of five Japanese prints which Kelly had bought at the Fine Arts Society in Bond Street some days before, four by Hokusai and an Utamaro. Kelly asked his opinion; Leonard Borwick was also present and was drawn in. Dinner, piano duos and Schubert songs with Maisie ended their evening. They began the second morning with chess in the garden but soon drifted to the pianos again to play through Tovey's Balliol Dances and Kelly's Bisham Waltzes. They explored Bisham Abbey next door with Charles Balfour[54] and Maurice Bonham-Carter, then took to the backwaters to see 'Mr Kearley's wonderful rock garden' on the way to Harleyford Manor and a party given by Sir William and Lady Clayton. Kelly and

Borwick played for their other guests, Borwick accompanying the contralto Murial Foster. Kelly's judgement was that she had 'a glorious voice', but 'overemphasised the sentiment'.[55] At the Grange again, Lady Nina Balfour brought in most of her party from the Abbey after dinner to hear Maisie sing, among other things, Kelly's *Aghadoe.* 'Borwick,' he wrote, 'very kindly joined me in Schumann's variations for two pianos (op. 46) and St Saen's variations on a theme of Beethoven'. (op. 35)[56] On the Monday morning Borwick was the last guest to leave, lingering to play Knorr's variations for two pianos with Kelly and to take a photograph of brother and sister at the piano. 'He is a delightful man and musician,' Kelly decided, 'and I only hope we shall be lucky enough to get him again.'[57]

A day later he heard Ethel Smyth's opera *The Wreckers* at Her Majesty's Theatre. He rushed lunch when he realised he was late, arriving only at the end of the first act and anxious at making a late entry to join Blanche Stanley and suffragette Bertha Lowenthal. He all but fell asleep but reported that: 'The prelude to the 2nd act struck me as being fine and I was surprised at the comparative excellence of the music. In the last act it has made good use of the dramatic possibilities but roughly speaking the libretto seemed silly.'[58]

The weekend of 11 July was spent at New College Oxford[59] taking part in the OUMC's three-day Bach-fest. During this Logan Pearsall Smith took Kelly off to lunch at Court Place, Iffley. There he met Smith's American mother, the Quaker reformist Hannah Withall Smith, an 'undergraduate named Huxley', and renewed his acquaintance with the American art historian Bernard Berenson and his wife Mary, Logan's sister.[60] Smith motored Kelly on to Newington where he introduced him to the painter and arts patron Ethel Sands, another American, and her partner Nan Hudson.[61] On the way there Kelly casually remarked that the riverbank they were passing was where an Aberdeen terrier had followed his canoe in 1902. He had adopted it. Ethel Sands turned out to be the original owner of 'Mossy' and proved it with a photograph. She thought the dog might have fallen into a trap in the woods and was delighted Kelly had found him. A friendship with the ladies developed, Kelly later buying several of Sands' paintings.

It was only now that his involvement with Tovey reached an impasse. A lesson at Northlands in late July again centred on structure in his newest work. There was lunch with Miss Weiss and afterwards Tovey accompanied his pupil in Beethoven's Emperor Concerto, and reversed roles for the Schumann Concerto in A minor. Tovey made objections to Kelly's tempi. There was a clash in Tovey's best style and, 'Miss Weisse who was with us put her oar in in rather a tactless way considering the strained relations on which we have been for the last three years or so. I never feel that she is the authority on pfte [*sic*] playing that she imagines herself to be.'[62]

Immediately after this Kelly was invited to a country house party at the Stanley estate, Alderley Park,[63] at Chelford in Cheshire. With sixty bedrooms on offer the

Stanley parties tended to be large and long, but in this case Lord and Lady Sheffield played host to family and a few friends, including Arthur Stanley and his wife, his siblings Oliver and Blanche, baritone Campbell McInnes; industrialist Hugh Bell (Lord Sheffield's father-in-law), Harold Baker (later Financial Secretary to the War Office), Conrad Russell (noted for his flirtatious letters),[64] his sister Diana, intelligence officer Aubrey Herbert, poet and novelist Herbert (Beb) Asquith, Violet Asquith and Violet's recent acquisition, Archibald Ian Hamilton Gordon. There were the usual distractions on offer: billiards, golf, bridge, Demon Snap, picture puzzles, 'Categories'[65] and musical guessing games; typical items on a house-party menu. As a precaution against boredom Kelly brought *War and Peace* with him and read it in bed.

Venetia Stanley kept a monkey, a fox, a penguin and several dogs, mainly as props. She took Kelly, with Diana and Conrad Russell, to see Lancelot, her bear, then only a few months old and named for Edmund Lancelot Warre. Kelly was entranced, more by the bear than Venetia. They shinned up trees hanging over the lake to see if the bear would follow, set it on one side of a high gate to get it to climb over to reach them, watched delighted as it fended off a cow, and fed it from a baby's bottle. When it later grew too big and was donated to a zoo, Kelly took to visiting it. At the time, Venetia was drifting into membership of the notorious 'Corrupt Coterie', fashionable, drug-ridden and much reported. She was also about to enter a relationship with Violet's father, H.H. Asquith, that scandalised parliament and was later said to have changed the course of the war. Kelly's involvement with her and her febrile circle was long-term but apparently peripheral.

There was, of course, music. Kelly accompanied McInnes in several songs and played the first two numbers of his Impromptu cycle. They argued, with McInnes claiming that modern composers did not 'take the same trouble to write for the voice as was taken by composers 100 years ago. Towards the end it became rather a heated argument when his tone was a little sarcastic about composers.'[66] This time Kelly let the matter drop; McInnes was too necessary.

At dinner the following night he sat between Lady Bell and Violet Asquith, 'the latter of whom taxed me with having mimicked her last weekend. It was true, but I can't imagine who told her. At all events she became extremely sarcastic and a regular little spitfire in manner for the time being.'[67] On the Sunday he walked to church with Blanche Stanley and Sir Hugh Bell to hear his son, the Rev. Hugo Bell conduct the service and preach. Hugo Bell and Kelly played through duet arrangements of the Beethoven 7th before lunch and the 8th afterwards.

That afternoon, at golf with Arthur and Oliver Stanley, it dawned on him that he had met Oliver before, vaguely remembering him from India. It turned out that Oliver was the quarrelsome officer he had encountered at Agra's train station one night in 1907 after the pomp and ceremony of a parade involving the Emir of Afghanistan. In front of an exhausted crowd Oliver was shouting abuse at the

Eurasian stationmaster after he discovered that the train they were all to take at 1am was delayed by three hours.[68] Kelly did not approve of this display of arrogance and remembered it only too well. The reformist Habibullah Khan was being courted by the British and appeared with his bodyguard of 1,100 cavalry and infantry to review the British government's 30,000 troops. The days at Alderley ended with more music pre- and post-dinner: Chopin and Bach, Brahms songs performed by Blanche Stanley and Campbell McInnes, with Kelly accompanying and finally his full Impromptu Cycle.[69] The incident with Oliver was not mentioned.

There were to be many more such weekends for him, trying out his evolving compositions as he went, but his preference was for house parties whose purpose was much more focused and demanding. High summer saw him at the Grange and in his element. At Henley he watched from Leander's enclosure with friends, from a launch on the river and kept pace with races on a bicycle. On 6 August he practised the Brahms Quintet, copied out the last two pages of his 'Lament', took his dog Speckles for a run and into the river with him to swim, sculled, watched crews training, noted that the apricots were beginning to get really ripe, and after dinner lay on the bottom of his dinghy mid-stream looking up at the stars and 'feeling thoroughly happy'.[70]

Yet in spite of an extraordinarily busy social life and relentless daily practice, his composition intensified, producing two piano works: *A Cycle of Lyrics* op. 4 -'Lament', 'Sea-piece', 'Idyl', 'Caprice', 'Choler', and 'Reminiscence' – (which Schott published in 1910, and which are dedicated to J.W. Warre),[71] and the Allegro de Concert op. 3 (Schott 1913). He began work on the *Orchestral Suite in E flat major*, (now known as *The German Symphony*) and the long gestation of his *String Trio in B minor.* There was a flurry of vocal music: *Six Songs,* op. 6 – 'March', 'The Sages' Dance', 'When the Lamp is Shattered', 'Music when Soft Voices Die', 'The Cherry Tree', and 'The Daffodils' – (Schott 1913, dedicated to Gervase Elwes), and 'Weep you no more', 'To the Daisy', 'Away! the Moor is Dark Beneath the Moon', 'Fulfilment', 'Harvest Eve', 'Mirrors', and 'The Pride of Youth'. He was still working over his *Theme, Variations and Fugue* op. 5 and the *Waltz Pageant* op. 2. dedicated to Donald Tovey (both published by Schott in 1913). Though a 'violin and viola duet' gets eleven mentions in Kelly's diaries around this time, no matching score has surfaced.

In mid-August he was in Bayreuth for the festival and not for the first time. Festival historian Frederic Spott says of this Wagner-fest: 'No one with any cultural pretensions could admit to not having been there, and for well-to-do British and Americans it was an essential part of the continental grand tour, a stop on the way to the picture galleries of Dresden and Berlin.'[72] The Foreign minister of the Weimar Republic Walther Rathenau wrote that German audiences were 'spellbound by the influence of Richard Wagner, not so decisively by his music as by the gestures of his characters, by his ideas'.[73] Not so for Kelly.

That year the conductors were Hans Richter, Michael Billing, Karl Muck and the director Siegfreid Wagner, whose musical reputation was as patchy as that of the festival itself. The singers included Ernst Kraus, Ellen Gulbranson, Walter Soomer, Alfred von Bary, and, in his only season at Bayreuth, Fritz Vogelstrom. What Kelly heard would have been uneven, at times mediocre, but occasionally riveting.

Kelly put up at 8 Schillerstrasse and began his stay by walking the town with parliamentarian Harold Baker,[74] then accompanying Viola Tree and Venetia Stanley to the swimming baths, where they looked in at the men's section. 'But,' Kelly wrote in disgust, 'the sight of countless old men plunging about in greenish-looking water put bathing out of the question.'[75] The opera for the day was *Seigfried,* which he thought well done but marred by an exhausted Kraus.

His party dined between the acts and ended with supper and musical games at Kelly's rooms. His guests included his sister, the Stanleys, Sir Ferdinand Mendl MP, Bertha Lowenthal, and Lord Howard de Walden, one of the wealthiest men in England. A London property baron, de Walden was a prolific patron of the arts. He was also a 1906 Summer yachting demi-Olympian.[76] They were joined by stockbroker Charles Van Raalte's daughter, Margherita (Margot),[77] whom de Walden was to marry in 1912. The composer Joseph Holbrooke was there, along with the commissioner of his Dramatic Symphony op. 51, the Irish poet Herbert Trench. Holbrooke later used De Walden as his librettist and retained him as his patron for life. His grandson sees this collaboration as an attempt to reshape Welsh legends to produce 'a grand new British opera in the Wagnerian manner' and dubbed Holbrooke 'the Cockney Wagner'.[78]

Kelly deals peremptorily with that afternoon's *Siegfried.* His attention was on Holbrooke, whom he challenged to identify six musical quotations which he played himself.[79] Money was involved. Holbrooke, humiliated, lost. Kelly, triumphant, wrote that: 'He seemed to have an excellent opinion of himself, rather of the type of Cyril Scott in his attitude towards anything good in music.'[80] Kelly's irritation with what he saw as a bumptious rival was apparently shared by others. Holbrooke was known for his skirmishes with the critics, attacking from the platform and in pamphlets. They thought him long-winded and pompous both musically and in person. After the war Holbrooke's star faded, De Walden's coveted patronage notwithstanding.

Gotterdammerung, Lohengrin[81] and *Parsifal* followed.[82] Though the diaries glance at *Parsifal*'s religiosity, Kelly's response was to the theatricality of the work not its ideology. Though he must have known it, he makes no mention of Nietzsche's famous condemnation: 'I despise everyone who does not experience *Parsifal* as an attempted assassination of basic ethics.'[83]

Back in England, Kelly holidayed at Brownsea Island in Dorset's Poole Harbour. The island had belonged to Charles van Raalte. His snobbish widow, Florence Clow, an amateur painter known in the family as Mrs van Royalty, ran the property. There she conserved her husband's extensive library, paintings and – (a magnet to Kelly) – his collection of 250 rare musical instruments.[84] Florence had befriended several members of the English and Spanish royal families, including Queen Victoria's grandchildren, princes Maurice and Leopold and their sister Princess Victoria Eugenie, there with her husband, Prince Alfonso of Spain.[85]

Brownsea's castle had been renovated and a nine hole golf course added. Entertaining was done on a lavish scale necessitating a small army of servants. At the end of a hard day a select few would don bandsmen's uniforms and play for guests on the castle terrace. For Kelly there was sailing, including a visit with Margot van Raalte to the family's neglected 150-ton steam yacht *Maruja*, swimming, golf, billiard-fives, demon-snap and hide-and-seek in the numerous passages, basements and seven staircases of the house. Evenings were given over to piano duets with Margot and Maurice van Raalte, playing 'bits of Wagner' for the company, Chopin and Beethoven for Princess Beatrice, and a particularly boisterous parlour game:

> After dinner we played Rabbits and Ferrets in the billiard room which was a tremendous success with the party, none of whom had played it before. There was a good deal of space between one end of the billiard table and the end of the room which was furnished with sofas, armchairs and a few tables. These made excellent barricades in the dark to prevent the ferret from pouncing upon one unawares. On one occasion there was a regular swarm of rabbits on the floor behind the sofas and in treading over a leg I tripped up and in falling down knocked a small table over with a terrific clatter which brought the ferret (the Princess) down upon us at once. The funniest part of the game were the suppressed giggles, occasional outbursts of laughter and the queer sounds people made in brushing by bits of furniture and occasionally knocking then over – I once knocked the sofa over backwards in trying to get over it [….] It was one of the jolliest days I have ever experienced, if considered in the light of pure childish enjoyment and excitement.[86]

This idyll was disrupted by a series of blunders, one of them major:

> At lunch the Princess gave us some personal reminiscences of bomb-throwing in Russia, which was very interesting as throwing light upon the question as seen from the point of view of the people aimed-at. A good many of her relations seem to have lost their lives by bombs. In discussing Catholicism I floundered into some questions about her marriage which showed that I had no idea that [….] it had been attended by rows with the Pope and the Spanish

> authorities who had turned Prince Alfonso out of the Spanish army for marrying a Protestant. Prince A seems to be very free thinking for a Catholic but perhaps that is not to be wondered after the difficulties of his wedding.[87]

In October 1909 Kelly revisited Eton and his old masters, 'Tuppie' Headlam and Dr Lloyd, the latter newly returned from South Africa where he had been examining. At critic Percy Lubbock's[88] house he tried a new Bluthner. Lubbock was in the Berenson circle, which may explain Kelly's connection. At Bisham, Kelly worked on his B minor trio and thought through ideas for settings of several Logan Pearsall Smith poems: 'March', 'Mirrors', 'Harvest' and 'Birds in a Garden'.[89] 'March' was published by Schott as op. 6 no. 1 in 1913. 'Birds in a garden' seems to have been discarded. The rest remain in manuscript.[90] He was to publish only eight songs. Musicologist Stephen Banfield has said of them: 'they show a fertile delight in technical invention', and that 'We have here an Edwardian style perfectly preserved, unravaged by any forebodings of linguistic crisis', and 'the op. 6 songs are too fecund and original to be dismissed'.[91]

Kelly took the trio to Tovey, who held forth at length on Kelly's use of modulations. *A Cycle of Lyrics* was examined. Kelly took down Tovey's instructions for revision without comment but noted that the older man broke off to play him the duet at the end of the first act of Cherubini's *Medea* as an oblique corrective. Kelly was silent, feeling pushed into agreeing with Tovey's less and less persuasive arguments. The manuscript of the B minor trio for piano, violin and cello survives in two early versions, one incomplete, and two others finalised at the Grange, one with corrections by Tovey dated 31 May 1911 on a score that was first signed off by Kelly on 4 October 1910.[92] Tovey's relentless fault-finding hit its mark. Kelly drew back and did not publish a work he considered finished. The corrections followed him to Australia while he was setting up what was to be his professional debut. It was part of Tovey's continuing attempts to destabilise his now antagonistic pupil.

Unable to disconnect, Kelly returned to the G minor trio, mentally composing as he walked the dogs and returning to Bramwell's methods to find a way through his blockage: 'I make suggestions to myself before going to sleep each night in order to bring on a musical frame of mind in the hopes that ideas will occur to me.'[93] Distractingly, H.M. Ferrer called to talk over his trip to Constantinople and Greece and, incongruously, his success at salmon fishing in the Tyne. There were telegrams to be sent to locate the Bonsai trees being shipped from Japan for Maisie. Felix Warre came to stay and James Grimson motored over from St Albans for dinner. He tried to work against this tide of socialising and failed.[94]

The Classical Concert Society opened its ten-concert autumn season on 13 October 1909 at the Bechstein Hall. Its executive committee is listed in the programmes as 'The Rt Hon. Gerald W. Balfour, Douglas W. Freshfield Esq.,

F.S. Kelly Esq., Sir Frederick Pollock Bart and Edward Speyer, Esq.' and as 'formerly the Joachim Concerts Committee'. [95] Kelly's presence was de rigueur. His name in this list suggests his influence was considerable, given his personal involvement with most of the performers and his propensity to argue a case. Leonard Borwick and George Henschel, who as usual accompanied his own singing, provided the first concert. Kelly wrote:

> Borwick was in good form and his performance of the Toccata [in C major op. 7 of Schumann] was interesting bearing in mind Paderewski's playing of it in Oxford 1902. Paderewski's was a magnificent 'Tour de force' and of the two it was the finer reading. Borwick's playing of it was technically faultless but he made it more reflective and was freer in his rhythm than Paderewski, who without being stiff played it like clockwork.

On 20 October on his way to the second CCS concert of the year Kelly called in at Augener's where he bought Alexander Scriabin's 24 Preludes op. 11, his Sonata no. 3. in F sharp minor op. 23, the Allegro de Concert in B flat minor op. 18, and his Preludes op. 15, 16, and 17. These were from Scriabin's early period and possibly all Kelly could get at the time. At Northlands a few days before, Tovey had played the Preludes to him from a copy sent to him by Timmy Jekyll.[96] Kelly had been impressed. During the weekend at the Jekyll home, Munstead House at Godalming, immediately afterwards, he played through the Preludes with Jekyll, whom he knew from Eton and Oxford. Jekyll was a pianist-composer and a folk song collector working with George Butterworth. Kelly's interest was roused to the extent that he went on to include Scriabin in his house and CCS programmes and introduced him to Sydney in his debut year there. At Munstead House he found Reginald McKenna who 'expressed his conviction that Frau von Grunelius,[97] was a German spy and nothing would disabuse him of the notion!'[98] Marie-Adele Tachard was in fact French. The First Lord may have brought a whiff of the coming war into the harmlessness of the weekend, but Kelly only found it amusing.

The following morning he drove Tovey and Casals the fifty-five cold and windy miles to Ridgehurst and the Speyers, two-and-a-half hours away. Through his composer-banker father, Edward Speyer had known Mozart's son Carl, and counted Rossini, Spohr, Mendelssohn, Liszt, Brahms, Joachim and Clara Schumann among the family's friends. Like his cousin Edgar, he was a distinguished patron of music long before Kelly met him, sponsoring the 1902 London visit of the Meiningen Orchestra whose programmes included Elgar's 'Enigma Variations'. His house was noted for its musical gatherings centered on its panelled 36ft x 27ft music room with its raised platform. Elgar is believed to have written 'The Smoking Cantata' there.[99] A visit to Ridgehurst was not just a social weekend, it was serious musical business. It may have housed a fine art collection, Mozart's viola and a formidable library of scores but it was far from being a museum, and though noted for its sports facilities, it was no gym. Casals probably got the balance right when he once announced on his arriving to stay with the Speyers: 'First we'll play six sets of tennis and then the two Brahms sextets.'[100]

The music performed included Tovey's B minor trio op. 1 with Marie Soldat and Casals who read at sight, seemingly without a mistake. They found the long-winded German minister at the Hague regaling the company with anecdotes. A bored Kelly was driven to filch Tovey's score of Schumann's Cello Concerto to read surreptitiously before the company rose. Among the guests was Jenny Cornwallis West, formerly Lady Randolph Churchill, Winston Churchill's American mother. Edward ('Eddie') Marsh[101] was there. Marsh was associated with the Georgian poets and the Bloomsbury set. He was, like Kelly, a friend of Rupert Brooke. When war broke out he was Private Secretary to Churchill and it was through Marsh's influence that Kelly was placed in the First Lord's Royal Naval Volunteer Reserves. Jenny Cornwallis West was a talented amateur pianist, a pupil of Chopin's friend Stephen Heller, hence her presence at Ridgehurst. She was also a society hostess and had been the king's mistress. She had turned playwright earlier that year with a Globe theatre production of *His Borrowed Plumes*.[102] Kelly left no record of having seen it – though it starred Mrs Patrick Campbell, who at the same time made off with Jenny's much younger second husband, as he would no doubt have known. In 1906, when Tovey first played this work to Kelly, he thought it original, but now he wrote smugly: 'there was a ground work of originality dressed up in some places in a very Brahmsish garb'. Casals, too thought it 'finely worked but being so much influenced by Brahms that it ought not to be published'.[103]

That afternoon there was a rehearsal of the Beethoven String Trio in C minor op. 9, no. 3 with Casals, Marie Soldat and Ferdinand Speyer taking the place of Frank Bridge when he failed to show. Kelly wrote that Soldat 'played disgracefully' and tried to persuade Edward Speyer and Tovey to replace her in the CCS concerts. Casals backed him up, 'saying he found it impossible to play musically with her'. Kelly won the argument, but mused,

> I can't understand why there should be all this false sentiment merely because she was a pupil of Joachim and because Brahms 20 years ago or so was enthusiastic about her playing. One can not do greater harm to the reputation of Joachim than by setting up poor players as exponents of the 'Joachim traditions'. There is, too, nothing in common between her playing and his.[104]

Two days later, on 27 October 1909, Kelly practised at home, paid a hasty visit to his dog, 'poor Blackie', at the vet's and took the train to London, reading 'Schubert's magnificent D minor string quartet on the way'. He thought 'The variations in it are about the most moving thing in the whole of string quartet literature.' At Steinways he tried two pianos for Mrs Hammersley in between 'hearing impossible passages from Liszt Rhapsodies played on the Welte Mignon piano by players like Carenno', and lunched with Leonard Borwick at 34 Wimpole Street, where they 'fixed up terms for the rent on my part of a sitting room and bedroom and share of spare room furnished at the price of £140 per annum to be paid quarterly'.[105] After which the pair went off to a CCS concert together. It was this move to shared quarters with Borwick that marked the end of Kelly's life as a grand amateur.

CHAPTER SEVEN

THE MATTER OF DONALD TOVEY 1909–1910

Kelly was late in getting to Northlands for a lesson on 28 October. 'Clara' had suffered a puncture. He had come unprepared. Tovey was in no mood to be lenient. He overrode his student's plans for the construction of one work and began to sketch out his own version. Kelly bridled:

> I suggested his letting me write down what was in my mind first and I think my request must have accentuated the slightly bad humour he was in. At all events he began to talk rather dictatorially and made most of his ensuing remarks in a loud flustered voice as though his authority were being impeached. I can never see what is to be gained in a lesson by a master screaming at his pupil and adopting a bullying attitude that terrorises by putting a lot of rhetorical questions to which no one could give any answers. There is a strong trait of this in DFT (though he would never admit it) and in this case I got so tired of being screamed at that I at last took him to task about it whereupon he adopted a *tu quoque* attitude and tried to make out that it was I who was trying to terrorise him! He has got queer old fashioned ideas of life floating about in his mind which come to the surface every now and then. We luckily got over the little outburst of hostilities very soon and discussed things quite amicably during lunch.[1]

Nonetheless the end was in sight.

Kelly drove off to Munstead House, Godalming, to appear with the Ackroyd Quartet. The house was half empty, the audience unenthusiastic. In spite of this he was elated and abandoned his recent tee-totalism for the weekend: 'I had a feeling that some principles might be relaxed after the conclusion of a successful concert at which I had earned my first fee (£5/5/0)!'[2]

Still in holiday mood, he joined old friends from Eton in a car chase at Louis Paulhan's pioneer aerial display at Brooklands in Surrey, marvelling that 'He flew 96 miles the majority of which I saw and about 5pm he rose up to about 400 ft [...] It was the first aeroplane I had seen – a Voison biplane and I was surprised at the noise it made. It travelled its 96 miles at an average of about 34–35 mph.'[3] 20,000 spectators watched.

He was at Ridgehurst for the weekend of 6 November. Speyer's events were a mix of works in rehearsal for the CCS, music from the repertoire – mainly Beethoven, Schumann and Brahms – and the testing of new works. In this case there was to be a second reading of violinist Karl Klingler's String Trio in C. Kelly thought it inferior but had to hold his tongue since Klinger was performing with Speyer's blessing. Somewhat unnerved at his own response, he went on to give the solo part of Tovey's Piano Concerto in G major, 'and accompanied (badly) from the score for the last movement'.[4] Klingler had been the violist of the famed Joachim quartet, and a close friend of the great man. His own quartet was founded to preserve the style of Joachim's. His only pupil was Schinichi Suzuki. Klingler's influence on both the Japanese Suzuki violin method and the development of British chamber music was considerable. For Kelly, it was another event reinforcing the conservative values of the Brahms-Schumann heritage embodied in his involvement with the CCS and his relationships with both Tovey and Borwick.

With the shift to 34 Wimpole Street now imminent, Kelly returned to London and Claridge's. He went shopping at Steinway's and, in a fit of enthusiasm, chose a concert grand, arranged for it to be moved into his rooms and went off to hear Hans Richter conduct the LSO in Ignace Paderewski's B minor symphony at Queen's Hall. At seventy minutes long, he thought it was one of the dreariest works he'd ever heard. Paderewski's new instrument, the Tonitruone,[5] reminded him of the Hydrophone in the 'Ode to Discord'[6] – capable of only one effect. The Emperor Concerto that followed he thought not good enough for the ostensibly greatest living pianist. Even the piano, an Erard, got a serve. It was deemed disgusting, 'and, as Borwick said, like a box of matches'.[7]

On the morning of 15 November Kelly finally moved in with Leonard. At Bisham he walked the dogs, packed hurriedly, lunched hastily and managed to just miss his London connection. There was a two hour wait. He had his String Trio with him so he closed the doors of the waiting room, settled himself before the fire and made 'considerable progress with it'.[8] Tovey and Borwick were at Wimpole Street to welcome him but both gave the thumbs down to Kelly's new Steinway. It was too big for the room, they said, so back it went. A chastened Kelly, making a very Australian gesture, had been put in his place by two very British gentlemen.

Wimpole Street was described in Tennyson's poem *Dark House* as a 'long unlovely street'. Society saw it as a very respectable address that attracted the banking and medical professions. Virginia Woolf made fun of it, branding it,

> the most august of London streets. The most impersonal. Indeed, when the world seems tumbling to ruin, and civilisation rocks on its foundations, one has only to go to Wimpole Street; to pace that avenue; to survey those houses; to consider their uniformity; to marvel at the window curtains and their consistency; to admire the brass knockers and their regularity … one has only to go to Wimpole Street and drink deep of the peace breathed by authority in order to heave a sigh of thankfulness that, while Corinth has fallen and Messina has tumbled, …. Wimpole Street has remained unmoved … as long as Wimpole Street remains, civilisation is secure.

Thackeray suggested it was 'as cheerful as the Catacombs – a dingy Mausoleum of the genteel'.[9]

At the time of the move Leonard Borwick was 41, Kelly 28. Both men had been students at the Hoch Conservatory in Frankfurt, Borwick from the age of 15 when he began piano studies under Clara Schumann. They shared a composition teacher in Iwan Knorr. The older man was long established as a soloist and chamber musician, notably with the Joachim Quartet. He played frequently for the queen at Windsor, and at one time was described as Queen Victoria's favourite pianist. In 1891 Brahms heard Borwick's performance of his Second Piano Concerto and remarked that it 'contained all the fire and passion and technical ability he could hope for'.[10]

He was to achieve an international reputation as a soloist, touring Europe, America and, in 1911, at Kelly's behest, Australia. He was to return in 1914. He had also been accompanist and associate artist with the Irish baritone Plunket Greene from 1893 to 1904 in the singer's pioneering solo song recitals in London. In spite of a lack of evidence and in the face of Greene's marriage to Sir Hubert Parry's daughter in 1899, it has been assumed that the relationship was intimate, an assumption also made about Borwick and Kelly. Reviews rated him as intense, technically perfect, even austere. There were references to his 'chaste expression', his 'Anglo-Saxon mind', his 'perfect clearness and masculine vigour', his 'splendid sanity' and his 'sound and wholesome' approach.[11] Kelly was in muted awe of it.

From the first night dinner Tovey, Borwick and Kelly progressed to Aeolian Hall for the premiers of Vaughan Williams' G minor Quartet and his song cycle 'On Wenlock Edge'. They focused on the quartet and missed the significance of the cycle, as did the reviewers. In this century it has been deemed a turning point in the history of British music.[12] Its subject, the untimely death of young men, brought it attention only as the war drew on. At this first hearing neither Kelly nor Tovey found it to their liking. They were scathing about the quartet. Though the concert also included recent songs by three of the Frankfurt group, Balfour Gardiner, Norman O'Neill and Roger Quilter, Kelly ignored them. By this time he was hearing several concerts a week, frequently two a day, and writing their programmes into his diaries with detailed critiques.

Some days later he arrived back at Wimpole Street after a weekend at Gorhambury to find an excited Tovey waiting for him with a proposal from Dr Ludwig Strecker, head of the Schott music publishing firm in Mainz, and wrote that DFT 'hesitated a good deal and behaved rather like a man preparing someone for the news of the death of a relative before he finally found the letter and gave it to me to read'.[13] To Kelly's surprise he found Tovey had been quietly urging publication of the op. 4 *Cycle of Lyrics.* Strecker apparently agreed with him that this was the work of a very serious musician, but thought it in-turned and too busy. The composer was to have fifty free copies ('heaven knows what I should do with them',[14] Kelly wrote) and further remuneration if the work sold well. Schott published it the following year.

In early December, with programming for the Schumann Centenary in April now urgent, he and Borwick risked driving 'Clara' through a snowstorm for a weekend of discussions at Ridgehurst with the Speyers. Inevitably, Tovey was there, annoying as ever.

> [He] gave us a continuous harangue about music some of which was very interesting. In these talks he is sometimes too anxious to prove other people fools – the fool in this case being Hadow.[15] It is not that he really thinks he's a fool so much as that he works himself up into an impatient state of mind and in developing his point of view and then proceeds to demolish what is in disagreement with it. In this case we were told that Hadow must be an ignoramus for thinking that Beethoven had failed in his late fugues by paying too much attention to fugal devices such as stretti, turning the subject backwards etc etc. I pointed out that he, DFT, accused Bach of failing in his bE min fugue in the 1st book of the 48 for the very same reason and then he had the usual explanations and sophistries uttered very fast and in a flustered voice in order to extricate himself from what seemed a hopeless position. DFT never admits that he is wrong and what's more I don't believe he ever thinks honestly to himself whether he has made mistakes of this kind.[16]

The Tovey matter went on festering. In the longest diary entry devoted to any of his relationships, a conflicted Kelly wrestled with his respect for his long-term teacher on the one hand, and his now white-hot resentment of Tovey's egotistical treatment of him both as a pupil and as a friend. Over lunch at Wimpole Street, Tovey confided that Liverpool was offering a series of concerts illustrating his lectures. He wanted to accept since it meant he could avoid Miss Weisse for at least part of the year. Kelly insisted that composition was more important than lecturing and that it would be a waste of time but DFT seemed to have retreated to his old ambivalence about any real break. The more Kelly pushed the more his mentor pushed back. To avoid a quarrel he showed Tovey his Trio, a work completed just short of the end of the development. Tovey now wanted to consider the work as a whole and proceeded to play it at the piano, asking Kelly to page turn. Kelly wrote:

> When he got to the new part (which is unplayable on the piano) he made a mess of it and got many of the harmonies wrong. He would have got a better idea of it by reading it away from the piano when half his attention would not have been centred on finding the right notes, but to be playing it himself is evidently the source of great satisfaction and I felt in a vague sort of way that I ought to be playing the part of the wondering pupil who will in old age tell how when he brought Tovey a new composition bristling with difficulties he played it faultlessly at sight! DFT's character is the most amazing mixture of generosity, genuine interest in other people's work and some very fine traits and on the other hand a childish vanity that is born of a musical egoism. He is at his happiest when he has people gathered round him turning over the pages of a score and vice versa he is visibly restless and uncomfortable when someone else is at the piano. He is also pretty deft at finding some excuse for illustrating something he had to say, if this is the case, and then establishing himself immovably in their place! I wish with all my heart, that one could eradicate this egoism out of his nature. Some of his gifts, such as improvising a cadenza to a concerto, playing from the score and the extent of his musical knowledge have probably never been surpassed in the whole history of music and yet at times they appear in the light of an intolerable bore. In conversation he has no give and take and if he is not monopolising it is generally silent. Lately he has been more tiresome than usual and for the time being he has got on my nerves. There have been pretty long stretches of time, though, when his society has been a source of almost unalloyed pleasure and interest to me.[17]

The last CCS concert of the season was a Tovey-Henschel in mid-December. Borwick, Kelly and P.S. Long-Innes went together. Earlier in the day Kelly had shown Borwick Tovey's Trio for piano, horn and clarinet. It was a work Kelly had never liked and when Borwick looked it over he 'didn't like what he saw of it' either, endorsing Kelly's now entrenched views. 'There is,' he declared, 'something false about its ideas like the mock heroics of 18th century poetry and the piano writing is very thick and uninteresting.'[18] Tovey's part in the ensuing concert was condemned as 'one of the most depressing things I have ever heard'. In the Beethoven Sonata in E flat op. 81a,'Les Adieux', he fumed:

> There was a load of false sentiment about it. A total lack of rhythm and an absence of all beauty of tone such as any pupil would have been turned out of the room for. I suppose there is no one, probably, in the world who knows more about Beethoven than he does and yet one could hardly imagine a greater misrepresentation of all the beautiful and direct ideas of which this sonata is full.[19]

A list of Tovey's pianistic faults followed. Back home Ferdinand Speyer and Borwick sat down to discuss Tovey's playing. Kelly felt vindicated when both men found Tovey's performance 'almost worse than I thought it'.[20]

In Christmas week Borwick and Kelly arranged a musical party at their rooms. The Speyers, Mrs Hammersley, Mrs Neruda, R.C. Trevelyan and the Dakyn women were to be there along with Tovey. On the day, Donald arrived early with a lesson in mind but since Kelly had made no progress on his Trio, he offered his E flat study for criticism, which was only too willingly given. Afterwards, Borwick and a resentful Kelly lunched together at Pagani's. Kelly was very bad company and aware that Tovey's judgement was shared by Borwick. He threatened to tell Tovey what he thought of his last CCS performance[21] but Borwich warned him off such an indiscretion on the day of their party and he held his tongue.

A panto at London's *Hippodrome*, noted for its spectacular programmes, captivated audiences with a trilling polar exploration story featuring seventy real polar bears. A momentarily diverted Kelly went with Felix Warre. The plot involved a girl organising a relief expedition for her fiancé, led by a villain who loved her and sabotaged the mission. A climatic scene showed the ice breaking up, causing a panic and the appearance of the bears. A bear hunt ensued, culminating in all seventy bears sliding down ice-like ramps into a tank of water, seemingly unfazed and even playful. The Hippodrome specialised in spectacular aquatic events, boasting a massive arena tank that could hold 100,000 gallons of water which could be lit from below. It featured high-shooting water jets, floodable side entries for boats, and even dwarf acrobats who would dive from a gallery. That tank's floor could also be raised to create a dry stage, with the orchestra playing from the grand circle.[22]

Felix Warre[23] and Kelly were to remain close. Kelly was to lend his friend considerable amounts of money on generous terms and left a rider in his will that Felix was not to be urged to repay it. From 1909 to 1912 Warre borrowed a total of £9,300[24] which Kelly lent him at 5 per cent, probably to advance Felix's cause at Sotheby's, where he was an auctioneer. Warre was only obliged to pay the interest on this loan. The principal was to be paid back when his Sotheby partnership expired. Kelly was being more than generous. In 2021 this loan, not including the interest, equalled UK £764,853.

With elections looming, Kelly's attention momentarily shifted to politics. He records attacking Ferdinand Speyer over the relative merits of policies espoused by Lloyd George and Winston Churchill,[25] an altercation with Headington during the New College meet and a resumption of the argument with Speyer at Wimpole Street when they had done playing for the night.[26] He moved a fraction closer to the action when he had to negotiate the Morris Crawford insurance policy on his car, which was on loan to the Conservative party candidate for Rotherhithe and South Bucks, but politics was to remain a spectator sport for him. A general election was held on 15 January 1910 in response to a constitutional crisis brought on when the House of Lords rejected Lloyd George's People's Budget. As it turned out, the Conservative candidate for Rotherhithe, Assheton Pownall, lost to the Liberal candidate in both the January and the December general elections. Kelly and Borwick went into town to follow the results, standing by St Clement Dane's for two-and-a-half hours to see the figures from the *Daily Chronicle* projected by a magic lantern onto a sheet. The intervals were filled with pictures of cabinet ministers, caricatures and jokes intended to keep the crowd amused. Kelly's crowd was 'mostly Liberal' and a good deal of booing was heard whenever the Tory colours appeared. At ten to twelve he and Borwick went on to the Union Club, staying till the results were in. H.H. Asquith and his Liberals had to preside over a hung parliament.

In mid-January Kelly, Edward Speyer and Leonard Borwick met at Bechstein Hall to hear two pupils of Eugenie Schumann's lover, lieder singer Marie Fillungar. These were soprano Edith McCullagh and contralto Helen Anderton. Anderton 'sang like a great artist',[27] and though Kelly spoke against McCullagh for the way she opened her mouth and for her odd stance, it was decided to engage both for the CCS concerts. They duly appeared in the Schumann Centenary concerts. Kelly's presence at these decisive moments had now become a given – for all that he didn't always get his way. In the end, with his backing, five of Clara Schumann's former piano students also appeared in the three Schumann Centenary concerts of 13, 20 and 27 April 1910 at Bechstein Hall: Iona Eibenschutz (Mrs Carl Derenburg), Fanny Davies, Mathilde Verne, Leonard Borwick and John St Oswald Dykes. These names appear in Kelly's diaries as fellow guests in town and out and as performers with whom he worked.

At Balliol to rehearse the Emperor Concerto under Hugh Allen for the 3 February OUMC concert,[28] he asked the conductor what he thought of Tovey. If Kelly was indeed still looking for confirmation of his own growing aversion he got it:

> Like everyone else whose opinion is worth having, he thinks his playing is awful and as far as his composition is concerned he thinks he cares more for the framework etc then the musical idea to be expressed. I think that in this DFT gives an erroneous impression in talking so much of technicalities so that such criticisms are exaggerated. A great many people, however, think the same and there is certainly some truth in it.[29]

On the 5th Kelly drove the four d'Arànyis[30] to the Northern Polytechnic Institute in Holloway Road where he was to accompany the excitable Adila in some Brahms in a People's Concert Society programme. He found she played 'like a runaway horse' and that the demonstrative family was disconcertingly entertaining: 'All the d'Arànyis talked at once, there and back in a semi-intelligible German and it was a task far beyond my powers to try to answer all their questions at once and follow the trend of their thought.' He was pleased to be able to add: 'They all loathe Miss Weisse with a cordial hatred and Adila in the morning told me of an incident in which, in retailing something stupid Miss Weisse had said about him to Joachim, she had surprised him into giving expression to his feelings by calling her "die alte Hexe".'[31] Which is to say 'the old witch'.

In March Schott's began to send proofs of Kelly's *Cycle of Lyrics*. These went back and forth, London to Mainz, for many weeks,[32] delaying publication until the following year. *A Cycle of Lyrics* op. 4 for piano finally appeared as six numbers: *Lament, Sea-Piece, Idyl, Caprice, Choler* and *Reminiscence.* By April he was working on a setting of Logan Pearsall Smith's *Cherry Tree* and another of Shelley's *Music when soft voices die.*[33] At the same time he continued refining at least some of his Etudes and the songs *March, Mirrors, Fulfillment* and *Harvest Eve.*

On 7 March he gave the Bruno Walter 1909 Violin Sonata in A with Marie Soldat[34] at 2 Cambridge Gate, the London home of Margaret[35] and Helena Deneke, daughters of the German Banker Philip Deneke. Kelly thought this early work inferior but felt obliged to attempt it since the sisters knew Walter. Margaret had studied with Eugenie Schumann. She was at one time president of the Oxford Ladies' Musical Society, founded to correct the exclusion of women from the OUMC. As a musicologist, the Mendelssohn family had entrusted her with Felix Mendelssohn's letters and MMS. Kelly could not refuse, and in fact turned the concert to his advantage by supporting Soldat, a Brahms discovery and a protégé of Joachim. His own claims to the Frankfurt heritage were now incontestable.

Meantime Borwick's reputation was on the rise again. When tickets for his and George Henschel's forthcoming February concert sold fast, their agent pressed them to follow up with a concert at Queen's Hall. Kelly was delighted and urged Leonard to come out of his shell 'and gain a great name as a pianist especially now that there is a chance of touring with Henschel to America'.[36] It was a decisive moment. By the end of the year Borwick was locked into an international tour and Kelly was making plans for his professional debut in Sydney where the two men were to meet. The Aeolian Hall concert on 19 February was a sell-out. Kelly was there with Mark Bonham-Carter and later gave Borwick his frank opinion. Though he thought Leonard's playing was 'about as good as one could wish to hear',[37] he had registered Borwick's nervousness, his hesitancy over tempi, cantabile that was a little pale and a failure to move the audience at times. Borwick heard him out but Kelly did not record his reaction. A lesser man than Borwick would have been as annoyed as Tovey. Kelly was there again for the Queen's Hall concert a month later and was enthusiastic: 'All of his playing,' he wrote, 'was pretty well faultless and I have never heard such good sustained playing throughout a concert.'[38] Yet afterwards, over dinner, he was ruthless in going over every note with an exhausted Borwick.

Undeterred, Kelly went off to witness Thomas Beecham conduct the first London performance of Richard Strauss' *Electra* before an audience primed by its still recent notoriety – its Dresden premiere the year before had caused a furore. Kelly was impressed, though he thought there was:

> a sense of decided deficiency in the text. There seemed to be nothing but blind animal hate and I got no sort of idea of the treatment of revenge as a moral and religious obligation. The music was not so out-of-the-way as I expected it to be and in the duet between Orestes and Elektra there was quite a touch of early 19th century Italian opera. I found my attention caught most in the scene between Orestes and Elektra and the depictment [*sic*] of Elektra's feelings while Orestes was committing the murders. There seemed to be a perfect mastery in the style of the music but when it was meant to be moving I just got a touch of the sweetly sentimental about it. It is difficult to recall one's actual impressions as everything was so strenuous and one's attention was often led off on a wrong scent by queer phrases and sounds which kept me laughing about a third of the time. There were some splendid chords on the brass (at Clytemnestra's entry I think) which suggested a sort of refinement in the vice of ugliness. The performance, as far as one could judge of it, seemed quite excellent. I remember being agreeably surprised to find that Elektra, after having made queer sounds and grovelled all over the stage for about an hour, possessed a beautiful voice when, towards the end, there were some good vocal phrases written for her.[39]

The singer was Edith Walker. At the time the modernist score, to Hugo von Hofmannsthal's harrowing text, was considered emotionally draining, sexually daring and generally repulsive. Hardly a laughing matter. Kelly later read the text, began to have doubts and changed tack. He went to a second performance with Borwick and Dr Allen and wrote:

> We were all struck by the old fashioned character of some bits of the work. At times it was almost like Italian opera. I like the sentimental bits (notes) or whatever it is. My first impression, on a first hearing, that it was all wild hate and nothing else, was certainly a false one. It is decidedly dignified towards the end.[40]

In early April he heard Serge Koussevitsky conduct the English premiere of Scriabin's *Le Poème de l'extase* op. 54 at Queen's Hall and thought it 'unhealthy music'.[41] In spite of this, he was to introduce Sydney to Scriabin in his debut season. A few days later he heard Richard Strauss conduct his own work with the same orchestra in the same space and wrote: '"Don Juan" appealed to me a good deal more than hitherto and "Tod und Verklarung" which I followed in the score made me enthusiastic.' He sat with Borwick who 'worried me by his habit of breathing loud when listening to music'.[42]

The Tovey matter now deteriorated rapidly. Kelly, still dutiful, went with Leonard to hear the premier of Donald's Sonata for Violin and Piano in G major with Marie Soldat as the soloist in the Chelsea Town Hall Concert of 2 March 1910. Late at night his pen scratched out a damning critique: 'What struck me most about D.F.T.'s work was the ugliness of the piano-writing', and, after an analysis of this he accused Tovey of 'doubtful taste', adding:

> I got the unpleasant sensation from these passages that I often get in D.F.T.'s playing – a sort of egotistic brutality. […] It has singularly the same effect upon me that D.F.T. has personally. One is struck by the grip, learning and mastery, by the total lack of charm, and finally, in such places as slow variations, the tedium is exactly what one experiences when in conversation, he spends ten minutes in spinning out what you have guessed in the first few sentences – especially when he is enunciating commonplaces. As is usually the case on the production of his new works, he had to sit up Saturday, Sunday and Monday nights, according to the Speyers, to finish the Trio and Percy Such complained of the unfairness of expecting him to give a proper account of the finale on a day's acquaintance especially as he had gone to Ridgehurst for the weekend in order to rehearse and was busy giving lessons

> on Monday and Tuesday. L.B. felt about the works in the same way I did.[43]

The Tovey contretemps was still unresolved when DFT came to lunch at Wimpole Street on the 21st. Kelly tried to turn the conversation to Tovey's Concerto op. 15, which he was practising in readiness for the performance at the Petersfield Festival on 20 April. Tovey would have none of it, becoming uncomfortable when his student (the first to perform it other than its composer) suggested giving him a detailed criticism later:

> It will be interesting to see if I can break down this aversion to hearing any sort of criticism. Others like Allen and Mrs Speyer have given it up as hopeless. I asked him what Joachim had said of it but I couldn't get anything out of him except that Joachim in his later years was very puzzled by anything new! I mentioned [notes] to him as a passage which seemed to me bad and immature in instrumentation but I got a hasty assurance that 'that' was alright and just gave the colour he wanted (as though I had just pitched upon about the best bit of instrumentation in the whole work!) I am determined to conquer this aversion to discussion as it makes any sort of intimacy impossible. The moment any question of his own work is raised which is not mere praise he becomes out of sorts.[44]

In spite of this friction between the pair, Kelly kept on with his lessons, noting Tovey's instructions in ever increasing detail.[45]

He was at Ridgehurst again for the weekend of 9–10 April when he, Edward Speyer and Leonard Borwick finalised the CCS autumn season programmes.

> Mr Speyer began by reading us out a letter from DFT in which he displayed some bitterness as to the small share that was allotted to him in the rough draft of the scheme which Mr Speyer had sketched on his own initiative. He had some justification, as in one concert for which he was definitely put down the programme consisted entirely of Bach like the programme of his last Chelsea Concert and in the only other programme which his name appeared in he was only to play supposing Cortot was unable to come. His letter, however, displayed too much ill-feeling to rank as a mere dignified protest.[46]

Alfred Cortot's reputation as a pianist far outstripped Tovey's yet this role as his virtual under-study must have rankled. Tovey had added: 'The Brahms C minor Pfte [Pianoforte] quartet oughtn't to be at the end of the program, and it would suit

Borwick 50 times better than Fanny [Davies]. I suppose Kelly doesn't approve of the way I play it.'[47] Speyer suggested Tovey raise the matter with Kelly but Tovey refused. Even Kelly's attempts to win him over later at Petersfield were rejected. 'He has been extremely critical of me lately,' wrote Tovey, 'and his lessons in composition have been almost a contradiction in terms.'[48] Tovey seems to have been aware that his own performance was erratic and he did not thank Kelly for pointing it out. Kelly noted, as an aside to the day's misadventure: 'The party was a curious collection of descendants of great musicians with Miss Schubert, Eugenie Schumann and young Wach[49] who is a grandson of Mendelssohn.' Geissler Schubert was a grand niece of Franz Schubert. Eugeine Schumann was a daughter of Robert and Clara Schumann.

Kelly's 1909–10 social calendar remained crowded with fashionable events and people. These ranged from seats at the *Follies* to the sobering new John Galsworthy offering, *Justice*, (on prison reform), and Harley Granville-Barker's *The Madras House* (on the vexed question of equality for women). He entertained large after-theatre parties at society cafes or at his club. He dined out frequently and thought nothing of cultivating fellow guests, among them the French novelist-critic Andre Beaumier who, he said, 'bullied' him into attending his barely understood lecture on Baudelaire, compelled solely by social convention. Patrons were to be courted which is why he was at Lady Ottoline Morell's weekly receptions at 44 Bedford Street, and at one point dined with her and her husband at Ethel Sands' and Nan Hudson's house at 42 Lowder Road. He moved lightly in political circles. A dinner at Charles Mead's house, for example, ended with the guests leaving for the House of Commons in order to congratulate Harold Baker (Liberal) and Arnold Ward (Conservative) on their recent election, Kelly among them. He also cultivated anyone able to advance his musical or social standing and thought nothing of going with Borwick to Steinway's to choose Welte-Mignon rolls for Mrs Berenson, who had recently bought a Steinway reproducing upright piano to be shipped to Florence and the Berenson villa. Recorded by electricity, these paper rolls replicated direct performances by famous pianists[50] Kelly was doubtful about the worth of the performances – Paderewski, D'Albert, Pugno and Busoni – saying: 'on the whole it was a lamentable exhibition of playing'.[51] At the time these performances were thought more authentic than the early cylinder and disk recordings. In spite of this there is no trace of Kelly having ever cut such rolls, possibly due to Borwick, who was opposed to recording of any kind.

On 12 April 1910, Timmy Jekyll invited Kelly to meet 8-year-old Christian Victor Hely-Hutchinson, a son of the last Governor of Cape Colony. Hely-Huchinson was a child prodigy and one of Tovey's pupils. A pianist-composer, he was already published by Novello. Kelly was charmed, played duets with him and began to circulate his compositions.[52] Two months later he heard from Walter Parratt that Tovey had given a three-and-a-half hour lesson to Hely-Hutchinson and so exhausted the boy that he took to his bed.[53] Kelly was angry and confronted

Tovey, who protested that he had only given Victor the agreed three half-hour lessons as arranged, but, Kelly wrote:

> as I was leaving he mentioned something about 'I was just showing him something' which explained a great deal! Possibly, as usually happens in such cases, he played the boy a couple of Bach's Cantatas, with the Ninth Symphony and an act of an opera thrown in without being in the least conscious of the state of mind of his victim![54]

It marked a further unravelling of the Kelly-Tovey connection. Hely-Hutchinson went on to become Professor of Music at Birmingham University and was later Director of Music for the BBC. He left some 150 works, some still occasionally aired.

On 19 April Kelly gave up wrestling with the ending of the first movement of his B minor Trio, a work begun in October but which had taken, in his view, 'an incredibly long time'[55] to complete, and drove to Oxford to rehearse Tovey's concerto for the Petersfield festival which was scheduled for the next day. He was billeted at New College with Dr Allen. They dined with the Olympic eight. On the drive to Petersfield Kelly and Allen discussed the concerto, Allen saying to a smug Kelly that 'there was not a tune in it for which he could not point to the original in Brahms'.[56] They lunched at a Petersfield hotel with Campbell McInnes, there to judge the choirs. Kelly had the singer cornered and asked if he might show him his newest songs. McInnes had no choice but to accept them.

The concerto did not go well:

> in the last movement I got confused for several bars in the first of the passages beginning (notes) by the imitation in the orchestra and in the Coda something odd happened by which I found that I ended the brilliant blind-octave passage a bar too late. DFT however hadn't spotted that anything was the matter and said very nice things about the piano part of the concerto. We should have had more rehearsals. DFT admitted that the bass was too low most of the time as far as the orchestral writing was concerned but didn't volunteer any further statement as to what he thought of his own work. The work received great applause and he and I were recalled several times.[57]

On the road home, Tovey looked over Kelly's songs, 'Fulfilment', 'Harvest Eve' and 'Music when soft voices die', and was scathing. Kelly, completely undone, was only too glad to see the back of him.[58] Within days, and with his attendance at the Schumann Centenary cut short, he was in Rome with the Berensons.

CHAPTER EIGHT

OUTWARD BOUND 1910

Bernard and Mary Berenson met Kelly in Rome and, on 1 May 1910, drove him to Palombara Sabina with American artist O.S. Field. This was only one of many Berenson expeditions in search of obscure Renaissance art. A Berenson authentication often led to private commissions. At dinner, Kelly met Scottish poet Douglas Aintree, who he thought pretentious. The following day, they continued through the hills with travel writer Carlo Placci. Kelly became increasingly alarmed by their chauffeur's reckless driving on the cliff-hanger roads. At Anagni, he was puzzled by the Berensons' excitement over crumbling frescoes in the Papal church crypt. Berenson was vindicated later when these were deemed of national importance. Their guest went on to admire a 'glorious Colonna palazzo' and the Roman viaduct at Genazzano.[1] At Palestrina he turned pilgrim and went in search of the composer Giovanni Periluigi da Palestrina's putative house, 'which is sadly fallen into decay and smelt of the farmyard'.[2] He also noted the Palazzo Barberini with its Roman mosaic of scenes of the Nile and a statue the Berensons pronounced as a genuine Michelangelo. Kelly declared that 'It was exciting as in a sense it was quite like a discovery; it being not generally known as a M.A.'[3] This time his hosts were wrong. A day later, Kelly was introduced to Eugénie Sellers, the assistant director of the British School at Rome, who took him through the Museo Barracco and the Museo Nationale Romano, sparking his enthusiasm for Egyptian art. It was this encounter that led him to start his own collection.[4] At the Villa Borghese, he considered Titian's *Sacred and Profane Love* the best painting he saw there, and afterwards took tea with Field and his mother at the painter's studio on Via Margutta, where the Berensons joined them. Novelist Truman Capote was later to occupy the same studio.

At Veii, some twelve miles out of town, the party was shown wall paintings in its Etruscan ruins. Kelly was intensely moved at the way the city had been lost and overgrown. In the afternoon they visited Campagnano di Roma, Castlenouva, Prima Porte, the Villa Livia and the Castel Jubileo.[5] At the Villa Livia they saw a room with frescos of a wild garden which Kelly thought the most realistic paintings he had ever seen. The Berensons declared them to be 'very great art', but in spite of the uplift felt by the rest of the group Kelly's day was spoilt when, still five miles out of Rome on the way back, their car passed a cart at 30 miles an hour, killing a dog which:

> had its attention distracted by people calling it out of the way. I looked back and told our party it was dead expecting them to stop and apologise but only got an impatient rejoinder from Berenson to the effect that if dogs frequented the road they must expect to be killed. I felt very much disgusted but avoided showing any anger.[6]

A certain awkwardness over dinner that night was only saved by Ainslie stopping by to talk, his pretentiousness conveniently forgotten.

The last days in Rome were spent on the conventional tourist route. The diaries mention the Colosseum, St Peter's, Michelangelo's Moses, and Santa Maria Maggiore, where Berenson had a fit of rage when an attendant tried to show him a work he deemed irrelevant. It was followed by the Galeria and Palazzo Doria, where Berenson introduced him to Prince Doria 'who kindly showed me Filippo Lippi's Annunciation and one or two other pictures in his private apartments'.[7] Let loose in the public collections, he five-starred 'the Velasquez portrait of Pope Innocent X, Titan's daughter of Herodias and some of Claude Lorrain's landscapes'.[8] In the Vatican galleries Berenson got out of hand again and behaved 'like a spoilt child'.[9] Kelly moved past to the Sistine Chapel and new ideas for his B minor string trio.[10] He saw the graves of Shelley and Keats and went with Mrs Berenson to Tivoli for the ruins of Hadrian's Villa – the Villa Adriana – and the gardens of the Villa d'Este. His tour ended at the Forum 'in which,' he said, 'I spent three hours of the greatest enjoyment studying everything with the help of Baedecker [*sic*].'[11]

On 9 June Kelly and Mary Berenson left Rome by car, bound for Florence. On a descent into Orvieto the brakes caught fire; in spite of considerable alarm they managed to get to the town and an overnight stop at the Palace Hotel where Alfred de St Andre (described as 'everyone's pet Parisian')[12] and garden designer Geoffrey Scott joined them. In the cold and wet they pushed on to Florence, Settignano and the Berenson's villa, *I Tatti*, which Kelly had visited some five years previously. There, on a rainy day that drove everyone indoors, Kelly met architect Cecil Pinsent. Scott and Pinsent were commissioned to design the putative Renaissance gardens of the Berenson villa, using the connection to draw further Tuscan clientele. Kelly ignored the commercial motives of his host and his guests, politely played for the company as required, pronounced on the merits of the Welte-Mignon, described by Berenson as their latest 'pride and joy', and finally escaped with the excuse that he was obliged to visit the now retired director of the Hoch, Bernard Scholz. There he played his *Cycle of Lyrics* and the Scholz's new *Fantasia*, with only Scholz and his daughter as audience. This reprieve was not enough. Kelly's unease about Berenson and his frequent tantrums soon had the younger man packing his bags. By 16 May he was back in London.

That evening he went 'to see the Russian dancers of which everyone is talking so much'.[13] This was Anna Pavlova, Michael Mordkin and eight other dancers as the twelfth item on a very mixed programme at Alfred Butt's Palace Theatre of Varieties. It was billed as their first appearance in England. They opened with an elegant classical pas de deux that earned ten curtain calls, unheard of in a music hall, but it was what came at the end of the segment that caused a sensation: 'Gone were Pavlova's tutu and Mordkin's ballet costume, gone her pointe shoes. In Greek tunics and sandals, they flung themselves onto the stage in the "Autumn Bacchanal" one of the most tempestuous and passionate dances ever staged.'[14] Kelly admired 'the wonderful sense of movement' and was 'quite amazed' by Pavlova, but the thrill felt by the audience was not his. 'Lots of the music was charmingly orchestrated'[15] was all Glazunov's score warranted.

Three days later Borwick and Kelly were at the Hippodrome to see 'the Russian dancers in Tchaikovsky's ballet *Le Lac des Cygnes*, but found them inferior to the Pavlova troupe: 'the music was a little too facile and undistinguished. […] We also heard Yvette Guilbert (whose voice is horrible but whose gestures are remarkable) and saw an airship which manoeuvred about the theatre by means of wireless control from an electric battery – this was an astonishing feat.'[16] The innocent looking Guilbert, then 45, was in fact a raunchy French chanteuse, and an acquired taste. Toulouse Lautrec painted her as a worn-out lush. The airship's inventor, Thomas R. Phillips, demonstrated with a 20ft model of a Zeppelin dirigible. *The Sunday Magazine* went along:

> It looked like a toy balloon at the mercy of any gust of wind – purposeless, slow, and unwieldy. And suddenly – Cr-r-rack! Mr Raymond Phillips had touched a lever, and the airship sprang into life. […] Running his fingers from one key to another he stopped it dead, turned it about, made it rise and fall, made it turn figures of eight in the air, and finally stopped it again, motionless in the air, forty feet above the orchestra stalls. 'Now,' said he, 'just imagine that row of seats is a row of houses, and that instead of a model, with paper toys in its hold, I am controlling a full-sized airship carrying a cargo of dynamite bombs. Watch!' He pressed another key […] and the bottom of the box that hung amidships fell like a trapdoor, releasing not bombs, but a flight of paper birds that fluttered gracefully down on the seats beneath.[17]

The next day, 20 May 1910, some 5 million spectators turned out to watch the funeral of King Edward VII pass along a route lined by 35,000 troops. Kelly bought two scalped seats in Edgeware Road for 25/- each and presented them to his and Borwick's housekeeper Mrs Cooper, and Ethel the kitchen maid, but his own vantage point, though still in Edgeware Road, was at an upstairs window in Boot's chemist shop. Three hours later the procession reached Kelly's party, which included his sister. They found it a long wait:

> but the seething crowd and its struggles to break through the line of police and soldiers was an unflagging source of interest. I was very much interested in the pageantry of the whole procession and I doubt if there had often been such a collection of Kings as there were following the coffin, but the whole thing was not impressive from the almost total lack of music. There were massed bands but they didn't play as they passed us. It was a hot day and numbers of people fainted.[18]

In the cortege were eleven carriages bearing representatives of seventy states, Theodore Roosevelt among them. Nine kings, including the Kaiser, rode by on horseback, part of a contingent of nearly fifty royals. Within a few years most of the kings would be deposed. The late king Edward VII left behind an unresolved constitutional crisis and a parliamentary system in such disarray that there was talk of a class-based civil war. None of this seems to have shadowed Kelly's day, though he must have been well aware of it given his avid reading of the news.

With Henley at its height, Kelly moved back to the Grange. Guests sought relief at night from the summer heat by sleeping in the garden chairs where insects kept them awake. Kelly slept in the punt, though he feared that a swan might put its head over the side and bite.[19] It was there on the river that he was most at home. There he was aware of himself as nowhere else and could write: 'On an evening such as this was, all the fragrance from the riverside gardens hangs over the surface of the water and one sculls from one scent to another.'[20] He felt, as he seldom did, that he was at peace with himself and later wrote with great conviction: 'I felt completely happy. [...] I used to dislike the wind some years ago but now it seems to fill me with the joy of nature and the trees and water are all alive under its influence. I am vaguely groping for a musical expression of the wind on the river.'[21]

That summer Kelly's ambition to take on the role of patron became focused on the construction of the Haslemere festivals, which he discussed with the Daykins, and the proposed twenty concert season of the CCS, intending to stay upfront by performing for both. In pursuit of all this he motored to Oxford on 7 June to appear in an OUMC all-Schumann concert with Tovey; aware that he could not risk an open break with so influential a figure, he was determined to be obliging. Docker, his chauffeur, drove while Kelly read the score of *Fidelio.* There was a detour to hear Theodore Roosevelt give the Romanes lecture at the Sheldonian. It was billed as dealing with biological analogies in history. Kelly wrote: 'What I heard consisted of a number of biological facts (which everyone knew) and platitudes strung together in a laborious way. I got an impression, however, of a powerful bulldog character who would say whatever he thought ought to be said no matter who the parties interested.'[22] Roosevelt's lecture was delivered with 'vigorous utterances and forceful gestures' to a cheering audience.[23] Kelly left early to rehearse. If he took in the rest of it he seems to have been unmoved by a speech that opposed British disarmament in the face of a belligerent Germany and which also implied American aid in the event of war,[24] the cause of the cheering.

That evening Tovey, Kelly and several string players were due to open the OUMC concert with the revised version of the Andante and variations for two pianos op. 46. Not an easy opener. Kelly was to follow with the Études Symphoniques. Tovey kept them waiting. Though the OUMC had sent three letters to him in order to clarify times, there had been no reply. Kelly telegraphed to Miss Weisse on behalf of the president and had to report that Tovey was engaged for a concert at Northland that would prevent rehearsal, and indeed would make him ten minutes late for the Oxford engagement. Kelly was furious but went through with it, outwardly calm.

Pablo Casals was fetched from Northlands on 6 June and complained on the drive about the small concert fees in England, citing Miss Dakyn's offer of £20 for a Haslemere concert. His usual fee was twice that.[25] George Butterworth, then considered the most promising composer of his generation, arrived on the 21st. The two composers played through Hubert Parry's two-piano Grand Duo in E minor in readiness for the first Old Etonian concert five days later, and spent the evening looking over some of Butterworth's compositions.[26]

Most, if not all, of the performers and composers included in the concert of the 26th were Old Etonians. The event probably owed much to Kelly's organisation. It opened with his Bisham Waltzes Nos.1, 3, 5 and 7, played with Tom Spring Rice, and went on to include the first performance of George Butterworth's two piano *Rhapsody on English Folk-Tunes* performed by the composer and E.R. Speyer. Butterworth appeared again with Kelly in Sir Hubert Parry's *Grosses Duo für Zwei Claviere.* Thomas Arne's *Rule Britannia,* in Kelly's two piano version, was played by the arranger and Butterworth and sung by the audience with Parry conducting.[27] At the end of the programme, in a burst of nostalgia and with Kelly at the keyboard, *The Eton Boating Song* was given with the Old Etonians at full throttle.[28]

Six years later, three months apart, both Kelly and Butterworth were shot. Butterworth's body, temporarily buried in the wall of a trench, was never recovered. Of similar rank in very different regiments, both were wounded and both were decorated. Butterworth's orchestral *The Banks of Green Willow* is now read as an iconic hymn to the sacrifice of youth in war. Kelly's *Elegy,* also for orchestra, is gaining a similar status. Both evoke a deep sense of loss, but on this summer's day there was none of that.

The return to Australia was not yet in sight, though at about this time Kelly was writing to Knorr, Engesser and Golden in Frankfurt, pushing for a visit. This eventuated towards the end of the year as a prelude to what was to be his last voyage home and his professional debut.[29] He was looking for affirmation that he was ready, something neither Tovey nor Borwick would give him.

On 2 August, Kelly and Pearsall Smith boarded Sir Hubert Parry's 90-ton yacht *The Wanderer*, anchored at Cowes among 'a glorious fleet of steam yachts, racing cutters, schooners etc'.[30] Parry had circumnavigated the British Isles several times in her. His organ Toccata and Fugue 'The Wanderer' is almost certainly named after it. Smith, one of Parry's sailing friends, had leased it for the annual races. It came with a skipper, six crew and a cook to service six passenger cabins, and an 18ft x 18ft main cabin where its tenants dined. The skipper took the ship out to watch the big schooners manoeuvre before following the main race. But, unable to make headway against wind and tide they were obliged to return to Yarmouth with Aldwimple, the New College chef, seasick all afternoon. The next day was calm enough for Kelly to swim round the ship before the tide all but crashed them into a moored yacht. It was decided to head for Cowes, but again the tide marooned them for hours on end and they could only make it to Stokes Bay in heavy rain.

It was a brief *entre-act* soured on his return to the Grange by finding that:

> DFT had been to call at the Grange (from Windsor!) during my absence and not finding anyone at home had left a letter for MAK which consisted almost entirely of criticism of LP-S's poems and my settings of them, which interested me a good deal. It ran: 'P.S. Tom Spring Rice tells me that the discussion on Mirrors on the wall is still very vigorous. Let me take the opportunity, while waiting for my train, to pour oil on the troubled […] furnace by enunciating in my best Johnsonese my own humble opinion. I should be glad some day to know whether it agrees with yours – which I feel almost sure it does – which is cheeky of me, perhaps, but not surprising. […] It seems to me that LPS's poems are very charming in form and expression – but that – at all events in the case of 'Mirrors' and 'I built my house', they are not on poetic subjects. The fading of youth's ambitions is not subject for such easy-going charming egoism in poetry (– "bow-wow! Let me make a note of that" Cleg will say.): but it might do as a realistic prose study in University careers. As to the "appalling ghost" notion in Mirrors, one surely can't look at LPS. without suspecting him of fishing for future compliments: it's as clear as noon day that he will be a dear old composite photograph of Liszt, Leo XIII and Gladstone by the time he's ninety; and he has no excuse for pretending he doesn't know this when he's got his picturesque

> Quaker mamma with him in a beautiful house that was built to his desire ages before he was born. I believe that poetry is made of seeing things from the outset as they are and not of trying to get up a vein of melancholy on the subject of indefinite early ambition […] Cleg's music to his words puzzles me. He's rather put out (though he avoids the subject) because I told him that he didn't always declaim them right and made the general effect far too gloomy: but I believe that what's the matter is that he isn't inspired by the poems at all, but only ambitiously excited by his admiration of LPS. It's curious how differently and how firmly he writes when a poem has really got into his mind instead of simply rousing his ambition: long ago his 'When I compare thee' tackles formidable difficulties of declamation and melodic flow with apparent ease: and quite recently his 'weep you no more' made me feel that life would always be worth living if one always knew that there was someone who could do that. Meantime he continues to be a very severe pupil (I hope his criticisms don't produce quite the same effect of suicidal depression on you as they do on me!) – but I feel as if I was beginning to make progress in the art of conveying "tips" to him without getting my ears boxed; and I hope that you will understand that he has no more thorough admirer and no firmer believer in his genius than I am. Appearances have sometimes been against me: and a letter never does as well as a conversation, so *please* don't let Cleg take this chaff seriously – Hallo! I must catch my train – yours sincerely, Donald Tovey.'[31]

Beneath this Kelly wrote:

> I have copied this letter out because it will be very interesting to look back upon as a study of DFT's attitude and our relations to one another. It will also be interesting to see whether he is right about 'Mirrors' and 'Fulfilment'. At present I feel as though they represent my work at its best and I don't think he is right as to their being uninspired (that is to say in relation to my other compositions). I put down most of this kind of criticism on his part to the habit he has of trying to find subtle reasons for a particular point of view. He seems to be much more subject to this than to the genuine musical impression in judging of novelties. The letter, however, makes for good reading![32]

Late in September Egyptologist Hugh Whitaker[33] came to talk over 'the Egyptian trip', a Nile river boat excursion to which he invited both Kelly and Maisie. This was planned for December. The Whitaker family fortune, made from the Palermo based masala trade, financed his 'digs'. As something of a romantic African adventure curtain-raiser, Kelly re-read Rider Haggard's *King Solomon's Mines*. His travel plans were now fixed: Sydney via Frankfurt, Venice and Cairo. On 4 October he cabled Bertie that he would be in Sydney in January.

On 16 October Kelly and Casals took the train to Newcastle to perform together in the splendid Georgian Westgate Road assembly rooms. For once Kelly was not nervous and found it 'a great delight' to play with Casals.[34] On the 8am train to King's Cross, Casals and Kelly read the critiques of the night before:

> On the whole they were fairly just, but one critic said a thing which I foresee will be repeated wherever it is known that I was a sculler – i.e. my playing was perhaps a little too muscular for an interpretation of Chopin. When LB read the criticisms, he said 'You'll never be able to leave that behind.'[35]

Borwick was right. Kelly shrugged it off and on 19 October bought his ticket for Sydney on the Orient line's RMS *Orontes*.

A second Haslemere concert with Casals on 22 October went so well that Kelly's confidence returned: 'Steinway had provided a beautiful piano and I felt very much at home all through the concert. Casals had a great success with his suite and my lyrics also seemed to be appreciated. Several of them e.g. Seapiece and Lament went better than I have ever played them before.' Afterwards he met the art critic Roger Fry and motored some of the party over to Guildford for tea at Fry's house. They were shown the critic's own paintings. Kelly was much taken with them[36] and later drove back with Borwick. He arranged to buy 'a charming watercolour with a background of the downs when he has finished'. He was not in sympathy with Fry's 'up to date work', however, and resisted buying anything further.[37]

Four days later he was back at Northlands to show Tovey the now completed four movements of his B minor String Trio. He was looking forward to some helpful suggestions but Tovey talked in generalities and spent the better part of their hour together playing examples from Beethoven and Brahms that outstripped Kelly, who detailed the lesson in his diaries, arguing at length against Tovey and ridiculing his teaching methods:

> the whole incident is rather typical of his habit of having to lay down some law. In this case as there wasn't one to hand he had to invent one and then when it begins to appear that it doesn't fit in with the facts he is haunted by the fear of being found to be in the wrong and has to justify what he has said by any means at his disposal. I have never known anyone to be more afflicted with 'Rechthaberei' than he is.[38] ['Rechthaberei' translates as a know-all.]

Back in London, Leonard took him to the 'Manet and the Post Impressionists' exhibition at the Grafton Galleries on 7 November. This was the first of the two historic exhibitions organised by Roger Fry. The first was a disaster and ruined his reputation. In the long run it and its successor changed the course of art. The secretary of the 1910 exhibition wrote: 'Kind people called him mad, and reminded others that his wife was in an asylum.' Cezanne's paintings were deemed childish. Virgina Woolf remembered the public reacting with rage and laughter. The critic Charles Ricketts wrote 'Why talk of the sincerity of this rubbish?'[39] Kelly was with them:

> There were a great many pictures by Gauguin, others by Van Gogh, Cézanne, Maurice Denis, Picasso and Henri Matisse. Some of the Gaugin pictures I liked pretty well and Picasso had one or two good pictures there. Taken as a whole I didn't find it very enjoyable. In most cases there was no skill (such as one is used to) shown in the brush work and the colours in Van Gogh. [...] The two pictures by Matisse seemed to be absolutely crude both in colour and drawing. A lady, who came up to Borwick, put the feelings of a great many of the public into words by saying how awful everything was – for her part she found it simply laughable, but of course one must remember what the effect of it all would be on young untrained artists and that's where the harm would come. I felt convinced from this that the room must be full of original masterpieces! No one ever talks like that of mediocrity.[40]

Shortly before he left for Sydney, Kelly gave his Trio to Borwick for comment and was dismayed when Leonard shared Tovey's opinion of it. He was unseated: 'I had no idea how miserably weak parts of the last movement were until I had to relentlessly play one bar after another. The Coda is pitiable.'[41] Notwithstanding this setback, he and Borwick went to hear Elgar conduct the Philharmonic concert in a programme of English music, including the Elgar Symphony in A flat, and with Fritz Kreisler in the premier of Elgar's Violin Concerto which had 'a colossal success'. Afterwards there was a supper party for sixty guests at Frank Schuster's house in Queen Anne Street. 'It was all very well done and with the dessert 8 men's voices struck up Elgar's part songs op. 45 from a gallery which overlooks the room. I thought most of them and especially the first and the last extremely fine.'[42]

When Kelly left on the first leg of his journey to Australia he had finalised several more songs at 34 Wimpole Street: 'March' (dated 1 January), 'Mirrors' (6 Jan), 'Fulfilment' (31 March) and 'Harvest Eve' (13 April), all to Smith's words and, at Bisham Grange: 'The Sage's Dance', words translated by Pearsall Smith from Li Tai Po (25 May): 'The Pride of Youth', words by Sir Walter Scott

(15 August) revised 3 Jan 1915; 'Away! The moor is dark beneath the moon', words by Percy Bysshe Shelley (27 August); and two to words by William Wordsworth, 'To the daisy' (4 September), and 'The Daffodils'(15 October). By this time he had formed the habit of composing at the piano.[43] He thought the B minor String Trio was complete but Tovey's notes pursued him to Australia, causing a revision. The long projected Symphony in G minor had been revived mid-year but it remained at the conceptual level.[44]

On 12 November Kelly lunched with Felix Warre at the Union Club, went to the zoo to see the polar bear's new house and to visit Venetia Stanley's donation, Launcelot, the discarded Alderley bear. He settled the household accounts with Leonard over tea and said goodbye as Borwick was due at Ridgehurst, but made the mistake of asking if he really intended to take on an American tour and to add Australia to his itinerary as Kelly wanted. The answer disturbed hum: 'I wonder whether he will come to Australia after all!' he wrote. 'I have done my best to persuade him but he has a perfect genius for getting out of things! [...] I left Victoria Station at 8.35pm and spent a miserable night on the boat as something I had eaten disagreed with me.'[45] More likely it was Borwick.

He was headed first for Frankfurt to get an answer out of Engesser: was he ready? His old teacher heard him through the Beethoven Sonata no. 2 op. 111, his *Cycle of Lyrics*, and several Chopin pieces. The Beethoven was approved but Engesser seemed reticent about the rest. Kelly was baffled.[46] He played for Golden the next day and was told he had improved, but when he asked Golden what Engesser really thought of his playing, he was told: 'Well, you know Engesser's fearfully pessimistic'. He ran into Cyril Scott in the street and invited him to lunch. Scott had just received a contract from Schott's giving him an income for three years. Kelly was jealous. He dined with Knorr and found Roger Quilter there. They played for one another. Kelly thought Quilter's pieces lightweight, but 'found him a very pleasant character'. This was followed by a dull dinner with the von Gruneliuses, at the Marwitzes but he had nowhere to go that night and was grateful. He sat through the Cäcilienverein concert in the Saalban with Mengelberg conducting and was bored, went on playing for his hosts at a number of dutifully offered dinners, and heard Scott's String Quartet in F in rehearsal with both Scott and Quilter there and thought it brilliant, writing:

> Scott prides himself on his modernity, but a work like this does nothing towards solving the problem that awaits modern music – the invention of a new kind of movement that differs from the movement in Sonata just as its movement differs from that of the suite. There is an incessant flow that I found wearisome.[47]

On his final night he got drunk with Golden and left behind a very forlorn man, an underpaid and underemployed teacher stuck in Frankfurt envious of an old friend, albeit a highly frustrated one, bound for the exotica of Venice, Egypt and Australia.

The train to Milan offered fine views of snow-clad alps, Lake Garda and Verona. At Venice he was met by Hugh Whitaker 'whose gondola conveyed us along the grand canal to his apartment in the Palazzo Tiepoletto. I was delighted with the appearance of the Palaces and especially the Ca Dora.' He bathed, lunched, and left in Whitaker's launch to pick up several ladies and, at the Fondamenta delle Zattere on the Giudecca, Lord Kitchener, where he had been lunching with historian Horatio Brown who had a house in Venice. Herbert Kitchener then held the Command of the British Forces in the Mediterranean, operating out of Malta. Earlier that year he had been in Australia to report on its defences, advising that conscription should be introduced.

> Whitaker then took us out at the rate of about 16 knots an hour to a charming little monastery surrounded by cypresses – San Francesco in Deserto. We got a lovely view from there of Burano with its leaning tower and houses all reflected in the glassy surface of the lagoon. We returned by Murano and the cemetery. It was very cold when the launch was in motion and Lord Kitchener looked very blue and did not take much interest in the views, which were very beautiful. I offered him my second coat several times (which I was not wearing) but he preferred to be Spartan and wouldn't take it. He seemed to me under the present circumstances to be the very embodiment of the 'strong silent man'.[48]

Somehow Kelly managed to practise daily and offered nightly performances to Whitaker's guests. Whitaker played the violin, which may explain his encouragement of this. The rest of the Venice episode was occupied with sightseeing – the Doge's Palace, St Mark's, the Santa Maria dei Miracoli church, San Giorgio e Paolo, the Scuola and Bartolomeo Colleoni, the Academia delle belle Arti and San Stefano. He went with Whitaker to see the land he had bought on the Giudecca. On 22 November Kelly met his sister's train. They dined with Whitaker and Horatio Brown who 'was like a university don, talkative and pleasant, with a good humoured wheezy laugh and not at all distinguished. He argued against the excellence of Egyptian things at dinner and resented the contention that Egyptian art had influenced Greek art very powerfully.'[49]

In the evening a gondola took Maisie and Kelly to board their ship for Trieste, the SS *Metcovitch*. There Casals and his wife came to see them off.[50] Cholera prevented them landing at Brindisi; they reached Alexandria on 28 November, took the train to Cairo, found Whitaker's boat luxurious, and took tea at Shepheard's Hotel with Whitaker's other boat guests, Baron Alexander Meyerdorff and his wife, Princess

Barbara Shervashidze. Though he was from a German-Baltic noble family, Meyerdorff was a Russian civil servant and politician whose parents had been personal friends of Liszt. He was to serve briefly under Aleksandr Kerensky, head of the Provisional Government that took power after the overthrow of Tzar Nicholas II.[51]

Aboard the *Cleopatra,* Whitaker's 'dahabeah', Kelly tried out the resident piano and sorted his music before taking in the obligatory sights: the Cairo Museum at once, and the next day the Great Pyramid at Giza, climbing for the view. He visited a Coptic church and Rhoda Island, which set off sketches for a set of preludes.[52] The Sultan el Hasan Mosque, the Marmaeluke Tombs, the 'Virgin's Tree', Heliopolis and New Cairo ('a horrible mushroom city like the exhibition buildings at the White City') were reached by hire drive. The Meyerdorffs and J.M. Horlick of the Coldstream Guards (and of the family that invented the ubiquitous drink) came to lunch on board and afterwards Kelly went with Horlick to the polo ground to see him exercise his four ponies. In the evening they went to the Tombs of the Khalifs in the near-dark.[53]

Whitaker, the Meyendorffs and the Kellys set sail for three weeks on the Nile on 2 December. Their dahabeah was probably a traditional passenger boat, shallow-bottomed, barge-like and usually with sails, the kind still visible on the walls of Egyptian tombs. It may also have been hired via Thomas Cook, complete with staff and victualling. Prior to the 1870s when Cook introduced the steamboat to the Nile trade, these boats were the only way tourists could negotiate the river. With competition from trains, even steam boats were too slow. The leisurely dahabeah, now fitted out for Europeans, had become the prerogative of the rich.

Kelly took in the Gaza zoo and watched the chameleons being fed. He sat about on the boat reading James Breastead's *History of Egypt* (he thought it arcane) as boats gathered for the once-a-day opening of the bridges. He bathed in the Nile while Whitaker tried to solve the problem of fresh water for themselves and the crew, watched the sun setting, read scores and worked on his compositions while Maisie accompanied Whitaker's violin. That night and most others were spent moored by the bank. It was slow going in cramped quarters and the travellers soon began to get on one another's nerves. By the end of the first week Whitaker was unsettled by the constant barrage of Debussy and Ravel. Kelly admitted that: 'I think my playing so much modern music worries him as he is always coming to tell me of some view or a sunset to be seen!'[54] Neuralgia in his right leg and lower back set in. His attempts at a cure through auto-suggestion failed.

At the Assiut Barrage, some 250 miles south of Cairo, the party disembarked, took carriages into the city and followed Whitaker into the bazaars, but once back on board Kelly returned to work, much to everyone's annoyance. He wrote apologetically:

> The question of the piano got out of the realm of unexpressed feelings when I went on deck to see the sunset. I don't wonder they

> don't like my finding my way through piece after piece ever faltering over the more difficult chords and passages, but I can't get Whitaker to consent to the piano being moved to the space at the back of his cabin aft which we call the alcove.[55]

The dahabeah proved too slow. Whitaker and his guests took the train at Girgeb for Balina and made an expedition to Abydos. By then the Meyendorffs had had enough and left for Luxor by train. Kelly didn't like the way the baroness ordered her husband about and was glad to see them go. He went back to his books, Debussy and the death of Mrs Eddy as reported in the *Weekly Times.* Twenty miles out of Luxor, the becalmed *Cleopatra* had to be rescued by a tug. The breeze that had seen the main sail raised for the first time, much to Kelly's delight, had failed. For five days Whitaker and the Kellys were stuck in Luxor. More Debussy. Even Karnak by moonlight failed to divert him and he wrote: 'I felt in rather a matter of fact frame of mind and didn't experience any of the mysterious emotions that I ought to have felt.'[56] Ladies from Theodore Davis's dahabeah stayed for tea and music. Davis was sponsoring excavations that were to prove the most important ever carried out in the Valley of the Kings. The same day the book illustrator Charles Whymper came for a week's stay on the *Cleopatra.*

On 17 December the Kellys and Whymper left on donkeys to visit Whitaker's dig. This may have been the tomb of Men-kheper-re-seneb, a high priest during the reign of Thutmose III in the Valley of the Kings, close to the great tomb of Rameses. Kelly only wrote:

> and then we saw the tombs of Rameses and Khaembat and another less interesting tomb adjoining the latter one. The sculptures in the tombs of Rameses and Khaembat are the most beautiful reliefs I have ever seen [...] We were all enthusiastic and spent quite a little while in both tombs. We lunched in the temple of Medinet Habu with Miss Rathbone and her friend Miss Clive, both of whom were spending the day there sketching.

The Kellys went on to look at the queen's tombs and the two colossi, then took a boat over the river to shop. Cleg bought a necklace, two alabaster vases and a bronze head of a cat. In the evening:

> Carter the Egyptologist came to tea and stayed to dinner and as he had told me my necklace was not genuine I took it back after dinner but kept the other three things. Carter talked a good deal about his subject and I found him most interesting. Whymper told us he was the son of a gamekeeper and that he has shown very great perseverance

> since he was dismissed from his post in the Egyptology department in setting himself up by making use of his talent for painting.[57]

Howard Carter was in fact the son of the artist Samuel Carter. Though the fake necklace was returned, Kelly went shopping in town again and this time bought a genuine antique necklace from Mohammed Mohassib, a reputable dealer based in Luxor. This survived and is now in the Nicholson Museum at the University of Sydney, along with other items bought on this trip.

With the wind too strong to sail, a visit to Davis' boat occupied the time. The Kellys performed and Davis showed his photographs and antiquities. They visited temples in the night. The *Cleopatra* had to be towed round the reach the next morning to complete the run to Luxor. Their party left for artist John E. Nicholl's dahabeah at Karnak, where the Kellys performed and the artist showed them his pictures, one of which Davis had bought. Cleg found them monotonous and kept his purse shut. This social life of the Nile touring boats mimicked life in the country houses with temple visiting replacing the English garden and house viewing and the obligatory cottage pianos making do for the Steinways. At the time Egypt was a pseudo protectorate. It had been occupied by the British since 1882. British tourists behaved as they did at home, clubbing together, the natives kept at a proper distance, their sense of entitlement intact.

On 21 December the Kellys left for the SS *Nubia*. They had been three weeks on the *Cleopatra* and Kelly wrote:

> it has not been an altogether pleasant time. Wittaker is like a selfish child and with very bad manners into the bargain. He was continually giving an exhibition of petulant temper in his dealings with the servants and whenever anything went wrong whether it was the soup that was cold or the tug that had run aground – he would call in John, the dragoman [interpreter or guide] and abuse him in the presence of us all. His only means of diversion, as far as I could gather, were games of patience and inspecting his large jewellery collection. MAK and Whymper were just as irritated with him as I was. I regret having accepted his hospitality as I feel that I shall never be able to either like or respect him. The best point I noticed about him was an undoubted ability to, at all events, seem to take chaff well. His selfishness was the thing that worried me most. MAK the other morning overheard him giving orders that she and Whymper should be called at quarter to six in the future because she was at the moment in the bath when he wanted it himself! I think the only cure would be a candid friend – unfortunately as his guest one is not in a position to undertake the task.

He consoled himself by adding that sunshine and comfort made the trip otherwise enjoyable. He opened Robert Curzon's 1849 *Visits to the Monasteries of the Levant* and composed as he paced the deck heading for Edfu. Their party spent the night at the luxury Cataract Hotel at Assouan (Aswan) – one of the settings used in the 1978 film of Agatha Christie's *Death on the Nile*. They left the next morning on donkeys for Shelal and the island of Philae, left exposed by low water levels. They rowed out to the west end of the dam, which was being heightened some 20ft. Cleg found the scenery more interesting than in any other part of the Nile and went on alone to Elephantine.

On Christmas Day the Kellys were up before dawn to see the two temples at Abu Simbel by candlelight before the SS *Britain* left at 8.30am. The four colossi and the Osiride in the first hall seen in the half-light impressed them deeply and the former reminded Cleg 'of the great bronze Buddha at Kamakura in their repose.'[58] At Wadi Halfa Cleg walked the town, returned to the ship and spent the evening copying out 'March', 'The Sage's Dance' and four other songs to send to Gervase Elwes. Curiously, he makes no mention of anything to do with Christmas.

The day after that, in need of escape from the others, he took a sailboat through the black rocks of the lower second cataract and up to Abusir rock, the crew's faces and outlines reminding him of reliefs in the tombs. He climbed the rock for its views over the desert and the river to the north:

> I was conscious of being far away from civilization a feeling which the desert and the wilderness of the cataract stimulated, and as my mind was full of musical ideas (mostly concerning my set of studies for the piano) I passed an exceptionally happy day.' The illusion of being at peace and far from civilisation was shattered when he was invaded, first by drummers and singers who would not leave him alone, surrounding him with what he felt was deafening noise, and then by boys who rode bladder skins down the rapids and demanded money for a demonstration he hadn't asked for. Kelly refused to pay up and had to retreat to his boat.

He left the *Britain* at Shelal and went on to rejoin Maisie, Horlicks and Whymper at Luxor's Winter Palace Hotel. He was still mentally composing his studies and the piano sonata in F minor. Arthur Weigall, then Chief Inspector of Antiquities for Upper Egypt and based at Luxor, invited the Kellys to join him, his sister Mrs Rutter and 'an officer from the Coldstream Guards named Lawrence who was about 4 years younger than I am'. (Not, alas T.E. Lawrence.) They saw three new tombs – Rekhmara, Neb Amen and Ken Amen and returned to the tombs of Rameses and Khaembat, which Cleg had particularly wanted to see again.

> On the way back I had an interesting talk with Weigall about art generally and more especially Egyptian art. He laid stress on the tender side of the Egyptian character which came out in work such as the tombs of Rameses and Khaembat contain, and he quoted a very beautiful phrase from a hymn to Aton as an illustration of the same thing in literature 'Thy love make the hands to faint'. As he explained the work in the tombs he pointed out some details which proved that the stiff looking figures of Gods and other religious emblems were forced upon the sculptors of each generation as a fixed convention, so that one must not suppose this kind of work to represent the artist's point of view. Miss Rathbone lunched with MAK and myself at the Winter Palace Hotel and in the afternoon I paid a last visit with Miss Rathbone to the Temple of Luxor.[59]

Whitaker gave the Kellys tea on the *Cleopatra* later that day and came to see them off:

> and asked me to send him back my monument ticket when I left Egypt so that he or his guests should be saved the expense of buying additional ones! As the Antiquities department make a point of asking one to destroy the ticket when one has finished with it and as Whitaker apparently is in with many of the senior Egyptologists I thought it very indiscreet of him to announce his intention of cheating the department of a few pounds quite openly in the presence of MAK and Whymper. It seems curious too that a man who is as rich as he is should want to save a little money at the risk of being prosecuted for fraud! He seemed to think it unfriendly of me when I refused to send it to him and explained that he didn't see why he should have to pay a pound for every one of his guests who came to stay with him. MAK suggested that if they had money enough to travel to Egypt that they might probably be able to afford a pound from their own pockets! I wondered, when I saw him in the hotel last night, whether I hadn't formed rather an exaggerated view of his faults, as he was very pleasant and friendly to us both, but the above episode of the monument tickets is a thing which I imagine most people would find it difficult to put up with in their friends. A.E.P. Weigall travelled down in the sleeping-car train with us to Cairo and we had dinner together in the Restaurant car.[60]

On 1 January 1911 he wrote: 'I seemed to take it for granted that I shall get through a great amount of composition this year.' The last two days in Cairo were spent at the zoo and on an excursion to Sakkara. At the former Kelly discovered a bird 'that looked exactly like the Lory in Alice in Wonderland – which I had hitherto always regarded a figment of the imagination'.[61] At the latter he entered a pyramid for the first time, afterwards taking donkeys to the Great Pyramid. A final visit to the Cairo Museum and the city mosques, farewelling Maisie as she entrained for Port Said to catch a ship for Marseilles, and a visit to the tombs of the Kalifs ended with a walk to Cooks to ask for news of his own ship. He found there was no sign of it and went that evening to hear Verdi's *Falstaff* at the opera house. He had been looking forward to this as he didn't know the opera. He found the music undistinguished and the text adaptation upsetting.

On 5 January 1911 he reached Suez and embarked on the SS *Orontes*. He was about to turn 30, his competitive rowing days were done, his pleasant city and country life as an amateur pianist was at an end and he was turning his face to the challenge of making the transition to life as a professional by heading half a world away from his target audience to make his debut in the country of his boyhood. He was coming home in order to leave home once and for all.

CHAPTER NINE

THE SYDNEY DEBUT 1911

When he shipped out for Sydney in the New Year, Kelly had no idea that he was heading into a storm that would threaten to capsize his new career. He joined in the familiar shipboard games, read, studied the scores of Elgar's Violin Concerto and Debussy's *La Mer*, which he much admired, and rewrote his own B minor string trio in the light of Tovey's searing comments. He was shortly blown off course by three unexpected encounters. The first was with Colonel Hubert Foster, a friend of Bertie's and then Director of Military Science at the University of Sydney, who lent him Norman Angell's *The Great Illusion.*[1] Cleg was deeply impressed by what turned out to be one of the most influential books of the times, writing in his diary that: 'It is a very interesting treatise on the futility of modern warfare and disposes very effectively with most of the current talk of the necessity and moral value of warfare.'[2] Long discussions with Foster carried over into a hiking holiday together. Kelly was forced to seriously assess his own role in what was now a looming war.

The second encounter was with the Australian flautist John Lemmone, Melba's friend, manager and associate artist, who Kelly regarded as the only saving grace of an amateurish after-dinner concert he felt obliged to suffer through a week into the trip. Kelly set about composing a work for him, the five-movement Serenade for flute, harp, horn and strings, which Lemmone described as of 'transcendental beauty' and which would shortly feature in Kelly's Sydney concerts.[3] It took nineteen days to compose and he later wrote:

> I am not accustomed to being able to work quickly. It is not very original, perhaps, but covers new ground as far as I am concerned. I feel that originality will come to me after steady work in making use of ideas and working in a variety of forms so as never to cover the same ground twice over. Of course when ideas come in greater numbers I shall be able to select what I want and reject those that savour of outside influences.[4]

By 'outside influences', he implied Tovey.

The third encounter was with Lord Richard Nevill, a friend of both his brothers, who came aboard at Melbourne to warn Kelly of a running scandal involving them, their wives and the governor-general, William Ward, the 2nd Earl of Dudley. Nevill was Dudley's chamberlain, the officer in charge of his household. He reported that John Norton, the owner of the scandal sheet *Truth*, had been gunning for the extravagant governor-general and had made use of unfounded rumours that one of the Kelly brothers was divorcing his wife, naming Dudley as co-respondent. Kelly had heard nothing. He now had to face an awkward time as Bertie's guest and would have to ride out whatever storm blew up, loyal to both brothers if he was to find an audience. In fact, Norton's aim was to force Dudley's resignation, in which he succeeded.[5] His motive for dragging the Kellys into his poisonous web was political. His method was the smear which he had already applied to the first prime minister, several previous governors-general, an Anglican archbishop and the royals.

Cleg Kelly was on deck as his ship steamed into Sydney Harbour. He was struck by the number of new houses on the foreshores of Middle Harbour, Watson's Bay and Point Piper. Bertie Kelly was on the dock. Ethel was in India, escaping Norton. The difficult Sydney summer, brooding and sultry, was in full force. Glenyarrah beckoned. Cleg's Steinway, already installed after its journey out from 34 Wimpole Street, was put to use and the old rapport returned. They dined at the exclusive Australian Club and took in Edward German's operetta *Tom Jones*, then in its first Sydney production at the Criterion Theatre.

They joined Bertie's holidaying children, 6-year-old Beatrice, 4-year-old Tom and 3-year-old Patricia, together with their nurse, for four days at Medlow Bath's Hydro Majestic Hotel in the Blue Mountains, a deeply nostalgic reprise of Kelly's own holidays there. As the weather closed in the brothers went on talking and playing music together in their sitting room. With the rain easing they donned waterproofs to tramp into the spectacular Kanimbla Valley.

At this time Bertie was a Sydney Municipal Council alderman and an officer in the Australian Intelligence Corps. He had influence as well as social and musical connections and was quick to put them at Kelly's disposal. A committee member of the Philharmonic Society, he played first violin in Roberto Hazon's Amateur Orchestral Society and entertained lavishly, his circle including Nellie Melba. At Paling's music warehouse Kelly was introduced to the conductor of the new Sydney Symphony Orchestra and the Royal Sydney Philharmonic Society, Joseph Bradley, who had been deputy conductor and organist of the Hallé Orchestra in Manchester.[6] He found himself accepting an offer to appear as a soloist with the SSO in the Sheffield Choir concert scheduled for 17 June at the Sydney Town Hall. It was discussed over lunch at the Sydney Yacht Squadron where Bertie was a member. He persuaded Cleg to strike while the iron was hot and drove him out to Lewisham in his Albion to meet the violinist Henry Staell, who was in hospital there after surgery for appendicitis. Staell not only led Bertie's private string quartet, but Roberto Hazon's Sydney Amateur Orchestral Society and Ferdinand Aengenheyster's Pleyel Classical Concerts Orchestra.[7]

Willie's influence, on the other hand, was not to be had: he was at first too busy as the Liberal member for Wentworth in the young Federal Parliament, then located nearly 530 miles south in Melbourne, but he soon used his interest in defence as an excuse to travel to London, conveniently avoiding *Truth* and Norton.[8] He attended the coronation of George V and was at the Imperial Conference in mid-year.

In town, Kelly found himself alone much of the time and took to walking the old familiar trails around Woollahra and Rose Bay, distressed at the loss of a cherished landscape but composing as he went:

> I did a good deal of work at the first movement of my B min String Trio, but during the latter half of my walk my mind was filled with reminiscences of the walks and picnics we used to enjoy twenty to twenty-five years ago in the woods which are now so fast disappearing.[9]

At Bondi he hired 'some bathing things and joined the surf bathers'. Body surfing was still new; it was to be four years before Hawaii's Duke Kahanamoku demonstrated surf-boarding at Freshwater.[10] Later, Kelly rowed alone across the harbour and was reminded 'of old yachting days, both in the Thisbe and Electra and both that recollection and the extraordinary growth of the town whose suburbs are invading many spots that used to be virgin bush in my early days made me feel rather sad'.[11]

Kelly was still nursing an injury to the little finger of his right hand, damaged in a game of deck cricket just after leaving Colombo. With his debut still hovering, its increasing stiffness was a worry. He visited a Dr Charles MacLaurin, who recommended massage. The swelling in the second joint was no better. He tried auto suggestion. Still no response. MacLaurin then forbade piano playing. He was ignored. On 22 February Cleg and Bertie inspected the YMCA, the Town Hall, Centennial Hall and St James' Hall looking for a suitable venue. They settled on St James'. Cleg went on to Palings to see an agent, H.N. Southwell, to discuss his giving three recitals in the winter.

In early autumn he was back at the Hydro Majestic at Medlow with his family, exploring the Jenolan Caves and mentally composing as he walked the grottos and mountain tracks. Ethel's return from India sent them all bucketing out to meet her ship in a hired launch with the children excitedly shouting an endless 'Mummy'. At Glenyarrah Cleg tried to ingratiate himself with her, playing briefly only to find she was 'not naturally musical'.[12] He listened attentively to her Indian anecdotes.

A year later these appeared as *Frivolous Peeps at India*,[13] a book much ridiculed by Norton who was still pursuing Willie in *Truth*.[14] Bertie, Ethel and Cleg held an urgent discussion: what to do about Willie?

The fragile rapport with his family was finally shattered when he was told in no uncertain terms that his relentless piano playing made it impossible for the children to sleep. He had to move on and soon. As a peace offering he hired a small launch, assembled family and friends and went up-river to see the Parramatta Hundred, in which forty-one scullers competed for a £100 prize.[15] It provoked a dim memory of being taken, aged about 4, 'to see Beach race Hanlan' at the same spot.[16] This was probably the second match between the Australian Bill Beach and the Canadian Ned Hanlan at Parramatta. The first was for the professional sculling world championship in August 1884 when Beach took the title.[17]

Rehearsals at Glenyarrah went on in spite of the now subdued piano practice. Bradley had decided on the Beethoven Piano Concerto, no. 4 in G major, op. 58, for the fifth concert of the Festival of the Empire series to be given at the Sydney Town Hall on 17 June. The work was new to Kelly. The challenge was to get it up in time for what was to be his first Australian appearance as a professional performer. At Paling's a few days later he was interviewed by the former music critic of the *Daily Telegraph,* George de Carios Rego. He was obliged to take tea with him and to listen to his daughter Iris play before they could begin. The article duly appeared two days later on the same page as another announcing the impending arrival of Leonard Borwick for a series of concerts.[18] Kelly's own Festival appearance and St James' Hall performances were also listed, with the addition that he was to give three piano recitals and an orchestral concert in London in February 1912. Shortly afterwards he had his first chance to assess Bradley and the SSO in a Wagner concert at the Town Hall. They were deemed competent enough to entrust with his musical future.

On 2 April he escorted Ethel to dine with the Dudleys at Government House, Kelly sitting between Lady Dudley and Adeline, Duchess of Bedford, and playing for the company afterwards.[19] The duchess later lent him *Universities and National Life* by the then secretary of state for war, Richard Burdon Haldane.[20] Quite unusually, he made a note of several passages in his diary. Haldane, like William James, advocated the strength of the will and a single-minded passion for excellence. Kelly wrote:

> I find it very inspiring to find one's own half-blind impulses corroborated as my own were in reading these and other passages. From being uncertain instincts they become at once part of the bedrock of one's character and a new limit is transcended (to quote the book's phraseology).[21]

Later that month Glenyarrah played host to thirty guests for a private concert, a preview of the series now planned for July-August. Bertie, Staell, Grieves, Ornstein and Carter were to perform the Brahms Quintet in F major op. 88. Cleg was to follow it with eight Chopin works. He was not happy with the outcome and wrote: 'A sort of restraint descended upon me with the first note and I never got hold of my audience.'[22] On the spur of the moment he accepted Colonel Foster's suggestion that they go hiking together. Their goal, Mount Kosciuszko – the highest peak in Australia – was reached on 17 April. Nine days were spent immersed in a majestic landscape and in the morality and the practicality of war.

Back at Glenyarrah he resumed practice and score reading, had new publicity shots taken, worked on his String Trio in B minor yet again, rehearsed with his string players, and rowed Bertie out to look at the *Kainan Maru*, a ship of the first Japanese Antarctic expedition then wintering in Sydney Harbour. He thought it small for its purpose and noted 'a dog with a face like a wolf' looking at them over the bulwark, the sole survivor of its dog team.[23] On 10 May there was a meeting with his agent, H.N.Southwell, to make arrangements for the debut concerts. Kelly was as uneasy about him as he was about Ethel and the situation at Glenyarrah.

At Nicholson's music store he found there were no practice rooms for hire and no Steinways. He was promised the first available. He attempted to shift to the Wentworth Hotel but there was no immediate vacancy. He would have to 'make a nuisance' of himself at Glenyarrah for the time being.[24] By this time his sister-in-law had had enough and finally said so: 'Ethel hauled me over the coals at lunch (in quite a good humoured way) for my bad manners to guests in the house and especially to Miss Wynne who stayed here about a month ago.'[25] His thirtieth birthday on 29 May was celebrated with a small dinner party with Bertie's family and their friends, at which he broke his resolution not to drink. He regretted this, resumed work on the B minor string trio and, sober, finished it two days later.

On 6 June he rehearsed the Beethoven concerto with the SSO in the Lyceum hall but had to make-do with 'a wretched instrument that happened to be in the hall' when Nicholson's failed to deliver the promised Steinway on time.[26] He immediately dropped Nicholson's and went to Paling's with Bertie to order a Steinway, the same size as his own, for use when he moved into the Wentworth Hotel. He went on to see Southall to arrange advertising of his own recitals and his appearance with the Sheffield Choir. Still at Glenyarrah, he was in a fever, practising in the room below the nursery for as long as he dared and copying parts for his string trio at a table carried down to the tennis lawn and wrote:

> I am beginning to be alarmed at the close proximity of my concerts. I have never taken on such a large task as a series of 3 piano recitals before and as about a third of the things are new to me I am not feeling particularly bright at the prospect.[27]

With the move to the Wentworth on 10 June his asthma attacks returned. In order to sleep he self-prescribed Himrid's Asthma Powder, with some success. Ethel, now reconciled, invited him to lunch at Glenyarrah and to play for her guests, including Lady Dudley and the Duchess of Bedford, but he found that no one was particularly musical and that it was uphill work.

The Sheffield Choir arrived the same day on the Canadian steamer *Zealandia*. As it reached the Heads it was met by a 'fair sized fleet',[28] its steamers carrying 250 members of the Yorkshire Society, the Newtown Brass Band, the boys of St Andrew's Cathedral choir, members of the Royal Philharmonic Society, the Amateur Orchestral Society, the Sydney Liedertafel, a citizen's committee, the general public and the Acting Premier. On shore there were speeches, cheering and 'a great reception'.[29] In a fit of Empire enthusiasm, the *Daily Telegraph* declared: 'People may say what they will about the relations existing between the colonies and the Mother-country … it is impossible for men to argue that sentiment is dead, and that the dream of a great, united English-speaking race is gone.'[30] The 220–strong Sheffield Choir opened its Sydney season with *Messiah* at the Town Hall, its visit the centrepiece of the *First Musical Festival of the Empire,*[31] a touring propaganda exercise that came with the backing of the British Government, one of many attempts to shore up the failing enthusiasm for Empire. Kelly found the double basses of the SSO very shaky but thought that Sheffield Chior 'sang magnificently throughout and (that) it was the greatest delight to hear such clear part-singing and such clear pronunciations of words. What a glorious work!' The third concert in the series which included Elgar's *Dream of Gerontius*, made 'a deep impression'.[32]

On morning of the 16th he rehearsed at the Town Hall with an unsure SSO. Surprisingly, the piano was placed behind the podium, masking the soloist's importance. With Bertie's help he had a small platform placed in front of the first violins but it was a make-do situation. Later at the Wentworth he gave a tea party for a soloist with Sheffield Choir, Lady Norah Noel; her brother, Lord Camden, and his own social circle. He thought Noel's performances mediocre but he needed her support. The Sheffield Choir's concert that night opened with *Pan – A symphonic choric ode* by the festival's organiser, Dr Charles Harriss. Kelly was outraged, writing that: 'This was one of the most vulgar compositions I have ever heard and I felt that every bar I listened to entered into my soul like poison.'[33] Any thought of getting Harriss' backing was dropped.

The all-Beethoven programme of the 17th consisted of the Leonora no. 3, the Piano Concerto in G major no. 4 and the Ninth Symphony. He wrote: 'I felt pretty well at home in my Concerto and on the whole it went pretty well', and that was all.[34] The press gave this first concert wide coverage and went overboard in praise of 'the choir and the SSO. *The Sydney Morning Herald* thought the soloist brought needed lightness, technical precision and sympathy' to the op. 58 and had a success 'recognised in enthusiastic recalls'.[35] The *Evening News* thought: 'Mr Kelly's musicianly work throughout was greatly admired for its grace, positiveness, and brilliance.'[36] None of it added up to much, though local papers across-country reprinted the reports.

Meantime Southall, the over-worked agent of both Kelly and the Sheffield Choir, failed to confirm one of the St James' Hall bookings. Kelly was deeply offended and immediately went to Nicholson's to engage George S. Hoburn at an extortionate two guineas a concert. He went off to hear the Austral quartet at St James'. Everything sounded quite dead and lifeless and, he wrote: 'I don't fancy the prospect of battling with it next Tuesday'.[37]

On 2 July *The Sydney Sunday Times* was the first to advertise Kelly's six concerts in the St James' Hall, Phillip Street, to commence on the 4th. Three solo recitals would be followed by a concert for small orchestra and conclude with two chamber music concerts, assisted by the harpist Grace B. Barnett, with Henry Staell, John Lemmone, W.J. Grieves, T.H. Kelly, Bryce Carter and Guido Gervasoni. On the day of the first concert Kelly tested the piano at St James' Hall, went on to Nicholson's to check ticket sales and returned to his hotel for bed rest. At 8.15pm he went up to the platform to find a meagre audience. His programme included the Liszt arrangement of the Bach Prelude and Fugue in A minor for organ, two Scarlatti sonatas (in C minor and G major), the Waldstein Sonata, and what were classed as the 'novelties' of the night: Scriabin's three preludes in C, G, and E flat minor from op. II, and Kelly's own Studies in E flat major and in C minor. It ended with the Henselt Etude de Salon in E major op. 5, Liszt's Study in F sharp minor Gnomen-Reigen, for which Kelly was recalled again and again, three Brahms works, and Schumann's Etudes Symphoniques op. 13, with an encore of his Des Abends. He wrote: 'I didn't play badly on the whole and the little F ma [major] Romance of Brahms went better than I have ever been able to do it in practice, but the chill and reserve of a quarter-filled hall was very difficult to overcome.'[38]

The *Bulletin* was light hearted:

> Pianist F.S. Kelly's 'Lament' (his own composition) was booked for Saturday night, otherwise it might have been appropriate to his first recital, when a well-scrubbed platform slowly dried up round his piano legs. The piano – evidently his own, since it fails to praise its maker in a large printed advt, – is a perfect instrument, with a tone of velvety thunder and honey sweetness. Pianist Kelly himself is so quiet in his manner that he might as well be dead until he touches the keys. He slips across the platform, a slim figure with a shapely, close-cropped head, the black thatch so short that there isn't a hair left over to nod in musical frenzy on his brow. His square piano stool wheezed with asthmatic creaks, having probably caught cold in its joints, from getting its feet wet on the damp floor. […] He is one of

> the most delightful persons at a piano that this city has listened to for a long time. He lifts the sombre chords of Bach, and puts them on a short cut to susceptibilities of the multitude – if the multitude hadn't stayed away and left St James's Hall half empty at the first recital. A sprinkling of the Well Dressed hugged their fur-edged cloaks close to bediamonded bosoms.

John Lemmone, Bertie and Ethel were in the audience, Ethel in gold shoes and 'a gorgeous Japanese silk cloak'.[39]

In a much more serious vein, the *Sydney Morning Herald* categorised the debut as 'a classic entertainment' and 'a formidable programme, which he rendered entirely without recourse to the printed page – a mnemonic feat of no mean order – he proved himself an accomplished artist.'[40] Buried in a report on vice-regal goings-on, balls, the polo, and the lack of crowds and cheering as the Sheffield Choir left on the *Zealandia,* Sydney gossip columnist 'Phoebe' wrote: 'Mr F.S. Kelly is a musician, there is no doubt of that. He has a dreamy, sensitive face, and looks like somebody, professional in the artistic sense, yet with a dash of the man about town, rather a fascinating mixture.'[41] Kelly, puzzled, began to doubt himself: 'All the criticisms of my last night's concert were good and yet I don't feel somehow that I have any success with the rank and file here.'[42]

Sydney's entertainment scene that month included Sousa's sixty-piece brass band, French mezzo Antonia Dolores, the Sydney Symphony Orchestra, several other debut concerts, the Austral String Quartet, and a Welte reproducing piano demonstration concert sponsored by Nicholson's. Add to all this sporting fixtures and orchestra-accompanied public skating and the wonder is that Kelly got an audience at all, particularly after Leonard Borwick arrived in town. His first concert was given on 3 August, with four more in the next ten days.[43] Kelly's last two concerts were scheduled for 4 and 8 August. Though these were chamber music concerts, not solo recitals, Borwick's predictable draw was bound to suck most of the oxygen out of other concert rooms.

The *Sun* ran a long article on Kelly on 8 July but he searched the press in vain for the notices of his recitals with extracts from press criticisms that he had asked his agent to arrange. Holburn, it turned out, had forgotten. He spent time at Nicholson's trying to get a replacement for the creaky stool. He lunched with Colonel Foster and Professor Barraclough at the Australian Club, walked round Mrs Macquarie's Point, read poems by Dorothea Mackellar, slept, ate his dinner and set off for St James' Hall. His programme included the Bach Italian Concerto (BWV971), Beethoven's op. 111 piano sonata, his own *Cycle of Lyrics*, and several works by Chopin, Brahms and Schumann. The audience that awaited him was larger and warmer than for the debut. He began with perfect composure, but 'a silly nervousness took possession' of him halfway through the Bach and never left. It manifested as 'several ridiculous technical slips – sometimes in quite easy places', yet the audience was enthusiastic.[44] The critics were merely polite.[45]

The third recital on 13 July was advertised with eye-catching quotes from the reviews interspersed with Kelly's name in duplicate. [46] Holburn had done his job at last. The third and final solo recital programme for 13 July was another marathon, included Mozart's Fantasia.in C minor (K.475), Beethoven's Piano Sonata no. 4 in E flat, op. 7, Debussy's *Masques*, *La cathédrale engloutie*, *La Fille aux cheveux de lin*, and *L'isle joyeuse*, Bach's Preludes and Fugues in F sharp and C sharp major from Book I of *The Well-Tempered Clavier*, the Gluck-Brahms Gavotte in A major, Mozart's Menuet in D major (K.355) and Gigue in G major (K.574), Chopin's Barcarolle in F sharp major, op. 60, the Study in E flat minor op. 10 no. 6, the Nocturne in C minor op. 48 no. 1, the Prelude no. 23 in F major, op. 28, and his Scherzo op. 39 no. 3 in C sharp minor. The audience was small. Kelly blamed wet weather. He got flustered in the Chopin pieces but the Debussy went well and he relaxed. At the end of the concert there was 'a good deal of applause ... in spite of the Scherzo having gone badly'. [47] The reviews were warm if perfunctory.[48]

Two days before his fourth concert a letter from Borwick announced that he was unable to join Kelly on the proposed Japanese holiday. Kelly's plans were now obsolete. He began to think of travel that would take him north along the east coast of Australia and to Java.[49] The programme for the concert, which Kelly conducted, consisted of the Mendelssohn Octet played by Staell (violin), Grieves (violin), F. Mowat Carter (second violin), S.R. White (second violin), Bertie (viola), Hill (viola), Carter (cello) and Miss Brenda Deloitte[50] (cello). It was followed by the Grieg's *Holberg Suite*, Kelly's Flute Serenade for flute, strings, horn and harp op. 7, with John Lemmone as the flautist, and ended with Mozart's *Eine kleine Nachtmusik.* Kelly thought the Octet went fairly well, the *Holberg Suite* was 'not very satisfactory' but 'the Mozart didn't go half badly'.[51] The press murmured careful praise with *The Bulletin* describing Kelly's conducting style as 'a quiet beat, more like a pat'.[52]

There was another clash with Holburn on the 29th. Ten days before, Kelly had handed his own article on Borwick to Holburn who said he could have it published in the *Sydney Morning Herald,* the *Telegraph* and the evening papers. Instead, Holburn had only taken it to the afternoon *Sun* which meant the morning papers had no interest in republishing it. Kelly was left with 'a feeling of intense irritation' eased only by an afternoon on the umpire's boat with Bertie at the world championship sculling contest between Richard Arnst and Harry Rawson on the Parramatta river before an estimated crowd of 80,000.[53] The following evening he went to the office of the *Daily Telegraph* to see Paddy Norton, one of its music critics, in an attempt to reinstate his Borwick piece, but without success.

On 1 August Bertie and Cleg met the Melbourne train to welcome Borwick. At the Town Hall the next day Borwick spent an hour trying the piano. Cleg realised he was playing with more force and abandon, qualities essential for a popular success. He was moving away. Borwick's first recital, however, drew a disappointingly small if enthusiastic audience of a mere 600.

Kelly's fifth concert at St James' Hall on 4 August drew only 200. The players were the Kelly, Staell, Grieves, Bertie and Carter. On the programme was Brahms's G major violin sonata, Kelly's String Trio in B minor and Dvorak's Quintet for piano and strings. Kelly's Trio went well 'but the first movement dragged, and in this and in the other movements Staell was frequently out of tune'.[54] The press was as measured as before with the *Sydney Morning Herald* reporting that the new trio 'proved a clever and very intricate composition, exceedingly difficult to render, and really wonderfully well given, all three artists coming in with spirit, sympathy, and smoothness'.[55] The conductor Chris Latham recorded this work in 2019 and describes it as 'the rarest of all beasts, an Australian romantic "*War Horse*".'[56] Kelly went on rewriting it until the 17 June 1914, when it was performed by the English quartet at the Grange. Frank Bridge was its violist. Pablo Casals, Jelly d'Arànyi and violist Lionel Tertis would later perform it at a memorial concert.

The Kellys were at Borwick's second appearance at the Town Hall on 7 August, when the audience was not much bigger than for the first. Borwick was uneasy about it. There was a matinee the next day, and this time the audience had doubled. Kelly was delighted, particularly with the interpretation of the Waldstein sonata. He hurried down to the artists' room at the interval to congratulate his friend before leaving to prepare for his own appearance that night. This was his final concert with Staell, Grieves, Carter and Bertie on stage. The programme consisted of the Beethoven String Quartet in C, op. 59 no. 3, Bach's Partita in B flat, and the Brahms Quintet for piano and strings. Again, the audience was small. Kelly thought it a success and that he had not heard this group play so well before. His own performance was another matter. He was put out by the heaviness of the piano and 'never felt myself comfortably at home'. [57] *Truth* had the last word: 'But how can a pianist with a normal head of hair expect to become a prophet in his own country? He should court fame by calling himself Kellyorino, and growing his herbage like an infuriated Turk's head.'[58] Kelly settled his account with Nicholson's shortly afterwards and was billed for six concerts, fees for players, hall, staff and advertising 'in an amateurish attempt at presenting an account … It was a perfect nightmare'.[59] His total debt was £82.0.0. Today, at the most conservative estimate, this amounts to some A$10,000, or just under £6,000. His debut had not come cheap.[60]

With his own concerts behind him, Kelly turned his attention to entertaining the Borwicks, hiring a launch and showing off Sydney Harbour, ending with dinner at Glenyarrah.[61] He was at Borwick's fourth concert with Colonel Foster. It went well, in spite of the hall being only about a third full. The next day Kelly hired a motor, picked up Borwick at the Australia Hotel, took the ferry across the harbour

Above left: Thomas Herbert Kelly (left), William Henry Kelly (centre), Frederick Septimus Kelly (right). Circa 1893.

Above right: Eton Rowing VIII 1899. Eton College Archives.

Below: Postcard 1903.

The Olympic Regatta, Henley, 31 July 1908. Final: Leander for Britain about to be flagged winner over Belgium. Kelly 2nd from right.

Above: Olympic 1908 rowing team, Leander Club lawns. Kelly, standing, left, is wearing his gold medal.

Left: Maisie and Cleg Kelly's home – Bisham Grange, Marlow.

Above: Kelly with Bertie's children, his nieces Beatrice and Patricia and nephew Tom, at Glenyarrah, Sydney, 1911. The children are holding presents bought for them by Cleg on the journey back.

Below left: Frederick Septimus Kelly, charcoal drawing by Singer Sargent, completed 21 February 1914 at his Tite Street studio. Dated 1915. Owned by Kevin Gordon. Email: kevingordonportraits.com

Below right: Mary Australie Kelly, Kelly's sister, charcoal drawing by Singer Sargent. Dated 1915. Owned by Kevin Gordon. Email: kevingordonportraits.com

Above left: Kelly's medals were sold at auction by Dix Noon Webb, London, 12 December 2012. L to R: Distinguished Service Cross, G.V.R., hallmarks for London 1916, in its Garrard & Co. case of issue; 1914–15 Star (Ty. Lieut. F. S. Kelly, D.S.C., R.N.V.R.) listed *London Gazette* 6 September 1916; British War and Victory Medals, M.I.D. oak leaf (Lt. Commr. F. S. Kelly, R.N.V.R.), together with London Olympics 1908 commemorative medallion, generally extremely fine (condition). $6.500.

Above right: Kellys' grave, Martinsart British War Cemetery, Somme, France. Photo: Martin Cross.

Kelly with 1908 Olympics team. Leander Club, Henley.

Above left: F.S.Kelly. 1903 in Balliol College War Memorial Book 1914–1919 Vol 1 (Balliol College 1924).

Above right: Aboard the troop carrier *Grantully Castle* bound for Gallipoli. Rupert Brooke left, standing. Kelly is seated front right, cross legged. King's College Library Cambridge UK.

Daily Graphic.
23.11.16.

WELL-KNOWN SCULLER KILLED.

Capt. T. S. Kelly, R.N.V.R., one of the best-known amateur scullers of the day, who has been killed in action. The gallant officer was also an accomplished musician, and prior to the war gave a series of pianoforte recitals.

Death notice, *Daily Graphic*, UK, 23 November 1916.

Above left: Jelly d'Arányi, violinist, who loved Kelly and for whom he composed. Date unknown.

Above right: At Oxford circa 1901. Balliol College archives.

Royal Naval Division band 1916. Bernard Freyberg in light trousers, centre. Kelly is on his right.

Above left: Donald Francis Tovey with Sophie Weisse c.1900. Photo: Frederick Hollyer. Victoria and Albert Museum London.

Above right: Leonard Borwick. *Argus* (Melbourne, Australia) 21 August 1911.

Above left: Memorial Cross erected by Kelly's sister Maisie, at Marlow, UK.

Above right: Leander Club Olympic team medal 1908.

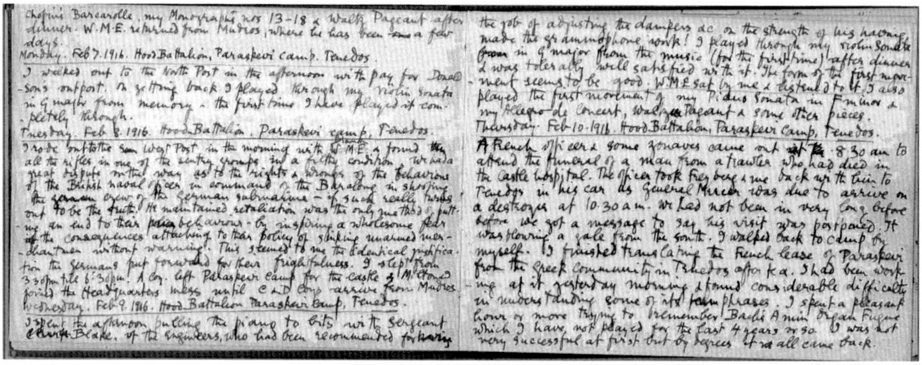
Chopin's Barcarolle, my Monographs nos 13–18 & Waltz Pageant after dinner. W.M.E. returned from Mudros, where he has been a few days.
Monday. Feb 7. 1916. Hood Battalion, Paraskevi camp. Tenedos.
I walked out to the North Post in the afternoon with pay for Donaldson's outpost. On getting back I played through my violin Sonata in G major from memory – the first time I have played it completely through.
Tuesday. Feb 8. 1916. Hood Battalion. Paraskevi camp, Tenedos.
I rode out to the West Post in the morning with W.M.E. & found all the rifles in one of the sentry groups in a filthy condition. We had a great dispute on the way as to the rights & wrongs of the behaviour of the British naval officer in command of the Baralong in shooting the crew of the German submarine – if such really turns out to be the truth. He maintained retaliation was the only method of putting an end to their behaviour – by inspiring a wholesome fear of the consequences attaching to their policy of sinking unarmed merchantmen without warning. This seemed to me the identical justification the Germans put forward for their frightfulness. I slept from 3.30pm till 6.30pm. A Coy. left Paraskevi camp for the castle & Mr. Ellwood joined the Headquarters mess until C & D Coys arrive from Mudros.
Wednesday. Feb 9. 1916. Hood Battalion Paraskevi Camp, Tenedos.
I spent the afternoon pulling the piano to bits with Sergeant Blake, of the Engineers, who had been recommended for the job of adjusting the dampers &c on the strength of his having made the gramophone work! I played through my violin Sonata in G major from the music (for the first time) after dinner & was tolerably well satisfied with it. The form of the first movement seems to be good. W.M.E. sat by me & listened to it. I also played the first movement of my Piano Sonata in F minor & my Allegro de Concert, Waltz Pageant & some other pieces.
Thursday. Feb 10. 1916. Hood Battalion, Paraskevi Camp, Tenedos.
A French officer & some Zouaves came out at 8.30 am to attend the funeral of a man from a trawler who had died in the Castle hospital. The officer took Freyberg & me back with him to Tenedos in his car as General Mercer was due to arrive on a destroyer at 10.30 a.m. We had not been in very long before we got a message to say his visit was postponed. It was blowing a gale from the south. I walked back to camp by myself. I finished translating the French lease of Paraskevi from the Greek Community in Tenedos after tea. I had been working at it yesterday morning & found considerable difficulty in understanding some of its phrases. I spent a pleasant hour or more trying to remember Bach's A min Organ Fugue which I have not played for the last 4 years or so. I was not very successful at first but by degrees it all came back.

Above: From Kelly's wartime diary written on the island of Tenedos, during the Gallipoli campaign, 1915.

Below: Final page of Kelly's Gallipoli sonata, 1915–16. The title page holds the words 'To Jelly d'Arányi'.

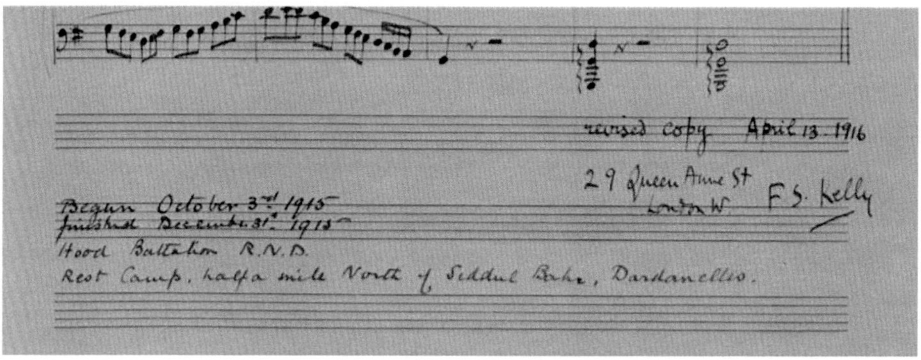

The Kelly family home *Glenyarrah*, Double Bay, Sydney, Australia.

and drove out to Narrabeen. Kelly was gratified when Borwick admired the coastal scenery that had acquired so much significance for the younger man.

Bertie and Cleg took the tram to town on 12 August to attend Borwick's last scheduled Sydney recital. This time there was, at last, a large audience with 2,000 seats occupied. The reception was very warm, but though Kelly found much to admire, he still insisted on giving Borwick a complete critique after supper that evening at the Australia Hotel. On 29 August Borwick gave his last Sydney concert before leaving for appearances in Bendigo and Ballarat. New Zealand, California and New York were to follow.

Kelly sold his Steinway for £120 through Henry Stael, not wanting 'the bother of carting it back to England', went through 'a volume of our early music' – pieces by Raff, Ascher Schalk, Blumenthal, 'and a good deal of other rubbish', shopped, packed, and was given a farewell dinner with friends at Glenyarrah.[62] The list of final visits grew long as he ticked off the calls on friends and the invitations he felt obliged to accept. Among them was a lunch at Potts point, at which Kelly talked to Dorothea Mackeller about her poems and pressed her to advance her cause in England. A day was spent on a motor launch with Ethel, Bertie and the children exploring the upper reaches of the Lane Cove river where the wattle was in full bloom and where the river was 'as broad as the Thames at Marlow'.[63]

In these last days in Sydney Kelly took to walking between the houses he visited, 'turning over a few ideas for a work for orchestra in E major in four movements'.[64] On 21 August he went into town with Bertie to pay for his music and a 'portmanteau' to be forwarded, only to find the usual Sydney problem: no one had bothered to do anything, not even to draw up a bill and those responsible could not be found. Shortly afterwards he left with Bertie and Tom for the railway station and his train to Brisbane, picking up Beatrice from her dancing lesson on the way. Ethel remained at home.

With Sydney and his debut behind him, Kelly was now on holiday. Dudley had resigned a month before. The scandal faded with him. Kelly took the steam train to Brisbane, and as he walked back to his hotel from sightseeing he:

> got an idea for a second movement of my G minor Symphony [...] As far as I can recollect, I have been in search of such an idea for the last two or three years – i.e. for a bright movement to relieve the gloom of the other three movements in G minor.[65]

He shipped north to Gladstone, had 'a dozen ideas for composition',[66] went to the races at Mackay, took the train out of Cairns to walk the Barron Gorge at Kurunda and visited 'the Butterfly Man', Frederick Parkhurst Dodd, to see his significant entomological collection from New Guinea. Further inland, at Mareeba, he stripped off to swim in a local waterhole and passed close to what he described as an Aboriginal camp: 'my sudden appearance over the top of the river bank seemed to scare some of the old women, who made off to their huts. Their whole appearance as well as their huts looked very squalid.'[67] Back in Kuranda he had an asthma attack and was so badly bitten about the face by bed bugs that he looked as if he'd been in a fight. Undeterred, he went on with his explorations along bush tracks, reading in the evening and working on a 'second Cycle or agglomeration of Lyrics or Lyrical Fantasia (I can't find a name for it)'.[68]

From Cairns he shipped north to Port Morseby, but was too afraid to enter the stilt houses with their fierce guard dogs. On Thursday Island he found Japanese and locals pearl fishing and, composing as he walked, 'got another idea for an impromptu'.[69] In Darwin he found himself strangely alert to a Chinese presence. As he sailed on to Java he composed a set of studies. At Surabaya he toured about with a Miss Keevil and recorded that he was sorry to say goodbye. She struck him as being very intelligent and well informed. He heard next day that she was a keen suffragette travelling to recuperate from a nervous breakdown. Gladice Keevil had recently spent six weeks in Holloway prison being force fed.[70] Now she was singled out by the press for her good looks.[71] Kelly was plainly attracted.

He was enroute for Mount Bromo when he left Surabaya on the 21 September, taking the train, pony carts and a three hour horse ride to the crater and, as always, composing as he went: 'I had a great number of musical ideas during my journey up to Tosari. They were mostly to do with orchestral work – lyrics, dances, a serenade and symphony.'[72] At Moengal Pass he could see:

> down onto the 'Sea of Sand' about 800ft beneath one and across it to the three volcanoes Bromo, Batok and Widodaren about 1–2 miles away. In the distance the right one seems to be Smeroe, the highest volcano in Java, looking very like Fujima in shape but without the snow.

His attempt to walk the sulphurous rim almost ended in an avalanche and he gave up. In the Sea of Sand wild dogs were said to hunt and kill horses. He was thankful to get back to the hotel to wash off the lava dust and wrote: 'I had several musical ideas (during the expedition and worked mostly at my set of impromptus).' In the distance 'There was a sound of music – mostly bells (sounding like cow bells – over a rhythmic drum bass) after sundown. I have got the little hotel to myself.'[73]

Djokjakarta followed, with a visit to the ruined Water Palace. His final stop was Batavia (Jakata) where he spent six days at the Grand Hotel Java Weltevreden,[74] joining the capital's expatriate society, with drinks and tennis at the English Club, discovering the Harmonie Club's excellent brass band, its gambling facilities and billiard room, and dining with a party of ten at the Hotel des Indes. He visited the museum with new-found English friends, dining with them and playing bridge and, inevitably, the piano. There was a visit to Parakan Salak 'a tea-estate about 60 miles away'.

On 5 October Kelly extended his fare to Genoa via Singapore on the SS *Grotius.* He boarded in a monsoonal downpour, and though most of the passengers were Dutch, he dined aside that night with English and Australian passengers. In Singapore he found his luggage had not arrived at Raffles Hotel and he remained on board, the only Englishman left, he said, in a rare moment of identification. At Sabang, an island off the northern tip of Sumatra, he was three hours ashore walking and swimming and admiring the town. On the 12th the ship berthed at Colombo, where he had tea at the Galle Face Hotel, now the oldest hotel east of Suez. He found that there was no one to talk to over the long meals and felt desperate. To pass the time he went on composing and correcting manuscripts. He revived 'a little piano piece of 1903' for use in a second flute serenade in F, toyed with ideas for this, intending to finish it before he left the ship, worked on his E major orchestral serenade, revised his *Allegro de Concert*, and composed three impromptus.[75]

By the 27th the *Grotius* was off Naples. Kelly woke at 6am to see Messina lit up and fairly close, a searchlight playing over it. The next day he disembarked at Genoa. After taking the train to Paris and Boulogne and enduring a rough crossing, he reached London. With his Australian debut – effectively a try-out – behind him, Kelly saw this homecoming as the beginning of a career as a London pianist; he was in fact at the beginning of the end. Fourteen professional concerts and quite a few private ones later, the war would bring it to a permanent halt after little more than two-and-a-half years.

CHAPTER TEN

THE LONDON DEBUT 1912

Early the next day Kelly set off for 7 Wigmore Street, the offices of Arthur Robinson Smith, Balfour Gardiner's concert agent. Smith's wife, Ethel L. Robinson, was Percy Grainger's agent. The Frankfurt group had obviously been consulted and Kelly was about to utilise it and every other contact he had to furnish the series of recitals he was planning for the New Year. The game was on. His first move was to discuss: 'the rather disagreeable question of getting someone to write me up in the press'.[1] The next day he felt bilious, cancelled tickets for a CCS-Casals concert, and sent for Dr Ernest Young who lived a few doors away. Young, an asthma specialist, sat him down and asked him to breathe deeply. Kelly fainted. This was attributed to 'the state of my liver' and the deep breathing. He was sent to bed. A strict diet was ordered. Cigarettes were discounted as a cause as he hadn't smoked for well over two years. With Young's consent, he returned to Bramwell and auto-suggestion in the hope of a permanent cure. A case of pre-concert season jitters was not considered. Yet here he was, primed but anxious, facing an audacious metropolitan debut: three piano recitals and an orchestral concert with other engagements to follow.

The musical London that Kelly returned to was booming. Choral, orchestral, solo and chamber music could now be heard, in addition to opera, for much of the year in its central district in purpose built spaces. These were well-appointed venues that ranged from the 2,500 seat Queen's Hall, where Henry Wood conducted its orchestra, to the showrooms of the keyboard manufacturing firms – among them Bechstein, Steinway and pianola producers Aeolian, whose halls were rented out to soloists and small ensembles. Other firms, notably Broadwood and Erhard, acted as promoters. There was a growing interest in orchestral music, the cult of the piano was at its peak, and celebrity soloists jostled for attention. The old subscription system was being replaced by the commercially driven single ticket. New forms of management were sharpening competition to supply outlets for the increasing cultural aspirations of an affluent middle class. Chamber music retained its aura of exclusivity. The Joachim Quartet's domination of the field ceased with its founder's death in 1907, but its work was continued by the Classical Concert Society (1908–1922), the group that Kelly was to chair towards the end of his 1912 London debut year.

For Kelly, practice was resumed with a vengeance. He now had less than three months to prepare an ambitious set of programmes, very little of which would rely on his Sydney lists. Most of the works performed would have been familiar to London audiences, but there was a smattering of the new: a single Scriabin, the early op. 8 no. 1 from the 1894 *Twelve Etudes* in the second concert, one work of Ravel's, the 1908 *Gibet* in the last concert of the year, and four Debussy pieces – *La fille aux cheveux de lin* from Preludes Book 1 (1909–1910) and *Mouvement* from *Images* (1905) in the third concert, *Masques* (1904) in the fifth, and the Toccata in C sharp minor from the *Pour le piano* suite (1894–1901) in the ninth. For Kelly, Debussy, Ravel and Scriabin were his moderns. His own work was to be represented by the *Cycle of Lyrics* in the first concert, his Studies in E flat and C minor (their first appearance in London) in the second, his Allegro de Concert in the third, the *Waltz Pageant* in the fifth, the Flute Serenade for small orchestra in the sixth, and his Study in E major in the ninth.

The friendship with Balfour Gardiner was renewed late in the year over dinner at Gardiner's Kensington house[2] with the two composers afterwards performing their own works for one another. Kelly recalled: 'I spent a very pleasant evening with him.' Which was all it was, adding: 'He is full of his scheme of four concerts in which he is going to produce numbers of works of English composers regardless of cost – in fact he is prepared to lose £1500.'[3] Gardiner eventually gave eight concerts at Queen's Hall in 1912–13. His aim was to raise public awareness of contemporary English music. They included works by Arnold Bax, Frederic Austin, Gustav Holst, Percy Grainger, Roger Quilter, Cyril Scott and Norman O'Neill. Grainger wrote: 'I realised how they changed the whole face of English music. Of course, the concerts did not alter the value of the music itself. But it altered the way the composers thought about themselves and the way the musical public thought about English music.'[4] Kelly was unrepresented in spite of his attempts to curry favour with Gardiner and Grainger. A great opportunity was lost. Nonetheless, Gardiner's example as a rich and generous patron intent on shaping public taste had its effect. Kelly was certainly moving in the same direction immediately before the war. On the 12 December Gardiner came to Wimpole Street to hear the *Flute Serenade* before the two men went on to see Smith. They agreed to save postage by having the circulars for their concerts sent out together. Kelly went off to buy the complete works of Mendelssohn, adding Gardiner's *Shepherd Fennel's Dance* to his order, for once very pleased with himself.[5]

Two days after Christmas Leonard Borwick returned to Wimpole Street, fresh from his American tour. He went over Kelly's projected programmes and showed him drafts for his own London return. Kelly played him his revised Allegro de Concert but though Borwick thought the revisions had improved it, his advice was not to publish.[6] On New Year's day Kelly was still rearranging his lists but took time for tea at Claridge's with Maisie, an excuse to pick up the proofs of his 'picture-post' at Smith's office. These he pinned up on the walls at Wimpole Street when his sister came to dine. Leonard brought out the souvenirs of their Australian tours. Kelly's were mostly Javanese, Borwick's Australian aboriginal.[7] Curiously, Kelly seems to have had no interest in the oldest extant culture on earth in spite of having spent his boyhood on 'country'.

Kelly and Borwick were still in Australia when Tovey's problems with the CCS came to a head. When he found that new CCS concert dates clashed with his commitments to Chelsea,[8] Tovey demanded the society change its dates.[9] He was refused and felt betrayed since he had deliberately positioned his close friends on its committee. He threatened to resign, then delayed, saying he would wait until Borwick's return as he was the mainstay of the CCS and he did not want to risk destabilising the group. In fact it was a declaration of war. Tovey wanted the chairmanship. He saw Borwick as his rival and failed to notice that Kelly was standing in the wings. About this time Weisse wrote to Trevelyan's wife that Tovey was seeing a good deal of Maisie Kelly and had written songs for her, obliquely suggesting a marriage was possible.[10]

Tovey then accused Edward Speyer of mismanagement and suggested changes to the CCS's constitution. Speyer, mightily upset, twice called on Kelly and Borwick for advice. It was decided Tovey had to be disciplined, but a week later Speyer called again to say he had changed his mind. Kelly was disgusted: 'DFT's correspondence gave me the impression that jealousy and an egotistic self-assertion were the prime motives which prompted his solicitude for the Society's Constitution and his proposal to reconstruct it. There was also an interfering and spiteful letter from Miss Weiss to Mr Speyer.'[11]

None of this deterred him from pursuing his publicity arrangements, sometimes to his own disadvantage. He decided to pay for a good deal of advertising, most of it through circulars sent to addresses he personally supplied. It had little effect. He dined at his club with the Warres and the publisher Gerald Chadwyck Healey, who proposed that Kelly join the young music publishing firm of Stainer and Bell. Parry, Stanford and Plunket Greene, he said, were all interested. Founded in 1907, the firm was dedicated to publishing new music by English composers. Though it was gaining a reputation, Kelly foolishly declined. A joint concert with Maisie for the Reading University Musical Club turned into a solo piano recital when she came down with a sore throat. Though the audience was warm and enthusiastic they didn't strike him as very musical and he was disappointed that he saw little chance of a flow-on to ticket sales.[12]

At the start of February the Tovey question burst onto Kelly's page again. Thinking that Speyer and the CCS were now conspiring to prevent him from engaging for the Chelsea concerts, Tovey tried to create a division between the committee members in order to discredit Speyer. Kelly wrote:

> He had written a long rigmarole to LB about his attitude to Speyer and the CCS and finished it up by saying he would refuse to believe LB disapproved of his action unless he heard from him to that effect. LB thus felt himself obliged to give his opinion and as he had been requested to hand the letter on to me he advised me to answer it too. DFT seems in a mood to snarl at anyone and everybody, feels himself misunderstood, justifies himself etc., and it is difficult to get a clear idea of what his grievance is. He has certainly behaved very badly to Speyer and the reams of explanation and justification seem to point to an uneasy conscience on his part.[13]

On 7 February a package was delivered to Wimpole Street containing two scores and a sixteen-page letter from Tovey. The scores were Mozart's Serenade in B flat and Dvorak's Serenade in D minor, which he was engaged to conduct for the CCS on the 21st. Since there was no payment Tovey felt free to accept Casal's offer of a concert in Budapest and asked Kelly to substitute for him. The only rehearsal was two days before Kelly's debut. Indignant at such short shrift, he refused to help and went off to perform in a Kensington Musical Club concert at Leighton House where Rhoda von Glehn was to give four of his songs. Even there the CCS had tentacles. Freddy Speyer was in the audience but he listened from outside through the closed door, insisting that he could hear better that way.[14]

With only a week to go, Kelly decided to ride the tube to see what sort of show his posters were making. A mixture of delight and anxiety had him writing: 'There is quite a lot being written about me in the press and I am hoping the advertisement may bring people to my concerts.'[15] Immediately before his debut the music critic of the *Daily Telegraph* fired a warning shot across his bows:

> 'Sculler as pianist' is all very well, but in these days it may be inconvenient. For if Mr Kelly's touch prove at his first recital in Aeolian Hall this afternoon to be too hard all kinds of things may be said. The winner of the Wingfield is, of course, a hero; but it is quite another matter to be a hero, because of this, in the concert room.[16]

One Australian newspaper added the indignant postscript that: 'Really, Mr F.S. Kelly must almost regret that ever he rowed a race to victory now that he is on the point of blossoming forth in the land of his adoption as a pianist.'[17]

On the morning of his first London concert, 20 February 1912, Kelly tried out the resident Steinway, went on to Bramwell for relaxation exercises, rested at noon for an hour, read *The Times* and at 3pm was on the platform. His programme included the Bach-Liszt Prelude and Fugue in A minor for organ, Beethoven's Appassionata, his own *Cycle of Lyrics* op. 4, the massive Brahms Variations and Fugue on a Theme of Handel op. 24 and a bracket of Chopin works: the F sharp major op. 60 Barcarolle, the E flat minor study op. 10 no. 6, the A flat major Mazurka op. 59 no. 2 and the C minor study op. 10 no. 12. Only the opening Bach-Liszt had been heard in the Sydney debut.[18] The hall was half full, the audience enthusiastic and the general opinion was that he had had a success. For the first time during a solo recital he felt fresh, but at the end fatigue suddenly set in. He gave tea to: 'Mrs Speyer, MAK, MELI, Miss Dakyns, Eddie Speyer, ELW and LB.' The gross taking was about £50.[19]

The following morning Kelly bought a dozen newspapers to read the reviews. Only three seemed to favour him and he wrote: 'Most of the critics seemed to be on their guard against being taken in by a sculler who has turned to music.'[20] He shrugged it off and went with Borwick to a CCS concert which, he said, he enjoyed. In any case, only one of these critiques really mattered – *The Times.* Henry Cope Colles, later editor of *Grove's Dictionary of Music and Musicians*, but then just beginning his thirty-two-year reign as the *Times*' chief music critic, was probably its author. His verdict was that Kelly's position as an amateur had secured him an appreciative audience on the day, but was likely to retard rather than to advance his recognition as a professional pianist. 'Yet,' Colles noted, 'not only the ambitious scheme of his programmes, but the manner of playing the first of them, entitles him to serious consideration.' It was in the Beethoven and Chopin items that,

> the pianist's limitations were most felt. In both, the tone qualities tended to be too distinct and to make one conscious that the interpretation had been closely studied in every particular; a stiffness of rhythm, too, sometimes held the imagination in check [...] But the completeness of his technical equipment became more and more apparent as the programme progressed.'

Kelly's *Cycle of Lyrics* was dismissed as a 'charming little work'.[21] The *Daily Telegraph* (probably Robin Legge)[22] was politely damning. It found the scheme of three recitals and an orchestral concert bold and extraordinary, referred to Kelly as 'an Australian and a first-rate waterman', found his touch 'rather hard', and was lukewarm about the pianist's own compositions.[23] *The Pall Mall Gazette* (possibly Edwin Evans) wavered about: 'There is no doubting the advanced nature of his technique, while it was quite evident that a successful handling of the oar had not interfered with the more delicate muscular efforts, for his touch and tone were alike singularly agreeable.' But it paused to question whether Kelly's 'artistic leanings' were of a serious enough order to meet the demands made 'upon the executive artist in these days of keen rivalry for recognition … there seemed to be in his playing none too much warmth and the driving force coming from the born executant.[24] *The Scotsman* assured its readers that 'Any doubt that might have been reasonably entertained as to a possible hardness of touch in such a renowned sculler was at once dispelled.' The six Kelly pieces were rated as 'not very interesting … It is, however, but fair to add that they seemed to please the audience, and in response to their applause Mr Kelly repeated one of the most attractive numbers.'[25] *The Globe* found his playing thoughtful, dignified and scholarly. It regretted that his rowing reputation had not drawn much of an audience. It found the six pieces: 'light, descriptive pieces for the most part, not by any means unattractive, but too indefinite in character to express fully the very definite ideas suggested by their titles'.[26] In the briefest of notes, the *Musical Times* summed it all up with this, some ten days later: 'Mr F.S. Kelly, of "Diamond Sculls" fame, who was well-known in his Oxford days as a pianist, gave a recital at Aeolian Hall on 20 February, and showed that in the interval he has added maturity to his characteristic refinement.'[27]

Kelly pressed on with recitals at the Aeolian Hall on 27 February[28] and 5 March 1912.[29] The first of these fared no better. This time it was the Bach Italian Concerto, Beethoven's Sonata no. 32 in C minor op. 111, Schumann's 'Inder Nacht' Kreisleriana nos. 6 and 8, Chopin's F minor Ballade op. 52, the F sharp major Nocturne op. 15 no. 2, the C sharp Mazurka op. 41 no. 1, the Prelude in F sharp minor, and the Study in A flat, op. 10 no. 10. The final group consisted of the Scriabin Study in C sharp major op. 8 no. 1, Mendelssohn's Study in B flat minor op. 104B no. 1, Kelly's Studies in E flat and C minor (their first performance in London), Henselt's Study in E op. 5 no. 4 *Ave Maria*, and finally Liszt's Study in F sharp minor Gnomen Reigen.

Kelly wrote:

> There is an [*sic*] universal complaint among friends and critics that I don't let myself go and that I keep too jealous a guard upon emotions (as one critic put it) and all the time I was thinking how warmly I had played and that if anything, some of the excess in that direction might have been curbed with advantage! There was a small audience of, at most, 150–175 but they were appreciative and applauded heartily. Henschel and his wife came and congratulated me afterwards – he seemed to have enjoyed the programme but what most excited his admiration was the fact of my having got through the evening without having to change my collar![30]

Cool as ever, he and his party left for supper at the Garrick Club.

The Times began to find fault, praising 'his capacity for maintaining an even touch of soft or *mezzo forte* tone through long sequences', but finding his execution hard in loud sections, his pedalling 'not sufficiently distinct' and his rhythm too mechanical. However, 'As the evening progressed the pianist seemed able to throw off a hampering nervousness which marked the earlier part of his recital, and he played out in consequence with increasing freedom and spontaneity.'[31] What Colles expected was theatre and a large stage presence. What Kelly gave him was a quiet gentleman with short hair, in conventional – if expensive – evening wear, expecting his audience to listen to the music without interference from a pianist trying to grab the limelight. There were no gestures. Kelly was ahead of his times and among the first of the modern precision executants.

The day after his second concert, the *Sketch* published one of the 'disagreeable' publicity articles Kelly had sought. Under a conventional portrait photograph it used the caption: 'A famous Oxford rowing "blue" turns professional pianist and composer. Mr F.S. Kelly.' It went on to list his rowing awards.[32]

The third recital on 5 March consisted of the Mozart Fantasia in C minor, the Beethoven op. 7 Sonata, Fugue no. 2 from Bach's 48 Preludes and Fugues, and a flurry of pieces by Schubert, Mendelssohn, Field, Debussy and Chopin. Though the reviews were as mixed as before, *The Times* tempered its disapproval with a grudging admission of Kelly's worth as a pianist if not as a composer.[33]

On the 17th he went to the Italian Futurist exhibition at the Sackville Gallery and found it, like the Post Impressionist exhibition, merely amusing, though he was aware of the Futurist's anarchist aims and the furore at the Paris-Berlin showings. Over tea at the Union Club he read the movement's manifesto, two angry pages that embraced the industrial, advocated war, and railed against museum culture.[34] Kelly and his circle may have found the paintings laughable but the manifesto was debated for weeks. At the time he made no attempt to explore the music associated with the Futurists.

The debut season ended with a Queen's Hall concert on 19 March, when he appeared with the London Symphony Orchestra in two concertos, Mozart's D major K. 537 and the Brahms B flat, with Henschel conducting. Kelly provided his own cadenzas for the Mozart and Henschel, (no doubt with Kelly's urging), added Iwan Knorr's Variations on a Ukrainian Folk Song op. 7. Ernest Walker wrote the programme notes.

A thousand free tickets saw the hall comfortably filled. George Henschel's conducting proved effective. There was generous applause throughout. Borwick said there was a great improvement in his playing compared to the recitals. Kelly's relief was palpable but there was a moment of high tension when Tovey stepped into the artist's room to find himself face to face with not only Borwick, but the Speyers. Leonard saved the day by making for Donald at once and shaking his hand. After which Kelly gathered up his guests, all thirty-two of them, and went off to the after-party at 18 Mansfield Street, the Sheffields' London house. He was saved from making a speech, which he dreaded, when Henschel rose in his stead to Lord Sheffield's toast.[35]

As usual, the reviews were mixed. *The Scotsman* admitted he had a 'limpid touch and general neatness of technique' with a 'simple directness of expression that delighted the audience' in the Mozart, though the Brahms needed 'a more strenuous treatment'.[36] *The Standard* thought 'Brahms would, without question, seem to be Mr Kelly's metier', praised his 'authority and power' and unfailing technique, but condemned his Mozart as 'facile'.[37] *The Pall Mall Gazette* found that though Kelly's playing might leave something to be desired emotionally, it had 'wealth and variety of tone' and 'a distinct stylishness', with 'no disturbing elements of … display or sensationalism'.[38] *The Daily Telegraph* detected 'a quite modern approach' in the Mozart: 'There was nothing that one could actually call outré in his method of playing' but it lacked fire. He detected a stiffness, something academic in Kelly's attitude. The new cadenzas he read as in the style of Cherubini 'and – at a stretch, of Dussek', and found 'there was vitality and a certain exuberance' in them. But he was genuinely puzzled: 'Stiffness towards Mozart and tenderness towards Brahms – it seems incredible in the same temperament!'[39] *The Times* offered no reprieve. It admitted that Kelly's grasp of the music was sound, his technique assured, but that 'the playing as a whole tended to become monotonous in its tone, and in Brahms' work particularly it lacked sustained quality and resonance.'[40] The *Musical Times* merely noted that Kelly 'gave satisfying interpretations of Concertos by Mozart (D major) and Brahms (B flat).'[41]

Mr Smith, being the agent that he was, snipped away at the newspaper reviews and with more than a little judicious cutting and pasting, produced a quite different Kelly than the one who read them. These tiny edited versions were published inside the advertised programmes for Kelly's concerts. They make for interesting reading. Not exactly lies, but not quite the truth either.

A mix of social and professional life kept the reviews at bay for a time: Putney for the Oxford-Cambridge boat race and its dinner – that year reserved exclusively for old blues;[42] Eton to visit the Provost;[43] and entertaining Miss Ball, by then Mrs Stack, one of the governesses from Glenyarrah days. He was touched that when he was shorn off into boyhood at 5, she had kept his curls. He played her *Idyl* and *Caprice* and talked 'of old times'.[44] At Wimpole Street he played an arrangement of twelve of the Bisham Waltzes to Leonard who thought there were too many and the writing rather heavy. A little startled, Kelly altered them to suit. He went to his agent to arrange two concerts in May and June, and to engage artists for the next CCS series.[45] On 4 April he took tea with Percy and Rose Grainger and left his Allegro de Concert op. 3, asking if he might dedicate it to his host.[46] Grainger accepted and Schott published it the following year. A week's holiday with Felix Warre was spent motoring to Bath, Wells and Glastonbury, but in the Lyn valley his car flipped over. No one was injured, though 'Clara' had to be conveyed to Lynmouth for repairs via a water-powered lift installed for cars unable to take the steep gradients and they were able to make it to Exeter, Salisbury and Stonehenge.

Mid-month Bertie and Ethel arrived and were shown about but Kelly's relentless practising soon drove Maisie to isolate him and the piano from the rest of the household.[47] There was a weekend at Shenleybury House in Hertfordshire, the home of Roland Nelson, then Private Secretary to the Home Secretary, Reginald McKenna, and known to Kelly from rowing days at Eton. He had been with Kelly on his world tour.

At month's end Kelly was back in town and working on the orchestral part of the Schumann concerto with Borwick.[48] Gardiner's fourth orchestral concert on 1 May left him snobbishly judgemental as had the third, but: 'Gurney Boyle took us off to the Garrick Club afterwards, and gave us supper. I started tea-totalling again after 2½ months wine-bibbing.'[49] With a recital of his own imminent it was about time, though the admission itself is telling; his critics were getting to him and he would have to pull up if he was to have any success at all.

On 15 May he gave his second orchestral concert with the Queen's Hall orchestra, this time under Henry Wood's baton, performing Beethoven's Concerto no. 4 in G major op. 58 with his own cadenzas, Schumann's Concerto in A minor op. 54 and the first performance in England of his own *Serenade for Flute and Orchestra* with the Dutch flautist Albert Fransella as the soloist. At the rehearsal on the 13th his *Serenade* did not go well.[50] There was a three-hour rehearsal on the day of the concert itself, half of it given over to the flute work because of this. According to Kelly:

> Wood has taken great pains in rehearsing and especially with my *Flute Serenade* but he has not got a sense of rhythm and nor has Fransella. Thus in spite of the careful preparation there was no feeling of conviction in the performance. Fransella's playing of my work was not as good as Lemmone's. I didn't have nearly such a success as in my last orchestral concert, but I believe that with Henschel as conductor I should have done just as well.[51]

Bertie, Ethel and Maisie were there.

The Times did an astonishing about-turn, praising his pianism in the Beethoven as:

> simple and stately and very much alive, with a careful but not obtrusive attention to detail. If technique has now moved on too fast for Beethoven's own cadenzas to be any longer as satisfying as they once were, Mr Kelly's cadenzas, modelled rather on Jadassohn's learned style than Reinecke's more allusive method, are a good substitute.

The Schumann was daintily picked over, but the Serenade was thought,

> to combine the grace of Robert Volkmann with the tenderness of Emmanuel Moor. […] there were some very happy conceptions in the part-writing of the Prelude, the gracious phrases of the Idyll, in the ingenious and airy Minuet, and in the Jig by 'Green Sleeves' out of 'The Carman's Whistle'.[52]

The rest of the press followed *The Times.* It was as if the critics met at interval and decided on what line to take together. In spite of Borwick's reservations about the *Serenade*, Kelly was determined to publish and took it to Schott's the next day.[53] frogpup.

On 19 May he performed at one of the weekly Balliol concerts, giving the Bach C minor Fantasia, Beethoven's Sonata in A Flat major op. 26, his own *Cycle of Lyrics* and Schuman's Etudes Symphoniques. As an encore he added Debussy's 'Mouvement', 'which,' he noted, 'seemed to strike the audience as strange'. The college made him feel at home and able to expand:

> I was in pretty good form and laid myself out in the Etudes Symphoniques to produce as large a volume of sound as I could since there seems to be a not inconsiderable body of opinion abroad that I excel in delicacy rather than in force and in restraint rather than in freedom of style. T.H.K. who was one of the carpers in my Sydney concerts about the smallness of tone seemed satisfied on this occasion and Walker, whom I consulted thought there was nothing in the charge and accused me of having got through the tone once or twice in the Schumann.[54]

He was still squiring the Kelly family about and on 21 May invited Bertie and Ethel to dine at Diendonne's with the Ferdinand Speyers, then took them to hear an all-Grainger concert before a large and enthusiastic audience at Aoelian Hall with Gardiner conducting, and wrote admiringly of his rival:

> Altogether it was a most entertaining evening. […] The Scotch Strathsprey and Reel savoured of the Taproom (L.B.'s description of it) but was full of exuberance rather than vulgarity. My whole impression was of a composer of a rather restricted emotional range, but of decided originality. There was nothing deep although there were moments (such as Willow Willow) that were genuinely pathetic and moving. It was the music of a grown-up child, immensely clever but which gave no indication of deep emotional experience. In a sense it was all playing with toys and not with the real things of life.[55]

The Kellys went on to Lady Sheffield's where the d'Arànyi sisters were playing. Henschel and Kelly accompanied and provided solos. Among the other guests was pianist Mark Hambourg and Edward Speyer's cousin, Sir Edgar Speyer, who was then a Privy Councillor and patron of the Proms. He was later to be accused of pro-German activity in time of war and his British citizenship revoked.

On 3 June Kelly gave a vocal and piano concert with George Henschel at Aeolian Hall. Two days before he had found his right hand too weak and stiff to play and had been forced to give up practising.[56] The reviews found that there was a striking contrast between Henschel's robust style and Kelly's, which was deemed sedate[57] and on the edge of primness.[58]

Now highly conscious of the need to adjust, he took on a recital at the Oxford University Musical Club on 18 June. It included his *Waltz Pageant* and the Schumann Novelette in F minor which went well enough for him to claim to be 'not in bad form … the Novelette went with sufficient warmth to cheer me up for the dull performance I gave of it in the Aeolian Hall on 3 June'.[59] Two days later he gave a recital with Rhoda von Glehn at an evening party in College Hall. After it Sir Walter Parratt asked for Kelly's *Flute Serenade*, with the intention of having it performed at court.[60] His mood lifted.

The rest of the summer was spent at Henley, the Grange, and friends' houses in the district, as usual, with brief London visits to take in concerts and theatre. He was there at Magdalene College to hear Bertie perform, but he found it all very amateur.[61] The day after this he took out his MA but left immediately afterwards to watch the crews at Henley.[62] On the final day of the regatta Cleg, Bertie, Maisie and Ethel were in the Grandstand enclosure to see the king and queen arrive in the royal barge 'looking like a medieval pageant with their beautiful silk standard and the red coats of the rowers'.[63]

As the summer drew on Kelly began to realise that his sister was finding it difficult to cope with him. It was all the little things. They argued over his wanting to sell a punt that she seldom used and which she had purchased when he was away.[64] When his dog Blackie 'flew for a swan' after breakfast one morning, 'MAK characteristically shouted at me as though it were my fault', adding: 'She is a good deal on my nerves at present and I imagine she must feel the same about me.'[65] Even making music together was no longer a pleasure. On a day when he had just returned from visiting Sir Walter Parratt to show him his Flute Serenade and some studies, Rhoda von Gheln and the Kellys went over 'several Brahms and Schumann duets in which there were the usual squabbles as to tempo between MAK and myself, and R.V.G. also had something to say. When MAK is reading and gets into difficulties she attacks me in order to cover her confusion.'[66] He was relieved when she left for Scotland two weeks later.

There was still the distraction of entertaining guests, visiting friends, composing and long hours spent sculling alone. He drove over to see Balfour Gardiner,

> in his cottage at Ashampstead Green which lies in very nice hilly country and is very typical of his tastes. […] He sent me away with several combs of honey from his apiary. […] When in good health H.B.G. is a very agreeable companion and today he was in good spirits and seemed to enjoy seeing me.[67]

The Speyers called at the Grange for the first time early in August and were rowed out to see the abbey from the water. They were shown the proofs of the autumn CCS programs, Kelly keen to impress the man he was replacing. [68]

On 13 August he met with Carl Volkert, Schott's co-manager, to discuss publishing his music. Kelly wrote:

> He was somewhat long winded but eventually offered me the following terms: The expense of producing the first edition (printing setting-up etc) of each work to be borne by me, after which he would give me 25% of the nett price on each copy sold. In case of a reprint he would undertake the cost of the new edition and still pay me 25% of the nett price, or else 50% of the nett price if I undertook the expense of producing the new edition. In return he would undertake to advertise the works in his catalogues. Of course he would thus have the best of the bargain, but on the other hand I should rest content in the knowledge that it was in the firms interest to push the sales of my works and of course I could seek new terms with each new work.[69]

The next day, with the Bertie Kellys and Joe Kelly in residence at the Grange, he composed 'a little jig for Beatrice to dance to – to Bertie's fiddling, and presented it to him to take away. In the afternoon I played it several times while Beatrice danced to it.'[70] Cleg was entranced by his nieces, Beatrice and Veronica, and nephew Tom, and played with them enthusiastically, 'rounders' out-doors and, when it rained, 'animal grab' in the house. Joe Kelly would become Cleg's brother-in-law three years later, but there was no hint of that at the time, just an old friendship renewed. On the 23rd he farewelled the Bertie Kellys, who were off to Paris, the Italian Lakes, Egypt and Sydney. He would not see them again. On the same day he delivered *Aghadoe* and 'Shall I compare thee' to Schott's for publication on the terms agreed to a fortnight before.

The following week was spent aboard a wherry on the Broads with Felix Warre, Francis Henley[71] and Philip S. Kershaw.[72] Bad weather sent them ashore. Kelly decided to join the Graham family at Airthrey Castle in Scotland where Lady Sheffield lectured him on his quarrelling with his sister. At Penrhos, the Stanley's house in Wales, Venetia Stanley tried to heal the three-year-old rift between Violst

Asquith and Kelly by seating the, together at dinner – only to make things worse. Kelly braved it out, playing a great deal and joining in the tenants' gathering for Welch choral singing to harp accompaniment. He tried to notate some of this but it proved beyond him. A riding incident further tested his relationship with Violet when she abandoned her horse, leaving Venetia to take it over. Kelly, who had only attempted such a thing once before, was obliged to take Venetia's untrained carriage horse back to base over jumps. He was in no mood to front Violet that night but found himself playing with her at Auction Bridge. Thereafter he wrote of her stiffly as 'Miss Asquith', the only expression of anger that he allowed himself.[73]

In London he plunged into concertising again. Borwick spoke against his programme for a proposed 5 November concert, saying there were too many familiar pieces. With no time to learn anything new, Kelly abandoned the date for one in December. On the 21st the proofs of *Aghadoe* and 'Shall I compare thee' arrived. [74] On the 24th he felt unwell. The next day he drank 'a little champagne'[75] at dinner at his club with friends, but was still not himself on the 27th when he went onstage for the Proms at Queen's Hall with Henry Wood conducting. The house was full. This time his nerves betrayed him badly. Resting pre-concert he found:

> for some reason or other my mind was busy making programmes for the 1913 series of Classical Concerts and I was much taken with the idea of inducing Ravel to come over and play his 'Gaspard de la nuit' and take part in some ensemble work of Faure (his master).

His preoccupation with the planning of this event took its toll. His memory failed just before the entry of the second orchestral *tutti* towards the end of the exposition. It took him four bars to re-enter. He confessed that:

> The rest of the movement in consequence was restless and lacked conviction – to say nothing of the bar I omitted in the passage leading to the recapitulation of the second theme! I was at my best in the slow movement and was in tolerable form for the last movement. I came out a good deal perturbed at the trick my memory had played me, and with a worrying sense of lost confidence.[76]

The following day *The Times* dismissed him in a single sentence:

> Mr F.S. Kelly's playing of Mozart's Concerto in D (K.537) failed where the orchestral playing succeeded, because by giving extreme care to the neatness of the scale passages and by just over-phrasing the delicate tune of the slow movement he drew constant attention to the mannerisms of Mozart's style.[77]

On 6 October, in what was to be his last orchestral concert under Wood, he gave the Schumann Piano Concerto op. 54. This time his memory held. He was elated. The days between this and the last concert had been given over to auto-suggestion and the result was 'complete immunity from any slips of memory, but there might perhaps have been more spontaneity in my playing. I don't think, however, I did badly on the whole and the audience seemed to enjoy the performance, as I was recalled three times.'[78] *The Times* reverted to its former position: he was accused of playing 'like a scholar', and that his rhythm was defective, and suggested 'that he should find a worse timekeeper than himself – and this will not be difficult – and conduct a Concerto to his playing'.[79]

Later that month, as he was going into Queen's Hall for a Borwick and Henschel concert, Kelly ran into Edward Speyer,

> who poured into my ear a story that seemed to me quite incredible, namely that DFT had been paying too much attention to Mme Casals when he was staying with them recently in Spain, and that when Casals took him to task and said one of them must leave the house, DFT took the line that he was a superman, that the ordinary rules of conduct did not apply to him and that he flatly refused to go! Mr Speyer said he had had an hour's talk about it on Saturday with Casals, who was very much depressed and worried.[80]

Over dinner a few nights later Hugh Godley relayed Tovey's own account:

> According to DFT Casals beat his wife while he was staying there so that out of natural human instinct he was obliged to interfere, where at Casals accused him of having an understanding with her. DFT has since been over to Holland to see Julius Rontgen, the composer, who is a friend of both DFT, Casals and Mme Casals and from him learnt (a) that Mme Casals is not Casals' wife, but his mistress [Guilhermina Suggia] (b) that both she and Casals are insanely jealous, so that it is a common occurrence for one or other of them to threaten their guests with revolvers! H.G. said he was convinced after talking to DFT and Coutts Trotter, who has been DFT's confidant, that there was no sort of foundation for Casals charge against DFT. Rontgen, apparently, is going to confront Casals and try to get him to admit the baselessness of the story he has been spreading broadcast – and we both agreed he has some courage![81]

Tovey later claimed he was taking a bath and was obliged to jump naked out of the window when Casals came at him with a pistol.[82]

The scandal undermined Tovey's cause with the CCS. Late in 1912 Kelly emerged as its new Chairman. Kelly was well aware that Speyer was ambivalent about the change: 'Mr and Mrs Speyer and I have changed our relative positions since the last series of concerts (which he arranged). I find I am the first and last to applaud now and they come in a very deprecating spirit full of pity.'[83] The first CCS concert fully under Kelly's chairmanship, given on 6 November, was a financial success. He was elated, though he thought Ernst von Dohnanyi, the night's attraction, unpleasant and smug.[84] Dohnanyi lunched with Kelly and Borwick at Wimpole Street six days later. Kelly wrote:

> L.B. threw out a feeler about the modern French School of Debussy and Ravel, whereupon Dohnanyi assured us both there was nothing in it and that it consisted entirely of mannerisms! [...] He amused us both a good deal by playing us a few extracts from Schonberg's three piano pieces op. 11. It was an interesting little luncheon party, but our talk might have been more interesting were it not for a certain egotistic obtuseness on our guest's part. He was too ready to put forward his tastes or his prejudices (as in the case of Debussy, of which he was evidently quite ignorant) as indisputable facts. There is, however, a good deal of charm and geniality about him.[85]

Dohnanyi may have failed to come up to scratch, but now nothing and no one seemed to please Kelly. He fussed over the proofs of his coming concert programme and over the construction of the CCS programmes. He consulted Edmund Lancelot Warre about the cover design for the title page of his op. 1 and wound up undecided between ten shades of paper. Nothing was quite right. When Mrs Hammersley sent him her translations of the poems that accompany *Le Gibet*, which Kelly intended to play in his 12 December recital, he amalgamated them with his own versions. Edith Sitwell came to plead the cause of her companion and some-time governess, Helen Rootham. Kelly paid no attention to Sitwell and found Rootham's contralto lacking. Anxiety sent him to Dr Maurice Wright, another advocate of auto-suggestion, 'to obviate the habit I have of contracting the muscles of the jaw'.[86] Ultimately, Wright's treatment, like Bramwell's, was unsuccessful. Not even buying paintings at the second post-Impressionist Exhibition helped. He felt nothing but distain for the French exhibits but bought two Russian pictures – Count Komarowsky's *Gabriel* for £50, and Dimitri Stelletzky's *La Genie et la vie* for £9.

The year ended with a return to Aeolian Hall on 12 December in a programme that included Handel's E minor Fugue, Mozart's A minor Rondo, Beethoven's Sonata op. 54, Schumann's Fantasia, the Brahms Variations on an original theme, Mendelssohn's Scherzo a'Capriccio, his own Study in E major, Ravel's *Le Gibet* and the Debussy *Toccata*.[87] The audience was small but enthusiastic. Smith had sent out 250 free tickets but in spite of this the hall was only about a third full. Bookings brought in about £10.8.0, by far the lowest total for any of Kelly's London concerts. In spite of this his nerve held and he 'felt very well satisfied as regards the warmth and spontaneity' of his playing, 'which,' he wrote, 'seemed to be borne out by the warmth of the applause, but the criticisms in half a dozen papers were far from appreciative and harped on the restraint, the painstaking but uninspired qualities of my performance.'[88]

He trained to Eton to ask Sir Walter Parratt what he made of the charges of coldness in his playing. Parratt thought them unjust, adding that the public was possibly misled by Kelly's 'motionless and self-possessed attitude to the piano'.[89] Two days later Kelly put the matter to Borwick again. Leonard avoided a direct answer but said his friend's playing was 'rather lacking in a sense of climax'.[90] It was a damning response from the one peer who knew his work best.

It had been a difficult year. His debut season had not drawn audiences, though those who came were enthusiastic. The critics were united in finding fault with his hardness of tone and lack of emotional impact, yet admitted he was technically brilliant and a musician to be taken seriously. His compositions were seen as trifles. How much of this negativity was rooted in the general bias against Kelly the muscular rower is impossible to say. Kelly the musician was at a crossroads. Should he have the courage to brave it out for another season or retreat?

CHAPTER ELEVEN

THE CLASSICAL CONCERT SOCIETY AND MAURICE RAVEL 1912–1914

The lease on 34 Wimpole Street expired late in December 1912. After three years living under the same roof Leonard and Kelly found themselves obliged to live apart.[1] A landlord who would accept tenants with two grand pianos and the need to practise at all hours, proved all but impossible to find. It wasn't until early in 1914 that the two pianists moved into a large Georgian house at 29 Queen Anne Street. Borwick held the lease. A telephone was installed, baize was applied to doors, a partition to baffle sound was erected and a visit made to the Omega Workshop, Roger Fry's venture into decorative arts. On 23 February 1914 Leonard and Kelly dined with Borwick's brother and 'broke a bottle of champagne over our first night together in our new quarters'.[2] Which would also be their last.

Leonard Borwick was thirteen years older than Kelly and by this time an internationally known concert artist. He dominated Kelly's world, teaching him art appreciation and the finer points of pianism, attending concerts and galleries with him, directing the younger man's career and introducing him to his influential friends. There are echoes of the Tovey relationship: the same deference to a mentor, the same seeking of approval, the same eventual rebellion against control. Possibly only the war prevented a similar ending. They were close. How close is not known, though the relationship certainly took time to develop. For one thing, it was not until April 1913 that Kelly was invited for a long anticipated weekend at Cooke's House, Leonard's country home at Westburn. Kelly had given up hope of being asked and enthused to his diary:

> Both garden and house are arranged in the most exquisite taste and everything is extraordinarily characteristic of L.B.[3] […] I enjoyed my

> weekend enormously. L.B.'s appreciation of good things is not only confined to art, as I don't think I have ever had better fare (though of a plain and wholesome character) in any house or restaurant I have been in![4]

One of the 'good things' Kelly was referring to was an early work by the Danish minimalist painter, Vilhelm Hammershøi, which he saw at Cooke's House. He had long admired another of his austere paintings, *Interior, sunlight on the floor*,[5] which Borwick had on display at Wimpole Street. Borwick came to regard the painter as a genius[6] and to act informally as his London agent, both promoting his work and trading in it.

He was now in the process of selling *Interior with an Easel*, which he had bought the year before. While he was about it, he introduced Kelly to Hammershøi and his wife and model, Ida. Kelly thought them like naïve children in need of protection. When he came home one afternoon to find *Interior with an Easel* being carried off to its new owner, Adam Black, he felt a distinct sense of loss and decided to acquire a Hammershøi of his own.[7]

In the spring he visited the Hammershøis at their rooms in 62 Guildford Street, where he saw two new interiors in progress,[8] one of which he bought ten days later, paying £250[9] for it – the current equivalent of well over £30,000. This he hung in pride of place in the dining room at the Grange.[10] He then bought Ethel Sand's *Blue Sofa* after which he ruefully admitted that: 'I have bought 5 pictures in the last five months and I am becoming rather alarmed as to how far the craze is going to take me!'[11] A year later he was still gallery hunting. He passed up Eric Gill's *The Boxers* when he realised he had nowhere to display it in town, but paid 120 guineas (almost £15,000) for a small still-life 'by Bovin'.[12] He was tempted by Hammershøi's *The Jews' College*, the view looking down into a fog-bound Brunswick Square,[13] but its owner, cellist Ethel Nettleship, had had it over varnished and the sale fell though. In spite of this exposure to paintings and painters, Kelly's compositions have no overt connection to visual art, although about this time his settings of William Blake's words in *Cradle Song*, and *Infant Love* ('I have no name') led him to take in the Tate's collection for the first time.[14]

By then his compositional process had settled into a pattern: the conception of an idea, a notational fragment or figure sometimes sketched into the diaries, its development into a form, an internalised musical working-through in silence and then, and only then, its transference to paper, occasionally at the piano. At this point he would go to a performer or composer to get an opinion, reworking the piece, sometimes for long periods of time, before dating and signing the score.

He looked to Tovey and Borwick for advice on his piano and instrumental compositions, but turned to Gervase Elwes and George Henschel for his vocal settings. This sometimes backfired. When he eventually decided to dedicate his

Six Songs op. 6 to Elwes, for example, he sent him a selection in manuscript and asked permission. Elwes agreed to run through them but kept making excuses when Kelly tried to pin him down for a verdict. This went on for two years. By that time, tired of waiting, Kelly was paying Henschel to give his opinion of the set. When Kelly asked Elwes to return his copy of the manuscript, the tenor gave in and made a hasty assessment. Far from taking offence at this off-handedness, Kelly quickly wrote a setting of Pearsall Smith's *Cherry Tree* for him, determined to keep his attention. It was later included in the published work. In both cases the aim was to reshape the material to suit his singers and to have them programme his songs, preferably as soon as they were written and without waiting for publication, providing an endorsement and the necessary publicity. The final process of getting his work onto the printed page, however, meant that Kelly was engaged in almost permanent exchanges with his publisher. He would deliver his scores to Schott in person as a rule but a multitude of proofs were exchanged by registered post, much to their composer's annoyance.

His publication list remained brief: *A Cycle of Lyrics* for Pianoforte Solo op. 4, the segments titled 'Lament', 'Sea-Piece', 'Idyll', 'Caprice', 'Choler' and 'Reminiscence' (B. Schott's Söhne, Mainz, 1910), dedicated to J.W. Warre, and *Two Songs* op. 1 (Schott and Co., London 1912) consisting of 'Shall I Compare Thee' (undated, words by William Shakespeare), dedicated to 'M.A.K.' (i.e. his sister Maisie), and *Aghadoe* (from 1903, words by John Todhunter), dedicated to 'Muriel Foster'. But in 1914 he brought out a further half dozen songs as well as three piano works, all with Schott's London: *Six Songs* op. 6 consisting of 'March' and 'The Sages' Dance' (both from 1910, to words by Logan Pearsall Smith), 'When the Lamp is Shattered' (1910–13, to words by Percy Bysshe Shelley) and 'Music, When Soft Voices Die' (1910, to words by Shelley), 'The Cherry Tree' (1913, words by Logan Pearsall Smith), and 'The Daffodils' (1910, words by William Wordsworth), all dedicated to 'Gervase Elwes'. The works for piano were *Theme, Variations and Fugue* for Two Pianos op. 5 (1913), dedicated to 'Professors Iwan Knorr and Ernst Engesser'; *Waltz Pageant* for piano duet op. 2, and *Waltz Pageant* for piano solo op. 2a (1913), dedicated to Donald Francis Tovey; and the Allegro de Concert for piano solo op. 3 (1913), dedicated to 'Percy Aldridge Grainger'.

In the eighteen months left before the war, Kelly was involved in some eleven public concerts. Only two of these were solo recitals; eczema on his hands was possibly forcing a retreat into ensemble work. Two concerts were for charities, and another was given with the d'Arànyi sisters in the regular Haslemere series. He took part in the annual Oxford Balliol Eights Week concert, a two-piano concert with Danish pianist Johanne Stockmarr, three CCS concerts the first with the Rose Quartet, the second with Maurice Ravel and the third with Pablo Casals and Jelly d'Arànyi. The last two of the eleven were conducting engagements. His last pre-war concert appearance was private, at a gathering hosted by him at the Grange, this time with the English Quartet.

One other private event stands out in this line-up. At Eton on 22 November, Kelly appeared as soloist in the Schumann Concerto in A minor with Charles Lloyd conducting an orchestra of fifty professional players personally hired by Kelly. His aim was to expose the student body to the highest musical standards by establishing an annual orchestral concert as part of the college music curriculum. In this he failed, in spite of an enthusiastic reception for this opener. He was to return to his old school to concertise many times before the war, driven less by nostalgia as a need to test his own compositions with an insider audience that included his old teachers.

The first of his last two solo recitals was given on 6 May 1913 at the Aeolian Hall. Bach, Beethoven and Brahms for the first half, then what he saw as modern works: Scriabine's Prelude in E flat op. 11 no. 19; Rachmaninoff's Prelude in G minor op. 23 no. 5; Dvorak's 'Auf der alten Burg'; his own Study in G sharp minor; Percy Grainger's 'The Sussex Mummer's Carol'; Henselt's 'Chanson de Printemps'; two Debussy pieces, '*La cathédrale engloutie*' and 'Bruyeres'; and Ravel's 'Albonada del Grazioso'. [15] In spite of papering the house he had a poor house partly due to the concert clashing with the Bach Choir performance of Brahms's Requiem in Westminster Abbey, Gotterdammerung at Covent Garden and a concert at Queen's Hall in which Casals was playing. He believed he had played well[16] but *The Times* called his performance 'a half-finished perfection'. [17]

A November concert at Haslemere featured Adila and Jelly d'Arànyi in the Mendelssohn Variations Serienses. He thought he played with considerable warmth but he failed to rouse the audience.[18] On the 27th he was with the sisters again, this time at the Aeolian Hall in his new role as conductor in the Bach Violin Concerto in E major, with Jelly as the soloist.[19]

His last pre-war solo recital was given at the Aeolian Hall on 19 March 1914. Empty rows had a depressing effect and he was not in good form. At supper at the Imperial, Borwick gave Kelly his criticisms, nearly all of which Kelly agreed with:

> He liked the Monographs and put two stars against those in F sharp minor, E minor, G minor, F major and B minor. Those in A major and F minor he thought worthless. There was a delightful wreath left in the artist's room by Mrs Street on behalf of Saighdeer, her Aberdeen terrier, whose photograph was enclosed. She had embroidered the head, tail and paws of an Aberdeen on the two ends of the riband with which the wreath was bound.[20]

A week later, on 26 March, he was back at the same hall in a two-piano recital with the Danish pianist Johanne Stockmarr, brother of violinist Lady Hallé. Stockmarr was teacher to the queen's sister, Princess Dagmar of Denmark.[21] Kelly was pursuing the connections and designed the concert to promote his own Variations for 2 pianos op. 5. The concert went better than was expected.[22] *The Times* found the Variations were 'cleverly written'[23] if not organically constructed. Kelly ignored the press and got on with doing the household accounts, wrestling with his tax return and settling the bills for decoration with Borwick who was departing for an Australian-American tour the following week. Leonard would be gone for a year.[24]

Kelly's three personal appearances in CCS concerts at Bechstein Hall were given in late 1913 and early in 1914. The first, on 29 October 1913, was an all Brahms concert with the Rose Quartet. The house was crowded and Kelly thought he did well when he was recalled several times,[25] but the critics were harsh, repeating that his tone was 'hard and unsympathetic',[26] and that he was 'only partially successful in his solos'.[27] The second and much more significant concert was on 17 December with Maurice Ravel. More of this later. The third was on 11 March 1914 with Pablo Casals and Jelly d'Arànyi. *The Times* declared his 24 Monographs formidable. Some were deemed to 'have a boldness of design which was unexpected', others to 'have great delicacy and charm; while others again explore problems of technique with considerable enterprise. The playing of them, too, was delightful, for with his own music Mr Kelly is freed from the sense of duty and the reference to precedents which sometimes cumber his playing of the classics.'[28] Progress at last.

On 14 May 1914 Kelly conducted for the d'Arànyi sisters for the last time. The Aeolian Hall programme included Handel's Concerto in F major for two violins and cello with string orchestra; songs by Schubert and Brahms, and some Russian songs; a work new to London, Dr Arthur Somervell's Concert-stuck in D minor for violin and orchestra, (published 1913) and the Beethoven Concerto for violin and orchestra (with the Joachim cadenzas) with Adila as the soloist. Rehearsals were shambolic: players failed to appear, the amateur double bass played so out of tune he had to be dismissed,[29] and there was a female drummer from the theatre who had no idea of how to tune her instrument.[30] Miraculously, the concert came together – though it was far from acceptable. Kelly got a mention in the reviews but that was all.[31] In his usual style, he shrugged off his setback, and went on to a party at Lady Ottoline Morrell's in Bedford Square.[32]

At the Balliol Eights Week piano and vocal concert on 23 May he gave the Handel Suite no. 8 in F minor, the Mendelssohn Variations Serieuses op. 54 and four of his op. 9 Studies (No1 in F major, the premier of no. 5 in B minor, No 10 in E major and no. 12 in D minor) and wrote: 'I didn't rouse the audience out of a respectful attention'.[33]

Ever since the September 1912 Queen's Hall event Kelly had been intent on having Maurice Ravel appear for the CCS but approaches from Kelly and other CCS representatives went unanswered. Kelly persisted, even consulting Vaughan Williams, who had hosted Ravel's 1909 visit. He paid for a hundred lessons in

French at the Berlitz School, just in case.[34] It wasn't until early in December 1913 that Ravel finally agreed.[35]

At Bechstein Hall on the morning of 17 December, Ravel, accompanied by Madame Gueritte, was welcomed by Hugh Godley to a rehearsal for that night's CCS concert which was to feature Ravel's work in a programme apparently negotiated by Kelly, who had been there for an hour. 'He is very small,' his host observed,

> but his features are clear-cut and have an air of cleverness and distinction that prevent him from looking insignificant. He was very smartly dressed and was very genial with us all – without a suspicion of superiority in his manner. He can't talk a word of English and I was thankful I had searched the dictionary for the terms and phrases I thought likely to crop up! After the Introduction and Allegro the English String Quartet played his string quartet to which he listened with me in the centre of the hall. He seemed to be quite genuinely delighted with their playing and assured me he had only once heard his work played so well. He constantly kept muttering phrases like 'mais c'est parfait' and he was also very pleased with their freedom. He told me there were no good quartets in Paris – not because of a lack of good players, but because they wouldn't rehearse enough for a good ensemble. He also praised their instruments and said that the cellos and violas in Paris were made smaller and consequently didn't have such a good tone.[36]

That evening Ravel appeared as both accompanist and conductor. The English String Quartet opened the event with Ravel's Quartet in F major followed by Rhoda von Glehn in Strauss and Reger songs. Ravel then conducted his own 'Introduction and Allegro'[37] with Gwendolen Mason (harp), D.S. Woods (flute), Charlesworth Fawcett (clarinet) the English String Quartet and Kelly as the pianist. Kelly followed with four Scriabin works. Von Glehn sang a further bracket of five Ravel songs before Kelly and the English Quartet performed James Friskin's 'Phantasy in F minor'. Ernest Walker provided the analytic programme notes.[38]

Kelly went into the body of the hall to hear Ravel accompany Rhoda von Glehn in two groups of his own songs. He was disappointed and wrote: 'Ravel's playing didn't mean very much to me'. He was nervous and began his own group of Scriabin pieces badly, racing through 'without giving them time to tell'. The final Scriabin sonata, however, he thought went as well as he could play it and had considerable success so that he had to add the Prelude in G major op. 11.no.3. All the shifting about of music stands between the items and the long applause for Ravel drew the concert out till 10.30. and it wasn't until 11 that Kelly and his party sat down to supper at the Imperial Hotel in the private room he had hired. The little gathering consisted of Ravel and Mme Gueritte (wife of Tony Gueritte, founder of the *Societe des Concerts Francais de Londres*) Hugh Godley and his sister, Rhoda von Glehn, Eddie Marsh, (then Churchill's Private Secretary), Leonard Borwick, the Scottish pianist-composer James Friskin, and Kelly.

Ravel was again very pleasant and discussed his musical tastes with Kelly without any restraint:

> Chopin he thinks one of the greatest composers and in passing he said something about Schubert being the first composer who had really explored the possibilities of harmony. He has the French prejudice again Brahms who, he thinks might have done better, if he had been content to develop his talent naturally along its Schumannesque bent instead of trying to be like Beethoven. He admitted it was a great talent, though, and he specially mentioned the Pfte Quintet as being a 'chef d'oeuvre'. The Symphonies he contrasted to their disadvantage with Beethoven's and he dubbed the bB Concerto 'très lunuyeux'! When he was finding fault with Brahms' symphonic themes I taxed him with the Rondo theme of the last movement of the first symphony and he admitted that was an exception and that generally speaking the 1st symphony stood out above the other four. He seemed to think highly of Schonberg's ingenuity, but he admitted that many of the harmonies remained 'unintelligible' and he finally neutralised all his praise by saying one must remember that he had set out to compose on a theory and that no good music ever arose out of such a proceeding! He talked very highly of Liszt and specially mentioned the end of the Dante Symphony and the A major Pft Concerto. He admitted there was lack of form about it, which gave me a ray of hope against this blow to my estimate of his judgement but he immediately extinguished it by giving high praise to St Saens as a master of form! Do they know in French music what form is, I wonder? He said Gounod and especially Chabrier were the two sources from which the modern French School came and after supper he sat down to an old upright piano (tuned half a tone low) and played us a pastiche which purported to be a composition of Gounod arranged by Chabrier. This amused everyone as did also an imitation of Borodin's music, though we were none of us sufficiently familiar with the originals to appreciate the humour. [note along the side – He also spoke very highly of Vaughan Williams' Song cycle 'A Shropshire Lad' on which he professes to see a style that is truly English]. He finally played us a piano piece of Chabrier which

> resembled many modern French pieces in that it was much too long. Ravel delighted everyone by his alert interest in everything and his pleasant manner. Friskin struck me, though, as not quite approving of it all. When I told him Ravel had confessed to writing everything at the piano he remarked that he didn't see how else that sort of music could be written! We were turned out of the restaurant by the light being turned out at 12.30pm, but L.B. and I went on and talked everything over in the Union Club and I didn't get to bed till 2am. Ravel told me he's writing an opera 'La Cloche engloutie', a piano concerto and a piano trio. The concerto interests me enormously as there doesn't seem to be a good modern concerto.[39]

The critics were universally surprised that the CCS would give a programme of works solely by living composers, exclaiming: 'One would as soon have expected a Cubist exhibition at Burlington House as a modernist programme at a concert of the Classical Society', and spoke of its centrepiece guest as 'that arch-modernist, M. Maurice Ravel'. Works by Scriabin – 'another troubler of the dovecotes' – were,

> played by Mr F.S. Kelly whose orthodoxy has hitherto seemed hardly less unimpeachable than that of Mr Donald Tovey. What is more, the audience seemed to like it all immensely, and gave M. Ravel a very cordial reception. Having so far trafficked with modernism, the society may, perchance, be found at no distant date entertaining Herr Arnold Schonberg and Signor Russolo, the 'inventor' of Futurist music.[40]

Kelly's audacious programming was vindicated.

The day following the concert he lunched with Borwick at the Bath Club before both of them settled in at home to wait for Ravel who was due at 2.30, when they were also expecting Rhoda von Glehn. Kelly took the opportunity to show Borwick his settings of Blake's 'Infant Joy' and 'Cradle Song', which he thought good, but when Kelly suggested filling in the remaining time by playing some of his Monographs he was received 'with a masterly silence'. After a somewhat awkward pause he asked Kelly to play him the Scriabin Sonata op. 53, which Kelly had played in the CCS concert the night before. Rhoda came in time to hear most of it, followed by Ravel who arrived with Madame Gueritte. Borwick began 'the proceedings' by playing his own arrangement of 'L'Apres midi d'un faun' very beautifully. Kelly then played Ravel's 'Aborada del gracioso'.

> My Tempo was much too slow for him and it was very nice of him to think of saying that the "esprit" was good, as it must have been

> very painful to him to hear it played so much slower than he wanted it. After I had done he scrambled through it at an impossible pace, using considerably less pedal than I thought it needed. Such passages as (notes) he played quite 'sec' with an idea of imitating guitars, I imagine. He played us some of the Valse Nobles et sentimentales and 'Le Gibet' and indicated the tempi of the 'Jeux d'eau' 'Ondine' and the 'Pavane'. He seemed very much at sea technically and at times it looked as though he were almost unfamiliar with his music! He evidently is not in the habit of playing his works and in such circumstances there was no possibility of interpreting them. It is curious that a man with such an original style of pianoforte writing and who has been brought up as a pianist should not be able to play his works! Even although he laid no pretentious to being a professional pianist one thought that, like Cyril Scott, he might possibly play his own music delightfully. 'Le Gibet' he played much slower than L.B. or I play it. He was again very pleasant and genial.[41]

Ravel's appearance marked Kelly's first year in control of the CCS as a success. It was neither an accident nor achieved solely though Ravel's presence. It was backed up by the choice of ensembles – the Gelesco, Rose, Klingler, London and the English Quartets in particular.[42] The soloists on his watch included pianists Leonard Borwick, Johanne Stockmarr, Fanny Davies, Percy Grainger, George Henschel (who also sang for the CCS), J.Campbell McInnes, and Mrs Carl Derenberg; the cellist Pablo Casals; violinists Jelly d'Arànyi and Maurice Sons; vocalists Meta Diestel, Julia Hostater, Jane Bathori-Engel, Gervase Elwes, Rhoda von Glehn and Muriel Foster. Maurice Ravel appeared as an accompanist and conductor.[43] Kelly himself plainly intended London's musical circles to take notice of him. He had no intention of accepting personal defeat at the hands of the press, yet he was soon to ease himself off the platform as a soloist as his eczema grew worse. What appeared to be time out while his hands healed proved permanent. He was to lend himself to the CCS and the usual round of private house concerts, but as a solo recitalist he was almost done.

The Borwick-d'Arànyi-Harrison CCS concert on 26 November drew a full house. Kelly gave a supper party at the Savoy for sixteen guests including the d'Arànyis, the Walter Jameses, Leonard Borwick, Maurice Bonham Carter, Violet Asquith, Hugh Godley and Viola Tree, and wrote in his diary afterwards with obvious pleasure at the success of his programming, that Jelly 'gave a remarkably fine account of herself in the Kreutzer and had a very great and well-deserved success'.[44]

Things were not quite as serene as all this might suggest. For one thing, Edward Speyer was finding it difficult to let go of the CCS chairmanship and was using his son, Ferdinand Speyer, to influence CCS decisions.[45] Kelly himself was to add to Speyer's distress when he learnt from Smith that Casals had put up his fee from 60 to 80 guineas and Kelly was obliged to inform him that the CCS would have to do without its favourite cellist.[46] In July he invited the Speyers to the Grange in an effort to resolve their differences, even showing his six songs op. 6.to Mrs Speyer, (soprano Antonia Kufferath) along with his second setting of *A Slumber did my spirit seal* and later playing his Studies op. 9 for both of them 'which they seemed genuinely to like'.[47] Nothing worked.

When Karl Klingler wrote to every member of the committee claiming he was being treated inconsistently, Speyer took his side. Godley, Borwick and Kelly found themselves in opposition. This correspondence was considered so serious that it was gathered together and compared with letters from Ferdinand Speyer to Hugh Godley and Kelly. When Borwick was shown all this he endorsed Kelly's interpretation of Klinger's letters as 'being full of arrogance and insolence. He also found F.C.O.S. letters extremely priggish and silly.'[48] Speyer was sidelined.

Then in early 1914 the English Quartet took offence at being asked to play Haydn's Quartet in D minor op. 42, which Kelly thought 'quite one of his best'.[49] This was followed by violinist Maurice Sons refusing to play the scheduled Schubert C major Fantaisie for violin and piano D.934. His pianist, Fanny Davies, sided with Sons. Kelly was outraged and insisted on his right to dictate programming.[50] They were asked to cancel but went on with the concert, giving a deliberately lacklustre performance and risking their own reputations.[51] During the war Arthur Asquith found Kelly's over-management as an officer disturbing but it was already on show well before the war. Rebellion in his ranks may not have been new either.

Throughout all this he stuck to his routine of intense musical activity, though there were holidays threaded through the pre-war months as well. In late summer he joined Pearsall-Smith aboard his 20-ton yawl, *Varani*. From Gosport they sailed into Southampton Water, taking in Hamble, Poole, and Weymouth where they passed fourteen warships at anchor, many of them Dreadnaughts. They visited the Royal Dorset Yacht Club where Pearsall Smith was a member, before moving on to Lymington through St Alban's Head and the Needle, ending at Southampton via Cowes. For a time Kelly toyed with the idea of out-doing his host by buying either an 80-ton yawl or a 120-ton schooner but his enthusiasm soon evaporated along with the sea mist. In September he was one of twenty-five guests at Dumfries House at Old Cumnock, Ayrshire. His host, John Crichton-Smith, the fourth Marquess of Bute, was offering attendance at the Scottish Grand National steeplechase by day and a great deal of dancing by night. Kelly took the floor only once but allowed himself to be inveigled into playing for the dancing on 'an atrocious Bechstein', incongruously choosing the Chopin C sharp minor and E flat major Waltzes.[52] He followed this concert-less, and what he saw as fairly mindless partying, with three days at Penrhos, Anglesey, yachting, prawning and playing poker.[53]

The following April, unaware of the extent of the confrontation that was about to divide him from his German teachers and friends – though one suspects, because of it – he decided to go to Frankfurt and wrote to Knorr, Golden and Engesser to arrange meetings.[54] The week he spent there was balm to Kelly's nostalgic soul. His former teachers were warm and generous with their invitations and their interest in his compositions. There were small musical parties arranged where he played his Studies and Monographs, visits to one house after another, time spent listening to music at the Conservatorium where he played his Flute Serenade for Knorr and Engesser.[55] Against all logic, he remained unaware that his friends were about to become the enemy and that Germany was already mobilised. On the train to Mainz he 'had an excellent view of an airship, the Viktoria Luise, in motion. For some minutes', he said, 'it flew in the same direction at a height of about 300ft. I don't remember to have seen one before'.[56] LZ 11 *Viktoria Luise* was the first of the two G-Class Zeppelins built and was originally used to carry passengers and post. It was requisitioned by the German military during the war and used for bombing, reconnaissance and, later, as a training airship.[57]

Visits to the opera, ballet, cinema and the theatre took him through most of the notable events of the fashionable London scene right up to the brink of war: *Elektra, Ariadne in Naxos, Pelleas and Melisande, Boris Godunov,* (with Chaliapin) *La Khovantchina* (in Ravel's arrangement), Stravinsky's *La Rossignol*, Strauss' *La legend de Joseph,* Steinberg's *Midas* and at a performance of *Traviata* at Victoria Hall he met the legendary Lilian Baylis He saw the Ballet Russes with Karsavina and Nijinsky at Covent Garden and Drury Lane and Pavlova at the Palace Music Hall. At the cinema there was the serialised swashbuckler *Don Q,* 'some ludicrous scenes from Dante's *Purgatory*' at a Cinema Palace in the Strand',[58] and a piece on African wild animals. He was horrified by a scene of a trapped hyena and a lioness and felt for the cheetah and lion set on by a pack of hounds. He found *Potash and Permutter*, (using characters from a Broadway Jewish comedy) 'very entertaining'.[59] But it was still the theatre that occupied much of his social life, visits that often as not entailed a party of friends and supper at a fashionable restaurant or café afterwards. He was at J.M. Barrie's *Rosalind* with Stanley Houghton's *The Young Generation, Little Tich* at the Palladium, *Twelfth Night* at the Savoy, Forbes Robertson's *Hamlet* at Drury Lane, George Bernard Shaw's *The Doctor's Dilemma,* and just before the war, Shaw's newest play, *Pygmalion.* The night before the Ravel concert he took in Ibsen's *Wild Duck* but on a first encounter didn't think Ibsen was the great writer he was cracked up to be. At Christmas there was Maurice Maeterlinck's last play for marionettes, *The Death of Tintagiles*, (with Vaughan Williams' score) and Galsworthy's *Silver Box.* The Galsworthy was much talked about but failed to take. He saw the Strand Theatre productions of the melodrama *Mr Wu* and *Hullo, Tango!*. He was unimpressed. Kelly's dislike of dancing left him unresponsive to the attractions of popular music, which was then being transformed by ragtime and the tango. Jazz and the foxtrot were already coming into town. This revue was in the vanguard. In quite a different direction, his attention was caught by,

> Hagenbeck's Wonder-Zoo, in which there was a circus performance from 7.45 to 10.30pm. What most interested us [he was with Felix Warre] was a collection of young lions, bears, hyenas, polar bears, two dogs and a girl all apparently on the best of terms. We also saw a great collection of Polar bears being put to bed by a girl and a man who treated them just as though they were dogs. Chimpanzees riding bicycles and even a tandem bicycle was a complete surprise to me.[60]

The owner of this display was the inventor of the cageless zoo, Carl Hagenbeck. The show, purported to demonstrate humane captivity. As a consciousness raising exercise it was highly successful but Hagenbeck was also responsible for the human zoo, the display of 'savages in a natural state'.[61]

Only one of these theatre events seems to have seriously engaged Kelly musically. This was John Masefield's play *Nan*, then in repertory with Moliere's *Le Mariage forcé* at the St James' Theatre. Kelly recorded that: 'Nan made a great effect on me and struck me as though it might do for an opera. I had a few musical ideas, including one [notes are sketched on the page] which suggested itself as a motif for Nan herself.'[62] *The Tragedy of Nan*, as it was later known, was acclaimed on its premier in 1908.[63] The play is a rural tragedy in the same vein as Hardy's *Tess of the D'Urbervilles* and today could hardly be more outmoded.

His opinion of his peers grew more and more dismissive as the year progressed. He walked out of James Friskin's piano recital at Steinway Hall. Arthur Somervell's *Thalassa Symphony* in D minor with its Elegy on Scott's death in the Antarctic[64] and the Queen's Hall premier of his Symphonic Variations, 'Normandy' for piano and orchestra, with Tovey as the soloist and Arthur Nikisch conducting, he found tedious.[65] At a small party at Mrs Deneke's house,[66] he heard the violinist-composer Adolf Busch. Kelly dismissed him as tame. His real interest in being there was Tovey's presence. At Kelly's suggestion they played Tovey's *Balliol Dances*, a gesture of reconciliation.[67] A few days later, after he and friends had been to Tovey's last Chelsea Concert at Aeolian Hall, he argued over supper that his former mentor was 'untouched by modern influences' which, coming from Kelly, was damning.[68] By December he had mellowed. He was to hear Tovey's String Quartet in G major op. 23 and went over the score beforehand with Borwick who dubbed it '"Kapellmeister musik", but this seems to me unfair' Kelly wrote, 'or at least an exaggeration'.[69] On 2 September he and Felix Warre heard the Jean Sibelius' early tone poem *En saga* op. 9. Kelly knew the Finn's music from his score reading but this was the first time he had heard any of it live. It was thumbs down to both:

> Vaughan Williams as usual displayed great command of the orchestra but the music seemed to me an incongruous mixture of English folksong against a very modern background and it is difficult to see why it should be considered apt to express Greek ideas. There was a note of commonplace in some of the dance-rhythms. I felt sure, when I should hear a work of Sibelius, that I shouldn't like it. And I was quite right. En saga is a weak bit of music.[70]

Sibelius said of *En Saga* that 'in no other work have I revealed myself so completely'.[71] Kelly's response to both works was untypically very wide of the mark.

Things did not improve in the New Year. He heard Dohnanyi's Suite for Orchestra in F sharp minor op. 19 at Queen's Hall. Kelly felt it was:

> like most of his music that I know, not quite first class. He doesn't always wait for his best ideas to come but good and mediocre jostle one another throughout the piece. It is a talent waster, as the wherewithal to make first class music is there and the one thing needed is a really strictly critical sense to only allow the best to pass muster. Kol-Nidrei, [Max Bruch] which I didn't know, struck me as boring and the Ballet music to Henry VIII [St Saens] was quite awful. P.S.L-I came to see me at 5.45pm and I said something about a handful of sentimental and very immature songs which he had sent me.[72]

Florent Schmidt's recital sponsored by the *Societe des Concerts Francais* at the Steinway Hall a month later fared no better. He found the music empty and formless and that its composer looked 'an unassuming and uninteresting little man with spectacles'.[73]

Only two concerts by Alexander Scriabin could brighten things. Kelly heard him play at Queen's Hall under Sir Henry Wood's baton in his own Piano Concerto in F sharp minor op. 20 and in his symphonic poem *Prometheus: The Poem of Fire* op. 60 on 14 March: 'Scriabin's playing displayed an excellent schooling and there was a very precise sense of rhythm about it. There seemed to be warmth, but delicacy was a more marked characteristic. The concerto didn't seem interesting though it contained some pretty writing.'[74] Scriabin's Bechstein Hall recital of his own works on the 20th fared somewhat better. Kelly was with Borwick and both pianists were electrified. Kelly wrote that he had:

> never heard a more constant beauty of tone nor a greater technical mastery. Once or twice as in his study in D sharp minor he completely carried me away with his fire and some magnificent climaxes. Usually such ebullitions were preceded by a curling of his lip and an expression on his features as of one possessed. Otherwise his manner was very quiet.[75]

The mood evaporated when he heard the Spanish pianist Ricardo Vines y Roda. This was a pianist with an international career and a reputation for interpreting new French, Spanish and Russian music. Kelly would have none of it:

> L.B. and I found his playing completely incompetent and without life or rhythm. He played everything but the Islamey [Balakirew] from the music and by his manner as well as by the results one would judge he was playing the things at sight. However, when he played without the music it was just as dull and incompetent. Bax, all honour to him, refused to come to the concert after he heard him play his pieces. He, too, had the impression that he was playing them at sight. I was interested to hear Vaughan Williams Quintet [Phantasy Quintet for strings] which I had read last summer. It isn't quite first class though in places it is excellent [...] Neither [F. Austin] nor H.P. Allen who sat next to me, nor Vaughan Williams seemed to have any idea of what wretched pianoforte playing it was.[76]

More importantly, he found Gardiner's 1913 British music concerts dull, though he admired Grainger's wind ensemble, *Green Bushes*, and the Delius piano concerto. Frederic Austin's Symphony in E major drew a sharp rebuke for the programme notes accompanying it: 'a sententious and rather ridiculous dissertation as to the supposed fetters of the Classical Symphonic form'.[77] The second set of Gardiner concerts at Queen's Hall in 1914 irritated him start to finish. Bax's *Festival Overture* (1911) and the first complete performance of his *Four Orchestral Sketches* (1912–13) were dismissed as 'undistinguished', and George Butterworth's now famous *Rhapsody, A Shropshire Lad* (first performed 1913) and his *Idyll, The Banks of Green Willow* (1913) as 'rather charming if somewhat formless'.[78] Boring, awful, immature – Kelly was sounding thoroughly soured again. Nothing seemed to please him. The normally cheerful response was turning acidic. He went to a concert of the *Societe des Concerts Francais* and found that:

> Except for the Ravel quartet it was a dreary programme. Gabriel Dupont's Poème for Piano quartet seems to be the usual formless and meaningless music that nearly all French chamber-music consists of

> and neither his nor Chausson's songs were much better. The fact that Bizet, Debussy and Ravel should have sprung up in such a soil seems like a miracle.[79]

The last Christmas before the war was spent, as usual, at Gorhambury, with music, parlour games, bridge and hockey in the rain and mud. Lady Verulum invited twenty guests to hear Kelly play, but it was an audience of friends and a programme of the undemanding. He went to church on Christmas day but came out before Communion and avoided church for the rest of his stay. He turned his back on the shooting parties, pleading composition requiring attention. Alderley Park and the Sheffields followed, with more bridge, bell ringers (whom he found tedious), golf, chess, playing for the children's dancing at the Christmas tree party and dancing himself, 'a little' at the tenant's ball.[80] He allowed himself to be drawn in to Sibyl Grimston's cataloguing of the house's collections and later agreed to edit her text. This evolved into 'type-written lives of the Gorhambury portraits', which annoyed him: 'They were extremely badly written and to put them into shape has been a fortnight's work on an average of about an hour a day or perhaps more.'[81]

Summer brought more than the usual number of visitors to the Grange, Denis Browne and Eddie Marsh among them. Browne 'played us Percy Grainger's arrangement of the *Londonderry Air*, a Rondeau of Couperin, the Varsovilune from his Ballet', and accompanied Maisie's singing. Kelly responded with Grainger's arrangement of the *Sussex Mummers' Carol* and other pieces and wrote: 'W.D.B. plays rather charmingly.'[82] The next day Browne,

> played E. Marsh and me his ballet 'the Comic Spirit' which has some rather charming music in it and shows some talent for dramatic writing. It has weakness of structure, however, and might be considerably improved. It would, too, be all the better for having some of the more obvious signs of the influence of Stravinsky taken out of it. I made him play it through twice.[83]

Balfour Gardiner came in July, Kelly returning his hospitality at Ashampstead the month before. They played tennis and rowed. Kelly played his Monographs for Gardiner's approval and finished making a fair copy of his 12 Studies while Gardiner went on with work on *April*, occasionally asking Kelly 'to suggest improvements in the pianoforte arrangements of the orchestra'. Over dinner they quarrelled: 'We disagree fundamentally about music,' he recalled, 'and we seem to drift into an argumentative statement of our views.'[84]

Summer somewhat restored his temper but his health was taking a turn for the worse. He consulted Dr Maurice Wright, looking for 'some treatment by suggestion' to rid him of 'a tiresome habit I cannot control – of sometimes tightening the muscles of my jaws and those at the back of the mouth'.[85] The treatment was ineffective. The day before his first recital of the year he was driven to visit Bramwell again not only for the facial tic but for the return of his asthma.[86] He decided to diet and exercise over summer and was pleased with the results,[87] taking to the water in earnest again, though not to row at high pressure and rarely at a racing stroke.[88] In the previous winter he had to see Dr J.F. Woods for 'the kind of eczema which in cold weather sears my hands and fingers with deep cuts'. Woods method differed from Bramwell's in that he said nothing while laying his hands on different parts of the body,

> in my case the solar plexus, the forehead and the hands. When his hands touched me I experienced a pleasant tingling of the nerves and altogether I spent a very restful three-quarters of an hour. He held out hope of being able to cure me, as he declared he had just treated a lady successfully for the same trouble.[89]

Wood failed. In January 1914 Kelly thought the cracks in his hands were somewhat better, not because of Wood's manipulations but from the application of a cream he told his patient to apply at night. Stress and exposure to the sun are now thought to trigger this condition but there is still no cure. On 28 March he attended Mr Gunn, one of the dentists renting the basement below Kelly's flat. There was an exposed nerve. Cocaine was applied. Kelly fainted:

> and on coming to I was completely unconscious of my where-abouts and had the impression that the strange man who had his hands at my throat (trying to undo my collar) was trying to murder me! I was not up to much for the rest of the day but attended the boat race [at Putney] and the boat race dinner at the Grand Hotel.[90]

He returned to Wood in May 'to have my nerves "tuned up" in warm weather and to avoid chapped hands in cold weather'.[91] He also saw Dr Young again, with an ongoing 'septic' leg and a 'septic' swelling in his left nostril.[92] Young had treated him for a 'poisoned' little finger in summer the year before. He developed a boil on his leg which the doctor lanced. Kelly was so ill that he was obliged to telegraph his apologies to Lady Bute for having to turn down her invitation to Cardiff for Whitsuntide.[93] By July he was suffering from boils and blisters again. He took to his bed and sent for a Dr Downes. He was bandaged up for four days but by the 9th he was able to take off the dressings and get about: 'I still had to bandage my hand, however, and wear a glove.'[94] This at least allowed him time to correct the first proofs of his *Flute Serenade*.[95]

In April 1914 he spent a weekend at Robert Townsend Warner's[96] Bay Cottage at St Margaret's Bay, walking the white cliffs towards Dover and playing for his host. On the train back to town he read 'a most interesting article (covering two sheets) on the late Army Crisis with regard to Ulster and I was well occupied through the 2 hours of the journey from Dover to London getting through it.'[97] Two days before the government had found it impossible to prevent the Unionist smuggling of German arms into Ulster ports. It was suddenly alerted to the divided loyalties of the British armed forces and the realisation of its inability to control its borders. The Home Rule Bill was passed that month. It was due to be implemented in September but went into abeyance for the duration of the war.

At the beginning of the summer season and with only the newspapers to flash brief warnings of what was about to blow his world apart, Kelly shifted back to Bisham and went on with his life as if nothing could ever change. Ethel Nettleship arrived on 15 May to go through Camille Chevillard's cello sonata op. 15 in B flat major and another by Ernest Walker from 1913 and still in manuscript, neither of which Kelly rated highly. The Chevillard 'had all the characteristic French weakness of form' he concluded. 'As it bore the date 1896 I was rather surprised to find the whole-tone scale employed once or twice.'[98]

With the war now only weeks away, Kelly's life ran on strangely as if nothing was happening. He turned 33 on 29 May. There was champagne at dinner with his sister and May Long Innes, he played Ravel afterwards. He went back and forth between the Grange and Queen Anne Street frequently, went to concerts, plays and films with friends, wined and dined them in town and entertained them at weekends at the Grange, rowed and watched rowing, swam in the river and played a great deal of tennis. He conferred with his agent and others about the programming of CCS concerts to come, shopped for furnishings for his rooms, bought music, practised and performed in company and worked at composition and his French as usual. There was ongoing bickering over the CCS programming, with Kelly detailing every move. In the finish he wrote that: 'F.C.O.S. [Ferdinand Speyer] had consistently made a fool of himself on the C.C.S. Committee and has always assumed the role of heckling H.G. and me in everything we have done.'[99]

He sat with Denis Browne and Eddie Marsh at Walter Rummel's Aeolian Hall concert on 3 June to hear Debussy, and on the 4th with Browne to Verdi's *Otello*, a work which neither had heard before, though Browne had read it. Kelly wrote:

> It struck me as being remarkably dramatic and fine, though I wanted something greater in the last act – a touch of something like Shakespeare's poetry. I thought it the greatest work of Verdi that I have yet come across, though even so I felt doubtful whether it really ranks in the highest class of music. It has a never failing flow of melody and there is a splendid dramatic instinct at play. We met R.C. Trevelyan afterwards and took him back to the Union Club to talk

> over the opera. Melba sang divinely and Antonio Scotti was quite splendid as Iago.[100]

He went to Marshall-Hall's *Stella*, a Jacque Thibaud concert with a double quartet and to Drury Lane to see the first English production of Ravel's ballet *Daphnis et Chloe* on a bill that also promised Rimsky-Korsakov's *Scheherazade*. Both were given by the Russian Ballet:

> Ravel had sent a letter to *The Times* the same morning protesting against the production of his work without the chorus and certainly some of the piece's entr'actes sounded pointless. He had arranged it in the version it was given for provincial performances where it would be difficult to get a chorus. The music throughout interested me very much and the scoring too. It is full of characteristic refinement, but some of the dance tunes smacked of Russian influence.[101]

And then, on 17 June, in a fitting conclusion to his career (though he thought his career was still at its beginning), Kelly gave a musical party for forty-six guests at Bisham Grange. It was 'a hot sunny day of about 80 degrees in the shade'. He had hired the English Quartet – Thomas F. Morris and Herbert H. Kinze (violins), composer Frank Bridge (viola), and Ivor James (cello) – ostensibly to play Ravel's String Quartet in F major, but his real intention was for them to 'incidentally play' his new Trio in B minor. Kelly provided the solos: the Chopin *Barcarolle* op. 60, Percy Grainger's *The Sussex Mummers' Christmas Carol,* Mendelssohn's *Song Without Words* in F sharp minor *no.* 32 op. 67 no. 2, and Brahms' *Rhapsody in E flat major* op. 119 no. 4. He thought the solos went well and that his Trio was well played – he was agreeably surprised; he also thought it was too long and that the first movement 'contains scratchy places'.[102] He gave his guests tea and when they were gone he took the quartet out in the punt to show them the abbey. Not a cloud in his sky.

On 30 July he wrote that 'M.A.K., M.E.L.I. and I were completely absorbed at meals by the news of Europe arming. It looks as though there must be a large war.'[103] He went on the following day: 'We were all in a great state of excitement over the European situation and I motored into Marlow after breakfast and came out armed with the Sunday papers. Late at night we got a special Sunday edition of *The Times* and *Daily Mail* and I sat up reading them.'[104] Five days later he was genuinely disturbed:

> I spent some 2½ hours reading the papers in which Sir Edward Grey's speech on our obligations as regards Belgium neutrality and the French entente. H.G. brought with him the news that England

> had delivered an ultimatum to Germany demanding an answer by midnight. I am wondering whether I ought to join the Territorials. I rested from 5–6pm and went sculling at 7pm. Dr Downs gave me a 3rd inoculation for boils.[105]

In the morning he woke to a world at war.

CHAPTER TWELVE

GALLIPOLI 1914–15

On the morning of 4 August 1914, Kelly could hardly tear himself away from his newspapers. *The Times* that day contained accounts and analysis of Sir Edward Grey's compelling speech to the House of Commons the day before. On page 6 the Foreign Secretary's arguments were set out in full.[1] They suggested that Britain could not stand idly by while the German army violated Belgium en route to its invasion of France, with whom it had declared war on 3 August. Grey's arguments on Britain's obligations to Belgium in the face of unprovoked German aggression had not only resonated with those in the house. They also struck a powerful chord with Kelly. The resonance was enough for him to consider if he should join the part-time territorial forces.

But it was not until September that he had any success in finding a unit he could join. On 7 September Winston Churchill made an appeal for men of: 'high character and education'[2] to join the newly created Royal Naval Division as officers. The age limit was set at 35 – and Kelly came in just under this limit. And, as luck would have it, Rowley Nelson – Kelly's rival for the stroke seat at Eton – was one of those charged with selecting men for commissions with the new division. Kelly contacted him on 12 September. Two days later he had received a commission as a sub-lieutenant in the new force.[3]

A 'Churchill connection' was important in the decision of Kelly's friends and acquaintances to join the RND. Most prominent among these were Arthur 'Oc' Asquith. The 31-year-old was not only the third son of the prime minister, but was already known personally to Kelly. Asquith received his commission to the RND on 25 September. Eddie Marsh, Churchill's long-standing private secretary, helped arrange many of the appointments in the RND on a personal basis. The patron of the arts was also well known to Kelly and had already spent a weekend at Bisham Grange in mid-July of 1914. Marsh's fellow guest on that occasion was the young gifted British composer and music critic, William Dennis Browne. At Bisham, Kelly and Browne had both played for Marsh.[4] Just eight weeks later, Marsh was arranging a commission for Browne in the RND. And it was Marsh's connection that had secured a commission for the most famous of all the RND's officers: the charismatic poet, Rupert Brooke – a man whose life and death would stir Kelly to create one of his most celebrated compositions.

Kelly began his military career in the coastal town of Walmer. And though some of the RND were thrown in unsuccessfully during October, to try and prop up the defences of Antwerp against the German surge, Kelly was not among them. But on 21 October, Kelly was finally given command: 3rd Platoon of A Company, Drake Battalion was now his. And Kelly soon learned how frustrating command could be. His Petty Officer Ellis had been taught naval discipline for twenty-seven years and according to Kelly: 'Isn't going to take up with any new-fangled ideas at his time of life.'[5]

Though Kelly was to become a good commanding officer, he initially found the going tough. These tensions were to become more apparent when he was posted to Scotland, where he would complete both his training and that of his platoon. It was there that at one stage, Kelly's commanding officer asked him to become a quartermaster to the battalion – rather than command a platoon. Later in the war, Asquith perceptively recorded how Kelly's rigidity could adversely affect his relationship with those he commanded. Asquith noted that Kelly 'combined something of the recluse's ignorance of the thoughts and feelings of all sorts and conditions of men with something of the artist's exacting austerity'.[6]

Kelly, somewhat reluctantly, accepted his new role. But he was determined that he should not miss out on service overseas. By the last week in February 1915, when the division had finally relocated to Blanford in Dorset, it had become clear that they were going to be sent to fight in the Dardanelles. But it seemed that Kelly would be left behind again as surplus to requirements. So, on Monday 22 February, Kelly swung into action when he heard of a possible gap in the Hood battalion. Rather than wait for official channels to unfold, Kelly used his connections with the officers of the Hood, including his fellow musician, Browne. The next day, on Browne's suggestion, Kelly visited Colonel Arnold Quilter, the commanding officer of the Hood, to press his case to be transferred. It so happened that Quilter's battalion was short of officers. By 6pm that day, Kelly had formally joined his new unit.

Kelly's arrival added the final ingredient to what was already a remarkable mix of officers. The Hood's commander, Lieutenant Colonel John Quilter, was a former Grenadier Guards officer. He'd served with distinction in the Boer War, trained his men effectively and crucially, his men liked him. Moreover, it seemed that Quilter's personality helped attract some of the RND's 'brighter sparks', whose personality might have clashed with officers from other battalions.[7] Already by Antwerp, the remarkable kiwi,[8] Freyberg, had joined the Hood. The American,

Johnny Dodge, had transferred from the Anson battalion. Through marriage, his wealthy family was related to Churchill.

In November came Arthur Asquith. Brooke had heard from Asquith that there was a vacancy in Freyberg's company – he got the news of his successful application for a move via a telegram from Marsh.[9] Browne, Brooke's friend from Rugby, joined the Hood, following a posting that Brooke had arranged.[10] It was clear that the Hood's mess was the: 'place to be'. Added to that list of stellar characters were two brilliant Etonians: Patrick Shaw-Stewart and Charles Lister. While serving in the Gallipoli campaign, Shaw-Stewart would write one of the war's most memorable poems: 'Stand in the trench, Achilles'.[11]

These were the men who were to become known as the 'Argonauts',[12] Jason's band of mythical Greek heroes, who set out on a quest to find the Golden Fleece. Once it was known that the Hood was to fight in Gallipoli, it was not hard for scholars like Brooke and Shaw-Stewart to identify themselves as latter-day warriors, cast in the mould of their ancient Greek heroes.[13] During classical times, Gallipoli had been at the centre of momentous events. The city of Troy, once besieged by the Greeks, was situated at the western end of the Straits. The legends of the famous Greek warriors involved, like Achilles or Odysseus, were part of Homer's epic poems: the *Iliad* and the *Odyssey*, the study of which formed an important part of the education of many of the officers in the Hood.

Though Kelly was more measured in his prose, as soon as he knew the Hood's destination, Brooke, in a letter to Violet Asquith on the 22nd, expressed both his and others' sense of excitement at the prospect of the Hood fighting on sites of ancient battles. 'Shall I loot mosaics from St Sophia … & Turkish delight? & Carpets. Shall we be a turning point in History? Oh God! I've never been quite so happy in my life … to go on a military mission to Constantinople.'[14]

But just a few days later – just before the division's embarkation – Brooke reported that a decision by Kelly to share some Brooke's poems around the mess caused him to be 'terribly upset'. On 25 February, Kelly received a copy of the magazine *New Numbers*, in the post. It contained a collection of Brooke's most recent work, *Poems 1914*. The six works, which spread Brooke's reputation to an even wider public, included his memorable War Sonnet V: 'The Soldier', which opened with the unforgettable and prescient lines:

> If I should die, think only this of me:
> That there's some corner of a foreign field
> That is forever England.

Kelly read the poems, was impressed, and then decided to pass the magazine round the Hood's mess. In a diary entry for 27 February, written in Marseilles some three months later, Violet Asquith takes up the story:

> Rupert joined us later very tired and the bubble of excitement momentarily gone off him … He complained bitterly that Kelly had got hold of his sonnets and was spreading them among his mess-mates.[15]

Some historians have subsequently sought to add further colour to Asquith's description. In his biography of Brooke, Nigel Jones wrote that on the 27th, Violet Asquith had found Brooke in a 'foul mood'. Jones then went on to write:

> One of his fellow officers Frederick 'Cleg' Kelly an Australian born Oxford 'hearty', who had thrice won the Diamond Sculls at Henley Regatta had got hold of a copy of his sonnets and shown them round the mess with Antipodean ribaldry, much to Brooke's dismay.[16]

It might be understood why Jones painted an unforgiving picture of Kelly's involvement in this episode. But Jones' description of Kelly does not align with either Kelly's character, or what he'd felt when he read Brooke's sonnets for the first time. Then, he'd written: 'I received a copy of *New Numbers* in the afternoon and found some poems by Rupert Brooke (of this battalion) which struck a sympathetic note in me.'[17] And, as we shall see, Kelly continued to underline their impact on him during the voyage to Gallipoli.[18]

By the time Kelly embarked on the 28th, he understood a new chapter of his life was about to unfold. That sense of history, with which Kelly and his fellow officers of the Hood Battalion begun their Odyssey to the battlefields of Gallipoli, was not misplaced. Gallipoli's eastern coastline faces the Asian shoreline just 5 km away. Along that eastern side of the peninsula ran the famous 'narrows', or Dardanelles Strait. If the Ottoman Empire controlled the narrows, seaborne access to their capital city would be impossible, so Constantinople would be safe from naval attack. But once Gallipoli's forts were subdued by British land forces, which included the RND, then the narrow's minefields could be swept clear. It would then be relatively straightforward for the British and French fleets to break into the sea of Mamora and bombard Constantinople, which lay less than a day's steaming away. Thus, a deadly blow would be struck against the Ottoman Empire.

The boat that would carry the Hood there, the 7,615-ton *Grantully Castle*, was a relatively new ship, and there were few complaints among the Hood's officers about their cramped quarters. A confidence about their ability to complete their task no doubt added to the upbeat mood in the mess. This was especially so among the men of the Latin Table. When Brooke, Asquith, Shaw-Stewart, Browne, Dodge, Kelly and later – after he joined the ship at Malta – Lister, met for dinner, high spirits, wit hand *joie de vivre* were the order of the day.[19] Their exploits were renowned throughout the ship and membership of this elite group was extended to

Freyberg. In a letter to Marsh, Brooke, in his own inimitable way, described how he experienced the characters of those in the 'Club'. 'Patrick is the life and soul of the party – the life, anyhow. Denis is competent, Kelly silly, Johnny inquisitive & simple hearted, & Oc OC-like. While Freyberg … often makes rushes across the room to say "I say do you think this is going to be a good show? I do."'[20]

Expectations of the scale of the military task that awaited them were not high. But on 12 March, while anchored off their initial destination of the island of Lemnos, Kelly received some information which may have just dented the confidence of the Latin Club a touch. The little harbour at Mudros had been placed under British control and was intended to be the main staging point for the Gallipoli landings. As such it wasn't that much of a surprise that Kelly saw HMS *Dublin* anchored there. The light cruiser had been in the Mediterranean since 1914. Though he didn't know it at the time, its captain, John 'Joe' Kelly, was soon to become his brother-in-law.

That day though, the talk was mostly about the war in the Mediterranean and the strength of the Ottoman defences on the peninsula. The accuracy and strength of the artillery had particularly impressed the captain and the *Dublin* bore the scars of Ottoman shells that had hit home. And that night, when the Australian returned to the Grantully Castle, it was clear that his friend had swept away any illusions about how easy it might be for the Allied task force to clear the Turks and their German allies from Gallipoli. Of his friend's views he wrote: 'He was rather depressing about the task that awaits us in clearing the Gallipoli Peninsula of Turks and German. He thinks there are a great many of the latter and that they have made excellent preparations.'[21]

Five days later, complete with 200 rounds of ammunition per man, the RND's transports, along with units of the Allied fleet, set sail for Gallipoli. Unfortunately though, the Allies' plan to force the narrows totally under-estimated the capacity of the Ottoman commanders and their German allies. Together, they had bolstered the land defences on the European side of the peninsula. Moreover, they had managed to lay more mines along the passage that Allied capital ships might take to engage the forts and force a passage through the strait. By the end of the day, over 700 allied sailors had lost their lives and three battleships had been sunk – destroyed by mines and guns. Three other ships were effectively crippled.[22]

In the wake of that defeat it became clear to the commander of the naval flotilla, John de Roebuck, that he would now have to wait for land forces to destroy the guns which threatened his ships and, more crucially, his minesweepers. These could not possibly sweep the narrows clear while under attack from heavy Ottoman shore batteries. Only when the mines were clear could the fleet proceed. But with strong British land forces, such as the 29th Division, still yet to arrive in the region, the decision was taken to wait a further six weeks before an assault was made on the Gallipoli beaches, so the *Grantully Castle* then headed for Egypt where the RND and other forces would disembark and await reinforcements.

It was 9 April, when the Hood finally re-embarked on *Grantully Castle*, once more en route to the Greek islands, that the Hood's Latin Table resumed their nightly discussions. This was despite Brooke having been taken ill in Egypt. Understandably, even though Kelly's focus was increasingly on the coming conflict, what is apparent from his diary is the pleasure he took from spending time with a convalescent Brooke talking about literature and, in particular, listening to the poet read out some of his poems.

It's hard to avoid the conclusion that in the last few days of his life Brooke had come to enjoy Kelly's company; both for the Australian's genuine fascination in his work and for their shared interest in literature. And one of Kelly's diary entries – that of 17 April – makes this clear. Quite apart from his evening encounter with Brooke, that Saturday must have felt like a particularly surreal day in Kelly's life. He had received a letter 'which gave me one of the greatest surprises I have ever experienced. Of all the incredible events!' Maisie had married 'Joe' Kelly in Malta. He was more than delighted.[23](Knighted in 1919, Sir John Donald Kelly became an Admiral of the Fleet.) While his mind was still trying to digest this news, Brooke walked into his cabin at 8.45pm. Kelly was in the process of preparing for bed but Brooke wanted company and he knew that Kelly loved to talk about 'literary matters'. After a while, Kelly asked his fellow sub-lieutenant to read him his five sonnets. 'I enjoyed the sound of his voice and the way he read them a good deal,'[24] he wrote afterwards. Clearly their relationship had developed since that day back in Dorset, when Brooke was so annoyed with Kelly. Moreover, it mirrored earlier recorded literary discussions between Kelly and Brooke on 13 April and this, only the day after Kelly had re-read Brooke's sonnets.

The contrast between the imminence of combat and the peaceful idyllic atmosphere of Skyros, where the RND engaged in training exercises, probably only served to heighten the emotions of those in the Hood.

The next day – minus Dodge – the Latin Club had what could be regarded as its final gathering. Kelly wrote that Tuesday: 'I sit at table with Patrick Shaw Stewart, Denis Browne, Arthur Asquith, Rupert Brooke and Charles Lister and we're a jolly party.'[25] But by Thursday, the mood had profoundly shifted. By then, Kelly had discovered just how seriously ill Brooke had become and with that sense came depression. Kelly wrote. 'I have a foreboding that he is one of those like Keats, Shelly and Schubert who are not suffered to deliver their full message.'[26]

On 23 April Brooke was dead because of sustaining blood poisoning from an infected mosquito bite. Kelly's diary entry is one of the most emotionally charged that he was to write. It opened with: 'The events of the day made a deep impression on me.'[27] Because time was so short before the *Grantully Castle* was due to steam to Gallipoli, Brooke had to be buried on Skyros that night. A beautiful grove where Brooke had rested just a few days previously above the anchorage was chosen for his final resting place. Kelly was part of the burial party. The Australian tried to resolve what must have been a tumult of different emotions. His diary entry for that day concludes:

> The body lies looking down the valley towards the harbour and from behind an olive tree bends over the grave as though sheltering it from the sun and rain. No more fitting resting place for a poet could be found than this small grove, and it seems as though the gods had jealously snatched him away to enrich this scented island. For the whole day I was oppressed with the sense of loss but when the officers and men had gone and when at last the five of us, his friends, had covered the grave with stones and took a last look in silence – then the sense of tragedy gave way to a sense of passionless beauty, engendered both by the poet and the place.[28]

Within a few hours, Kelly and the Hood had left for Gallipoli. The inevitable preparations and focus ahead of the landings must have provided a welcome distraction to those men. But of course, it meant that the Hood's officers and crew would have to come to terms with Brooke's death as best they could. For many that would involve recollections, letters and obituaries. Kelly though, would reconcile his feelings with one of his most memorable and moving pieces of music, his Elegy, 'In Memoriam Rupert Brooke'. The voyage to Gallipoli was nearly over; the waiting complete. Kelly's first battle was about to begin.

By late April, the 75,000 British, ANZAC and French troops commanded by General Sir Ian Hamilton, had been assembled for the assault on the beaches of Gallipoli. Equipment had been a concern. In addition to Hamilton's force having no specialist landing craft, they were short of both artillery and high explosive ammunition.[29] But despite the death of Brooke, morale – at least on the surface of the Hoods – seemed to be high. At dawn on the 25th (poor weather delayed the initial assault) Hamilton therefore planned that his main force – the troops of the 29th division – would assault at five points, along a 6-mile stretch of coastline around Cape Helles. On 26 April, Kelly wrote that the RND had been ordered to steam towards Helles to: 'support the 29th Division'. But already word had begun to percolate to the troops that all had not gone well with the landings. After initial success at Anzac Cove, there were reports that the forces above the cove were now under heavy pressure.

The story was the same on the beaches further to the south of the peninsula. With the landing battalions so badly mauled, Hamilton had no choice but to throw in fresh troops, including the French, to consolidate the beaches. After digging in on the 26th, the British realised that the beleaguered Ottoman forces – now reinforced – had withdrawn to a new defensive line a few miles north of the beaches and in front of the town of Krithia. If the Allies wanted to secure the strategic hill of Achi Baba, they would have to launch a frontal assault on that line.

Kelly witnessed that offensive 2 miles offshore from on board the *Grantully Castle*. Launched on 28 April, it was to become known as the first battle of Krithia. A stout Turkish defence meant that there was no meaningful progress. Of the 13,500 troops with which the allies had attacked, 3,000 were dead or wounded.[30] In truth, the battle for Achi Baba had now turned into the kind of siege warfare that was had become familiar on the Western Front.

Even Hamilton knew that if he were to continue, he would need reinforcements. With them, he would have enough manpower to assault the Ottoman lines in front of Krithia once more. Until substantial numbers of new troops arrived, Hamilton turned to the only troops he had left to throw into his newly dug trenches: the brigade of the RND. So, in the early hours of Friday 30 April, Kelly and his platoon slipped aboard a tow to make landfall.

It wasn't long before Kelly and his battalion were in fierce action, in support of the larger units of French and Senegalese troops. During the nights of the 1st and 2nd May, the Turks made one of their many attempts to drive the exposed British and French back towards the landing beaches. In the small hours of the morning, of the 2nd, Kelly's platoon was charged with running along a half-mile stretch of trench line supplying ammunition to those holding off the Turks. Under fire from the attacking troops in front and snipers behind, the champion sculler moved so fast that by the time he'd run out of ammunition he noticed that only three of his platoon had managed to keep up with him.

There was little time for Kelly to catch his breath before the Hood – at 10am and without vital artillery support – was ordered to make a quick counterattack along a dried-up riverbed that led up towards Achi Baba. It was an action which revealed that Kelly did indeed have the qualities necessary to command men under fire – qualities that perhaps a previous commanding officer might have doubted. In preparation, Kelly had already sent six scouts ahead to protect his platoon from snipers hidden between the Ottoman and Allied lines. When the battalion got closer to the Ottoman front line, they were met with a hail of bullets and had to dig in.[31]

Undoubtedly, it had been a torrid baptism for both the Australian and his battalion. But though his combat skills, and those of most of his comrades were still in their infancy, he had proved to his platoon that he had both the courage and motivation to lead from the front. There would be little or no opportunity for the Hood to rest and worse was soon to follow. Another major assault was scheduled for the morning of 6 May. The second Battle of Krithia saw the Hood acting as part of a push that would involve most of the 25,000 Allied troops advancing across the 1½ mile width of the peninsula. This assault, supported by naval gunfire would – it was optimistically thought – finally push the Ottomans off the heights of Achi Baba.

Unsurprisingly, Kelly's diary entry for the first day of the offensive is one of his longest. Since then, much ink has been spilt about the poor planning and wildly

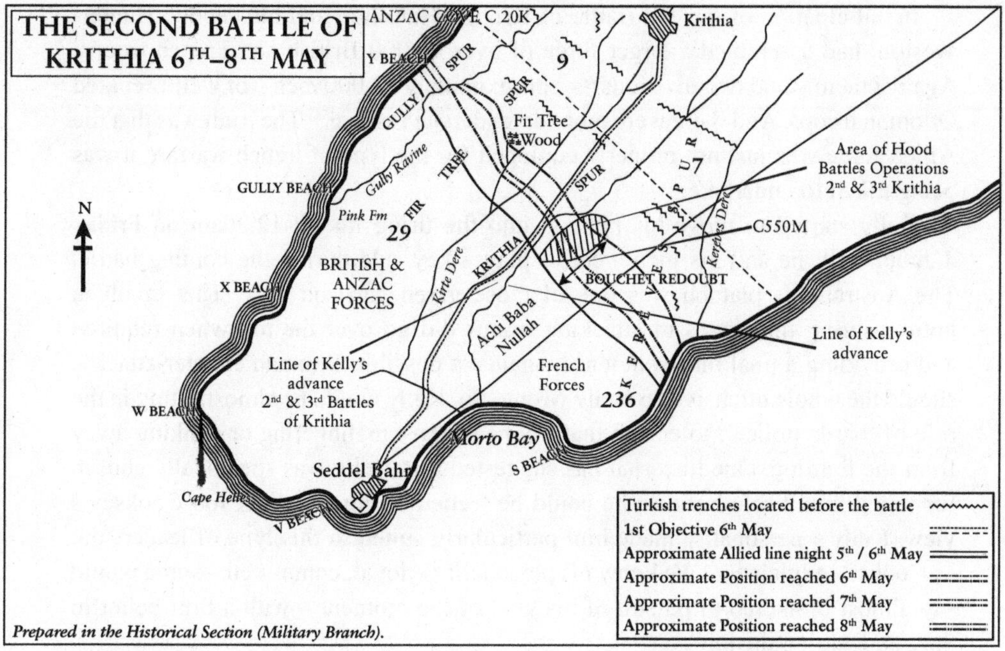

over-ambitious expectations that preceded the battle. Kelly called the original plan 'promising'. But then his company commander had only been able to brief him just after breakfast that morning.

Kelly's platoon – from B Company – was placed in the fourth wave to go over the top. Advancing 1,000 yards in a series of 'rushes', Kelly's platoon soon became isolated and pinned down. They had no choice but to dig in. Fortunately, an Ottoman counterattack didn't materialise. But between then and 8 May, when the attack was called off, Kelly's platoon had sustained seventeen casualties – a loss of around 50 per cent.[32] Quilter – the Hood CO – had been killed instantly while leading his men into action with an oversize walking stick. Moreover, over 30 per cent of the Hood's officers had become casualties.

It was inevitable that the men of the *Grantully Castle*'s Latin Club would suffer. Kelly ruefully reflected in his diary. Brooke had gone before the landings, now 'Oc' Asquith, Browne, Lister, Dodge and Freyberg too had been wounded. Just Shaw, Stewart and Kelly remained unscathed.[33] On 6 May, the Australian revealed his own frustrations at the organisation behind the attack when he wrote, 'our numbers were wholly inadequate'.[34]

The campaign had now developed into trench warfare – Western Front style. But for the forthcoming 3rd Battle of Krithia the ratio of allied guns to rifles was just 30 per cent of that normally used on the Western Front for offensive actions.[35] Furthermore, Hamilton's stockpile of artillery shells was low.

In anticipation of the 3rd Battle of Krithia, Hamilton and his deputy, Hunter-Weston, had assembled a larger force of over 40,000 British and French troops. Against them stood two divisions[36] – approximately 20,000 men – of well-prepared Ottoman troops. And there were more defenders in reserve.[37] The truth was that the Allied force was just not properly equipped for the type of trench warfare it was being asked to undertake.

Kelly started to move his platoon into the firing line at 12.30am on Friday 4 June. Both he and his men were to play a key role during the coming battle. The Australian's platoon was one of those given garrison duty. This involved both ensuring the waves of attacking troops did go over the top when required and providing a final line of defence, against a possible Ottoman counter-attack – should the whole offensive go badly wrong. So, Kelly would be almost acting in the role of 'battle police': to ensure that troops weren't malingering or slinking away from the fighting. One historian has suggested that Kelly was specifically chosen for this difficult role because he could be 'relied on utterly'.[38] In Jon Cooksey's view, Kelly's personality made him particularly suited to this type of leadership, as Cooksey explained: 'We know his personality – loyal, committed – some would say almost blinkered in pursuit of his goal of the moment – with a firm belief in duty and "doing the job".'

At noon, the order for the RND to go over the top came. Compete carnage followed. Kelly's platoon, now spread out along the trench, could only guess at the devastation that was taking place ahead of them. Kelly later wrote: 'I heard heavy rifle fire but had no conception of what was happening.'[39] Just to the right of Kelly, Joseph Murray later recounted what had happened to the first wave, of which he was a part, when it went over the top following their commanding officer, who was killed instantly: 'Many of those following him just fell back into the trench, or forward across the parapet. The Turks inflicted horrendous casualties: only half the troops got forward to the dead ground immediately in front of the Hood trench.'[40]

Incredibly though, a few RND men – including Browne – got as far as the Turkish front-line, and even the second-line trenches. Jerrold estimates that only 30 per cent of the 930 men in the first wave made it. And their numbers soon began to wither faced with determined Ottoman counterattacks and accurate fire into the trenches.[41] At 12.15, troops from the newly trained Collingwood battalion launched their attack from Kelly's trench. Now, savage enfilading fire cut them down. Soon, just over 40 minutes into the battle, almost all the officers of the Anson and Collingwood battalions had become casualties. Not unnaturally, faced with such conditions, men from those two battalions started to crawl back into Kelly's trench.

At this stage, it is hard not to imagine that Kelly's trench already contained significant numbers of dead and dying men, with more in a similar condition, on the parapet. But he obviously remained completely focused on his role to keep the RND's attack moving forward. So, a furious Kelly – 'my temper was not of the best'[42] – tried any way that he could to get these men, many obviously both shocked and frightened, back out in the open to continue the assault. Having no success while remaining in the trench, the Australian leapt up into the inferno above ground, braving the withering fire while he tried anything he could to stem the RND tide coming back to the trenches. Faced with a bellowing officer in full flow a few turned around. But there were too many retreating for Kelly's commands to have a significant impact. Given the scale of officer-casualties on that day, he was fortunate to have survived.

Kelly then decided to re-enter the trench to get those who had returned to take cover, to go over the top for a second time. There must have been quite a degree of physicality involved in this because during this period of some three-quarters of an hour Kelly wrote of 'pushing' thirty men or so back into 'No Man's Land'.[43] Unsurprisingly, once out of the trench, most of these men preferred to lie low and seek whatever cover they could on the edge of their trench. When Kelly eventually realised that none of the men were advancing, he now jumped up out of the trench for a second time. This time, he tried to lead the men forward to a bank, 100 yards away. Incredibly the men started to move. His job done, and conscious of his duty, Kelly turned to get back to his allotted station in the trench and at that moment, he was hit on the right heel by a bullet, which left a wound 2in long and ½in deep. Again, given the scale of casualties it's possible to argue that Kelly had been fortunate that the bullet struck him where it did. He managed to get down into the trench. But it was clear that his wound was serious enough to require proper medical attention.

Kelly was just one of the thousands of men who were wounded on that day – many of those died from their wounds. Twenty-five per cent of Hunter-Weston's corps – some 4,500 men – became casualties in the assault. The Hood lost a further twelve officers and some 300 other ranks. Among them, Kelly's fellow musician and friend Denis Browne – the man who, with Kelly, had buried Brooke.

Kelly – still able to limp – was evacuated back to a ship. There, he was left to recover from the shock of his wound and cope with the 'anxiety' that those on board all felt about the fate of their friends and comrades. While on the ship, Kelly had no inkling about what had happened to Browne beyond the news that he was among the 'missing'. The Australian was shipped off to recover in hospital in Alexandria, where he was to remain for a month.

On 12 July – the day after the now-recovered Kelly returned to the peninsula from Egypt – Hunter-Weston launched yet another frontal assault on the Ottoman trenches to take the positions that the RND had failed to hold on 4 June. By the end of the offensive some two days later, the line had been moved forward but was still short of the original objective. The battle of Achi Baba Nullah, thus became the campaign's most costly engagement yet. Moreover, the conditions that troops had to fight in were horrific. The action was launched during one of the hottest days yet experienced during the summer of 1915. With that season had come millions upon millions of flies; not only did they feast on the corpses in No Man's Land, they also settled on those men still fighting.

Dysentery had been a problem for the troops on the peninsula even before the July offensive. Kelly confided to his diary: 'The flies are thick over all the foodstuffs.'[44] This inevitably made everything more torturous – even sleep. On 16 July, after he'd moved up into the support trenches, Kelly wrote: 'The flies are very bad, but I got some sleep in the day by putting a muslin cloth over my head.'[45] Some idea of the impact of both dysentery and wastage from offensives can be seen from the fact that before 4 June the RND had consisted of 208 officers and 7,141 men. By 1 August that had fallen to just 129 officers and 5,038 men.[46]

With so few officers now present, Kelly was not only gazetted lieutenant, but also put in temporary command of B Company. The task of getting B Company battle-ready was already difficult enough but the unsanitary conditions on the peninsula were to make the task even more demanding. Nevertheless, Kelly's sense of duty kept him hard at work, trying to complete the burden of the company administration – including having to censor 135 of his men's letters home.[47] The meticulous and conscientious nature of Kelly's character would have in all probability made this task particularly time-consuming. Whatever the nature of the task, it must have helped both him and his fellow officers in their efforts to ensure the men under their command were looked after. In short, Kelly was becoming an even more effective commander of men. Asquith captured Kelly's leadership qualities as part of his obituary: 'Under him [his Company] became a model Company in matters of trench routine, discipline and matters of appearance.'[48]

But like the good commander he was developing into, the Australian instinctively knew that the demands being made of his men by the high command were both unfair and unreasonable. Moreover, the stress he was under trying to maintain his company as a fighting force under both shellfire and sniper attack was beginning to tell. So much so that the RND would play no offensive role in the forthcoming August Offensive. Hamilton's long-awaited final throw of the dice would begin on 6 August.

That this attack, like others before it, failed is of course a matter of record, though initially there was some cause for hope. The Australians' heroic seizure of Ottoman positions on Lone Pine Hill was a memorable achievement. So too were the initially successful landings at Suvla to the north of the peninsula. But poor leadership, seen most notably in the failure to rapidly exploit the landings at Suvla, combined with factors like the steep and torturous terrain, over which it was extremely difficult to pass – let alone fight to thwart the allies. According to one historian the breakout ultimately failed because the Ottoman troops: 'fought better, with stronger motivation and more desperate courage'.[49]

With that chance gone questions would inevitably turn to the viability of keeping British and French troops on Gallipoli. Finally, on 22 November 1915,

Kitchener recommended that forces at both Anzac and Suvla be evacuated. In truth, nothing could stop those left from being affected in some way by the unremitting misery of the conflict and the seemingly endless stream of death and injuries that accompanied brought by it – especially if they happened to a close friend. Despite being wounded twice, Lister's presence had been a real boost to the morale of the battalion after the casualties sustained on 4 June.[50] At the end of July, Lister had been appointed to B Company and become Kelly's second in command. That, if anything, made the friendship blossom even more. Kelly was to later write of Lister that 'He was the most individual man I have ever known, I think, and his sense of humour was exquisite … As an intellect too, he was remarkable.'[51] The two men had been together in B Company for just a month before Lister was wounded for the third time on Gallipoli. This time, he was hit by several pieces of shrapnel. Kelly recalled how Lister had seemed when he was brought down the trench. He was: 'looking a dreadful pale green colour'. Ominously, Kelly noted there seemed to be no exit wound and added: 'We're all anxious to know that the first piece has not got in too deep.'[52] Just four days later, Lister died of his wounds on board the hospital ship to which he'd been evacuated, but Kelly did not hear of his death until a fortnight later – and the news hit the Australian particularly hard. On 12 September an already below-par Kelly wrote: 'The news came as a knock-out blow. I was fond of Charles and his loss is a great a blow as Rupert Brooke's.'[53] Just four days later the strains of a new violin sonata began to ghost through Kelly's head.

The release from the dirt, grime and flies surrounding the trenches was complete when he and his fellow officers could bathe in the sea. Touchingly, while bathing in September, in his diary, Kelly used a line from Brooke's poem 'Peace' to express how he felt. 'After three days without washing in the trenches it was an indescribable joy diving in, "like swimmers into cleanness leaping".'

But back in the trenches, Kelly was as exacting on himself as he was with his junior officers and men. He was an old hand now; expected to take the inexperienced, new officers that arrived on the peninsula under his wing. As Company Commander, he was expected to apply the necessary discipline to the officers serving under him. Kelly took delight in the many shared interests he had in common with one of the more bohemian of his company officers: Sub-Lieutenant Ivan Heald. The two discussed literature, poetry and even sang songs. But despite what they shared together, Kelly was still prepared to call Heald to account over his slovenly dress. Of course, in the confines of the trenches, Kelly found it particularly challenging to administer a rebuke to his officers: 'Telling-off officers is not easy in these conditions as one can't get them sufficiently far away from the men to be able to raise one's voice.'[54]

By Christmas Eve, Kelly had just learnt that over 80,000 Allied troops at both the Anzac and Suvla fronts, had been secretly and brilliantly evacuated from under the noses of their foe without loss. Hamilton had predicted casualties of between

30 per cent and 50 per cent.[55] And, as the French forces began to withdraw from the Helles end of the peninsula, the RND moved across to hold their positions.

The evacuation of British forces at Helles – scheduled for 8 January – posed an even greater threat to its defenders, than those that had occurred further north at the end of December. Therefore, maintaining secrecy and spreading misinformation where possible were vital. While the British forces were being withdrawn, the Ottoman command had to be somehow duped into believing that they were still facing fully held front lines. Though all the time both men and supplies would have to be progressively withdrawn to the beaches over 4 miles away. This subterfuge was a challenge that brought the best out of the British officers and men. As one of the very last troops scheduled to leave the front lines, Kelly was to play a key role in this final act. It was one for which he would be eventually awarded the Distinguished Service Cross.

He was tasked with the responsibility of commanding one of the few control stations where the troops would be counted through as they finally left the trenches for good. Heald's own account indicates that just before midnight on Saturday, 8 January 1916, that part of the front was being effectively held by just three men: Kelly, Freyberg and Asquith. 'So we shuffled past the telephone station at the top of the communication trench, and there we left Freyberg, Asquith and Lieutenant Kelly, the Diamond sculler and musician. They were all the garrison of that part.'[56] As Kelly and the others left, they set minefields and closed gaps in the trenches with wire obstacles to make it more difficult for the Turkish advance that was sure to follow. Relief only came when the destroyer on which the he and 750 other men were stealthily embarked, finally steamed clear of Ottoman shellfire en route to the island of Mudros.

For the time being the future of the RND as a viable unit remained uncertain. For all, including Kelly, it had been an agonising odyssey. During that time, the perhaps naïve sub-lieutenant had now become a battle-hardened warrior, capable of command at the highest levels. While on Lemnos the lieutenant was briefly placed in command of the Hood battalion itself.[57] He could not then have known that, for him, the greatest test still lay ahead.

Brooke's death was the genesis of Kelly's Elegy: in Memoriam Rupert Brooke, the work by which he is best known. In a diary entry for 21 May 1915 headed 'Near headquarters at the White House' on Gallipoli, and with the nine-minute work for string orchestra and harp still forming in his mind, Kelly wrote: 'The modal character of the music seems to be suggested by the Greek surroundings as well as Rupert's character, some passage work by the rustling of the olive tree which bends over his grave.'[58] He completed its notation on 27 June while recuperating in Alexandria.[59] Two days later he wrote:

> It is so entirely bound up with Rupert Brooke and the circumstances of his burial that in a sense I feel myself the chronicler of its ideas

> rather than the composer. … The work is a true portrayal of my feelings on that night – the passionless simplicity of the surroundings with occasionally a note of personal anguish.[60]

The published version holds an epitaph chosen by Kelly from the works of the Hellenistic poet Callimachus,[61] and reads:

> Someone spoke to me of your death, Heraclitus, and it led me to tears as I remembered how often we two had put the sun to sleep with talking. But you, my guest-friend from Halicarnassus, long, long ago became a heap of ashes somewhere. Still, your poems live on; and Death, the universal Snatcher, cannot lay his hand on them.[62]

The nine-minute Elegy, for solo violin, divided strings and harp, is indeed modal, though the effect is muted throughout the slow build from calm mourning to the intense outburst of grief at the climax at the two-thirds mark and its long subsidence thereafter into a still contemplation. The use of doubled triplets supported by the single version creates an illusion of the glittering Aegean summer, and an unease so strong that the listener can't help but feel with Kelly a deep sense of loss made more intense by the knowledge that he wrote it as he himself faced death. It is no exaggeration to call this work a small gem of the highest order.

By 4 March 1916 Kelly was back at 29 Queen Anne Street, still on leave after a brief time at the Grange. That day Kelly played the *Elegy* as a piano short score for Leonard Borwick who suggested adding a harp part. On the 6th Kelly wrote: 'I had considered this addition to the score when writing it and felt that as it would play such a small part I should not do amiss to make myself independent of it – putting it in, if desirable, later on.'[63] The following day, the 7th, he played it at 10 Downing Street and later performed it again before the Gallipoli commander, General Sir Ian Hamilton. At Mesnil on 2 October, less than a month before his death at Beaucourt-sur-Ancre in the last phase of the Battle of the Somme, he wrote out a harp part and posted back to Borwick. It was incorporated in the 1926 edition of the work. The *Elegy* had its first orchestrally realised performance in the Rugby School Speech Room on 28 March 1919, with Frank Bridge conducting, at a memorial concert for Rupert Brooke.

The Elegy, however, was not the only work Kelly composed on Gallipoli. Throughout the campaign, at ease in the mess and in the stress of trenches under fire, Kelly went on composing, thinking through new works in detail. The committing to paper was usually only possible once he was behind the lines. The remarkable thing here was that he was able to compose at all. There can be few composers who had such commitment and such focus.

The first time the work now known as The Gallipoli Sonata (but then only termed 'the Sonata in G major') is mentioned in the diaries as a casual aside at the end of a dramatic day, 28 August 1915, headed 'Hood Battalion, Support trench behind "Worcester Flats"'. By then the piece was already well developed. He mentions working on the first movement on 4 and 18 October at 'Base Camp, near D.H.Q. Cape Helles.' He didn't begin the second movement until 28 November at 'Rest Camp, X Beach, N.E. of Cape Teppe', continuing it there on 13 December, and on 16 December, the day he received 'only a scratch on my neck' from a shell bursting 'a couple of yards away from me, covering my face with dirt'. He was still working on the second movement on 19 December at 'New Camp in French Area, high ground half a mile N.E. of Seddul Bahr [*sic*]' the day he heard that the Australians had successfully evacuated from Suvla during the night. On 21 December, still at Sedd el Bahr, he spent nearly the whole day: 'writing down the ground (last movement) of my G major Violin Sonata'. On the last day of the year it became apparent that evacuation was imminent. The last movement had to be completed in a hurry. Kelly wrote:

> It has been rather a race against time as I was anxious to get it packed up and sent off with my gear – which might, for all I know, be called for at any moment. The gear left at 6.30pm and I had put my manuscripts in the top of my tin box, but Freyberg very considerately suggested I should put them in the Orderly Room strong box, which is going off in the charge of two men. So there they went, the Violin Sonata and a red book containing the E minor piece I wrote at the Crystal Palace, two Organ Preludes, a setting of C. Smart's 'He sang of God, the mighty source of all things', and a revision of my early song, 'Rough wind, that moanest loud'. I am not displeased with the violin sonata, but its ideas are neither as distinguished nor as original as I should like. Perhaps distinction and originality are more likely qualities in forms in which one is most accustomed to write. I am still serving my apprenticeship in sonata form but in lyric form I feel I have every now and then said something good and original, e.g. my Monographs in E flat major, B minor, C minor and my studies in E major, F major and D minor. I had no time to put in phrasing nor expression marks and the indications of tempo are of the scantiest.

Kelly left Gallipoli on 9 January 1916. On 7 February, after the Hood battalion reached Paraskevi Camp on Tenedos, he was able to play through this sonata for the first time. It found its way onto paper on 28 February as Kelly's ship sailed en route for England. He tried it on HMT *Olympic*'s battered piano 'and was tolerably well satisfied with it. The form of the first movement seems to be good.' He began copying out the violin part that day, finishing it the day after.[64]

Thereafter, he performed the Gallipoli Sonata privately several times: after dinner at Felix Warre's for the first time with a violinist – Jelly d'Arànyi – on 6 March,[65] and for her friends, Mr and Mrs Fowler, on the 13th,[66] as well as together in a private concert given by the Bonham-Carters on the 10th.[67] On 4 April they played the Violin Sonata (with the Elegy) for the Speyers at Ridgehurst. Its first public performance was given by Jelly d'Arányi and Leonard Borwick in December 1918 in a Classical Concert Society programme 'and again at Balliol Hall'.[68]

The last known revised score of the Gallipoli Sonata is in the library of the Goethe University in Frankfurt. Thirty-five pages hold its three movements: Allegro non troppo, Adagio con moto, and Ground, Allegro non troppo. On the last page Kelly has written: 'revised copy 13 April 1916. 29 Queen Anne Street London W. F.S. Kelly. Begun 3 October 1915 finished 31 December 1915 Hood Battalion R.N.D, Rest Camp, half a mile North of Siddul Bahr [*sic*], Dardenelles.' The title page holds the words: 'To Jelly d'Arányi', also in Kelly's handwriting.[69]

Kelly's wartime output consisted of a setting of *Green Grow the Rushes O*, for voice, chorus and brass band written early in his service; Elegy: in Memoriam Rupert Brooke, which is dated 27 June 1915, Alexandria, with the harp part dated 27 October 1916 and inscribed as written at Mesnil; the three-movement incomplete Sonata in F minor for piano, written at Bisham Grange on leave dated 27 April, and 1 and 3 May 1916; the Gallipoli Sonata 1915; and a theme for orchestral variations, preceded by an introduction, and dated 'Mesnil, near Thiepval 28th October 1916'.[70]

With France now his next destination, and with nine welcome weeks of leave behind him with all its attempts to reconnect with his former life, Kelly turned his face to his undoing: the notorious massacre of the Somme.

CHAPTER THIRTEEN

THE SOMME 1916

Just six days after having left Lemnos, on 27 February, 1916, Kelly once more walked through the front door of his house in Bisham Grange. In his time off there were many musical evenings with friends, where his newly composed Elegy figured prominently. He even dined in 10 Downing Street in the company of the Asquiths. Of course, the break was welcome but the war was never far away. Initially, there was some doubt as to the future of the RND. But by Saturday 29 April, Kelly found out that the division was to be reconstituted. Freyberg then told Kelly that he now would become the second in command of a new RND battalion – the 2nd Hood. Oc Asquith was to be its commanding officer, and on 30 May Kelly's seniority was reflected in his temporary promotion to the rank of lieutenant commander. His thoughts must have inevitably turned towards the job of rebuilding the men of the Hood into two new battalions, ready to fight on the Western Front.

The major 'push' that Kelly, Asquith and Freyberg had been so keen for the RND to be a part of was scheduled to happen that summer. Field Marshal Douglas Haig and General Joseph Joffre had agreed to assault German lines around the River Somme on 1 July – where the British and French held-trench lines met. The potential for the Somme offensive to become a grim attritional struggle lasting many months, into which the newly trained RND would ultimately be thrown, was there from the outset.

On 5 May, Kelly left for France and eventually by the 17th was billeted in the quiet, backwater village of Pont Remy, by the Somme, where he and the small cadre of officers waited for the main body of the RND to arrive. But soon, Kelly, together with key officers and ratings, had to leave their new battalion for two weeks of intensive instruction at an infantry training base near Rouen. Though small in number, the men of the Hood were to have a significant impact on the 5,000-strong camp. Sub-Lieutenant Jeremy Bentham, who accompanied Kelly, wrote: 'There was a stir when we arrived at the camp … nobody knew who or what we were.'[1] The reason for that, Bentham made apparent, was that not only did

Kelly look physically different from the officers surrounding him – by virtue of his full moustache and beard, but also that he was absolutely determined to uphold the place of the navy as the senior service over and above the army.

Naval ranks were permitted to sport a 'full set', whereas the army were only permitted to grow a moustache. In the environment of an army training camp, that distinction may have reasonably passed most by – not with Kelly around though. He understood that naval ranks also had seniority over those of the army. And Bentham explained just how Kelly reminded the whole camp of this. 'Kelly stipulated that the navy took precedence on parade, much to the army's annoyance.'[2] The young sub-lieutenant must have understandably felt a sense of trepidation, as Kelly's relatively small group of new arrivals took their place at the head of what was most likely a parade of thousands. And Bentham concluded: 'we lined up behind the band and led the parade off the parade ground'.[3]

But Bentham wanted to add even more colour about the sort of man his commander was. He briefly referred to Kelly's illustrious rowing career and then he described what he saw as the Australian's unconventional behaviour: 'But he was very eccentric: he washed his teeth at least 12 times a day and loathed getting his hands dirty, so he was never without gloves.' Later, when the Hood battalion was back in the trenches, Bentham repeated his description of Kelly's eccentric behaviour: 'His constant calling to his batman for fresh water to clean his teeth got on everyone's nerves.' Just before this – as if to underline the point – Bentham described how Kelly was 'very eccentric and intensely keen on cats. We never had less than four of five cats in the line with us and when we went out to rest each platoon commander had to take one in a sandbag.'[4]

The possibility is that what Bentham described could indicate that Kelly was suffering from some kind of obsessive-compulsive disorder. Although this condition affects people differently, there is common ground with many other sufferers and it's possible that at some time during 1915 – or possibly earlier – Kelly may have developed a fear of contamination by dirt or disease. The stress of war can lead even people with relatively normal stable personalities to develop neurosis.[5] Before the war, Kelly had, of course, already sought treatment to cure a nervous condition that affected his piano playing. The conditions of the front at Gallipoli, including the appalling hygiene of those summer months of 1915, could have been enough for Kelly to experience a heightened level of anxiety. In that context, his repeated teeth cleaning and glove-wearing might be interpreted by some as behaviours that could have brought Kelly a brief but temporary relief from the anxiety he may have been experiencing. However, as we have seen earlier, Kelly's wearing of gloves is more likely to be explained by the fact that he suffered from eczema.[6] Dr J.F. Wood first treated him for this painful ailment in 1913. Bentham was unlikely to have been aware of his commander's condition – hence his comment.

But mostly, both Kelly's diary and the accounts of his fellow officers, like Freyberg and Asquith, suggest he was perfectly able to keep his mind focused on the demanding role of a senior battalion officer. Moreover, his mind can hardly have been wracked with anxiety, when, on several occasions, it was able to wander free and imagine what pieces he might compose. On 18 August 1916 Kelly recorded how his mind turned to music: 'During the evening stand-to-arms I found my thoughts turning to the set of organ preludes or Voluntaries … I got an idea for one in B minor.' This seems to indicate that if Kelly was suffering from OCD, his symptoms were both mild and containable.

And though Bentham puts Kelly's fondness for cats immediately after he has described him as 'very eccentric', there is no evidence to suggest that Kelly's undoubted liking for feline company was particularly unusual for an officer in the trenches. Asquith recorded: 'He was devoted to animals and especially fond of cats.'[7] Freyberg wrote that when the Hood was moved into a different sector of the front, 'every Company was carrying: a number of cats in sandbags, which they took out and fed during the halts'.[8] That Kelly – and others – undoubtedly found solace in the playfulness of kittens is as touching as it is understandable. Just a few weeks before his death on the Somme, Kelly uncharacteristically shared his emotions while watching the frolics of what he described as a 'house full of cats' behind the front lines. 'Their playing is a perpetual joy,' he explained. Such vivid descriptions of Kelly's emotions are rarely found in the pages of his diaries.

That Bentham does not explore that level of Kelly's personality is perhaps not surprising. The junior officer was not as close to Kelly as those like Asquith and Freyberg, both of whom showed in their correspondence that they had a more sensitive appreciation of their friend's emotional make-up.[9] Of course, Kelly was reluctant to write about his emotions in his diary. But there were exceptions.

On his 35th Birthday, just days before he left for Rouen, he penned a particularly poignant 'glass half-empty' passage. In it he left no doubt that, however others saw him, he viewed himself primarily as an unfulfilled composer.

> I reflected that another 35 years would probably see me out. Life seems suddenly to have ceased to be an eternity and I must disillusion myself of the fiction that I am a young man with a whole career in front of me! At the same age, Beethoven was writing his Fifth Symphony – a depressing comparison.[10]

Though it was written after Kelly's death, Asquith's description of him gave a sensitive insight into the personality of the 'frustrated composer' that dwelt inside the company commander. 'He was not, and I think would never have made, and enthusiastic soldier. He spent most of his leisure time composing music and reading.' Asquith then perceptively added what qualities he had brought to command first in

Gallipoli and then in Northern France. 'But he had a true artist's desire to perfect his Company. He was an uncompromising disciplinarian, spared neither others, nor himself and rarely turned a blind eye. Highly-strung and as brave as a lion … he commanded the respect of all under his command.'[11]

Asquith's description adds so much more to an understanding of Kelly's complex personality. And the prime minister's son concluded with a fulsome appreciation of some of the character traits that made Kelly such a fascinating friend and companion. 'He was contentious, always happiest in argument: interested in the psychology of his friends, highly critical of them, and warm-heartedly loyal to them; and violently intolerant of anything that bore the faintest tinge of cheapness, insincerity, pretentiousness, or bad manners.'[12] When Kelly returned from Rouen, the man 'who would never have made an enthusiastic soldier' would be tasked with passing on his newfound knowledge to the battalion in a series of lectures. And Kelly knew that when he rejoined the Hood, they would be nearer than ever to the front line. The section where the Hood were to be based was some 25 miles north of the trenches where the Somme offensive would be launched on 1 July.

This was the Hood's first taste of warfare on the Western Front, and for the next three months, they were to be based in this area. It was part of France's dour and grimy northern industrial belt. Kelly would be based close to Lens, one of the area's most important towns, then held by the Germans. Unfortunately, by this time the creation of a second Hood Battalion had been put on ice. That meant that Kelly returned to being a company commander in the original Hood battalion, although he kept his rank as a temporary lieutenant commander.[13]

Perhaps Kelly's most striking – and amusing – escapade in No Man's Land during his time close to Lens came on 28 August, when a short message came through to his position from brigade that both Italy and Romania had declared war on Germany. The message concluded with the directive 'Tell the Hun!' Kelly immediately set to work finding a blackboard, on which he chalked – 'in thick and legible type – 'RUMANIAN IST MIT UNS'. That night he and four men crawled out over 100 yards towards the German lines, till they came to a thick belt of barbed wire. There, they screwed in a metal picket, to which Kelly and one of the men attached the blackboard, ready for the Germans to view at dawn, or whenever the next convenient star shell lit up the landscape.[14]

Intriguingly, Kelly's command of German was used as a lure or bait to attract potential deserters over to the British lines. The incentive on this occasion seems to have been the offer of seven days' leave for any soldier who could identify the German regiment holding the trenches opposite. On 31 August, Kelly was called over to a point on a sap where a German sentry had been exchanging whistle calls with the men stationed there. According to Bentham, he tried a combination of both 'whistling' and greetings to try attracting the German over after darkness fell. In his diary, Bentham claimed that Kelly had also sung extracts from Siegfried and added that the sentry 'would always carry on where Kelly left off'.[15] Apparently the incentive of seven days' leave proved too much for Bentham and others to resist and a group of them ambushed the lone German and 'put him to sleep'.[16] They then took his identity papers, only to find out that another unit had secured the relevant information a day earlier.

Kelly had other strings to his bow as a wartime entertainer in France:[17] part songs. In July, at Aix-Noulette, he invited four stretcher-bearers who were all bandsmen to join the mess to learn H. Elliot Button's arrangement of *Annie Laurie*.[18] By September part singing sessions were attracting 'a large attendance'.[19] There are later references to part singing: *Green Grow the Rushes, O!*, *The Wraggle Taggle Gypsies-O!*,[20] *The Chafers*, *Maiden*, *Listen*, Vaughan Williams' *The Ploughboy*, Glanville Bantock's *Give A Rouse*, and choruses 'out of the Hood books',[21] as well as Elgar's *After many a dusty mile*[22] and a selection from Sullivan.[23]

But perhaps the most remarkable example of Kelly using his musical talents to good effect came in mid-September. Kelly had always been drawn to the potential boost that singing could give to morale. In his bag he carried a book of songs that he'd had printed for the Hood Battalion.[24] But in late August, Freyberg – who was particularly keen on the battalion's band[25] – had also asked Kelly to lead it. It was an assignment that the accomplished musician clearly relished. 'I find it amusing conducting the band,' explained Kelly in early September. And he went on to describe the exact nature of the ensemble. 'There are about 18 players (cornets, tenors, horns, baritones, trombone, contrabass-tuba). The men are interesting and quickly improve when things are pointed out to them.' This relationship was to bear fruit in a rather special way just a couple of weeks later, while both Kelly and the band members were enjoying a spell behind the lines in their Noulette Wood camp.

Kelly's aim had been to add to the band's repertoire ahead of a special post-dinner concert that was to be given in the battalion's mess on the evening of 16 September.[26] But the one selection that those present would remember above all[27] was an unforgettable rendition of Tchaikovsky's *1812 Overture*. According to his sister, Kelly had always wanted to play the piece 'to the sound of real guns'.[28] And that week, not only would he achieve his wish, but in the process also craft a performance that may have been unique in the history of music.

Freyberg was one of those who heard the band play that September. And in his memoir, the man who led the Hood explained both the unique nature of Tchaikovsky's composition and Kelly's wartime interpretation of it:

> It was originally written to be played in the St Petersburg Cathedral, to the accompaniment of cannons firing blank charges. At the last minute it was played without the cannon accompaniment for the fear of smashing the windows.[29] This time our band played it conducted by Kelly to the accompaniment of a 4.5–inch Howitzer Battery (a

hundred yards away) firing High Explosive Shells at an enemy; a performance believed to be unique in the history of music or war.

Part-singing and internal musings apart; Kelly's reticence to 'sing his own praises' about his band's performance of the *1812* meant, the Australian never recorded in his diary his satisfaction at achieving what had clearly been a significant ambition for him. But in a letter written to the Speyer's on 24 September – just a week after the event – Kelly did explain what had transpired. 'I have recently been taking the battalion band in hand and have been teaching it the '1812'! My idea was partly to be able to perform it with real guns as intended.' And in a comment that highlighted both his and the band's undoubted enthusiasm he added: 'It was different to the band's previous repertoire, but they really got very keen on it.'[30]

The concert that night had also included other works, including the battalion's parade ground tune *Cawe and Ray*. According to Kelly: 'Most of the programme went extremely well, but there were perilous moments in 1812 at which we have not had sufficient work … After the band had departed, we sang 'Green grow the rushes, oh!' [*sic*] It was a very jolly evening.'[31]

Part-singing and singing from his song book were easy enough to maintain, but keeping the band together soon became a problem. By October 'there were several important men – such as the euphonium player – on leave and 1812 was impossible.'[32] When a fifty-piece band from the King's Liverpool Regiment played in Forceville on the 11th Kelly was listening with Freyberg who 'was beside himself with excitement' and determined to set up such an asset for the Hood.[33] On 4 November Kelly wrote to Boosey and Co, London suppliers of music and instruments for such bands, on Freyberg's behalf. On the same day he felt obliged to record: 'Our present Band is hors de combat by reason of recent casualties.'[34] He was not to see what became of the remnants.

But at least that September, had brought its share of good news to Kelly. His main purpose in writing to the Speyers had in fact been to thank them for their congratulations following the news that he'd been awarded the Distinguished Service Cross for his part in the final stages of the Gallipoli campaign. The news had come a complete surprise to Kelly, who only learnt of the award when Freyberg passed on the news both to him and to Egerton on the morning of 8 September. Unknown to Kelly, the Hood's commander had taken umbrage that the names of both Kelly and Egerton had been omitted from the final Dardanelles dispatch. According to Kelly he 'has apparently given them no peace and the result is honours for both of us!' Tellingly, Kelly also noted that the award was generally associated with acts of bravery, 'and I have an uneasy feeling that I shall be expected to live up to the standard'.[35]

At the back of his mind Kelly must have been aware that the battalion was likely to take part in the ongoing Somme offensive. In fact, the performance on the 16th was a watershed for him in more ways than one. That afternoon Kelly received news that the battalion was going to be relieved: 'It looks as though we should follow the way of all flesh to the Somme'[36] to participate in the final stages of the Battle of the Somme. For now, the Hood would be withdrawn from the lines to train and ready themselves for an eventual assault on the German positions that ran north of the River Somme, close to a small tributary: the River Ancre.

Kelly's descriptions of the terrain the Hood were to assault are worth noting. On 26 October, on a second visit to the higher ground on the south bank which overlooked the path of the Hood's intended assault on Beaucourt, Kelly used some of the most deeply personal and foreboding language to describe his feelings. He described himself as 'Haunted by the sense of terrible tragedy. The triumph of death and destruction over life.'[37] Those comments were prefaced by a description of the terrain above Beaucourt. It was 'an indescribable scene of desolation. For acres and acres (as far as one could see), there was no sign of vegetable life, just a sea of lacerated earth with here and there traces of a former trench'.[38] And this was a landscape that had once been 'home' to thousands of men. But now, the remains of many of them served only to enhance the Dantesque nature of the scene. And Kelly described how he experienced these corpses: 'some of them horribly mangled and with glazed eyes, others trodden almost out of sight in the mud'.[39]

Once the RND had arrived at their billets at Forceville, near the Ancre, the realisation of what they were to be part of was apparent. Freyberg pointed out that it was then that 'we realised the magnitude of the operation … Every village was crammed full of troops.'[40] In fact the RND would eventually be asked to attack as part of an assault force that would number five divisions and two brigades.[41]

At least Kelly still had time to think about music. On 27 October he made his final reference in his diary about his compositions. It is striking that he was still able to compose – even after a day as demanding as he'd experienced, during preparations for the upcoming offensive. Conditions in the basements of Mesnil were cold and damp, and the only illumination was by candlelight, but Kelly wrote: 'After dinner I wrote a harp part for my "elegy in Memoriam Rupert Brooke" and made a copy of it.' That he was determined to get his ideas down on paper was clear from the difficulties he faced, as he explained: 'I had not a score and had to write the numbers of bar rests from memory.'[42] Though bad weather had temporarily postponed the offensive, it may well have been a sense that he might not survive the forthcoming attack, which prompted him to complete the part.

After the war, Borwick reflected on what might have driven Kelly to finish the Elegy at that moment. The concert pianist had received Kelly's altered score in a letter and in his programme notes to an Edinburgh concert of 1921 he wrote:

> it is not the discomfort of the trenches that bears most hardily upon him, nor the stress of and turmoil of life in the ruined village with

> high explosive shells and gas popping all around. What 'gave him no peace' was an impulse towards the ideal – an overmastering concern that his utterance might lack not one perfecting touch or last fine shade of expression.[43]

But the intense preparations for the offensive were always in the forefront of Kelly's mind. They also took place in an atmosphere of uncertainty. The dreadful cold and wet weather during the early part of November left the trenches 'with [according to Kelly] water more than a foot and a half deep and the mud such as to tear one's gumboots (thigh) off one's feet'.[44] In these conditions the offensive was repeatedly postponed. But by 6 November Kelly noted that it was 'W' day, which effectively meant that the attack would take place in three days.[45] But yet again, there was another delay. Then, finally, came the break in the wet weather that the high command were waiting for. In a comment laden with irony – conditions behind the lines still resembled 'a sea of mud' – Jerrold wrote: 'It was only on 9 November that the sun shone for one fateful morning, and all the staffs from all the headquarters … came out to inspect the wicket and decided it would be fit for play in four days time.'[46] 'Z' day would be on 13 November. Kelly's final three diary entries: for Friday 10th, Saturday 11th, and Sunday, 12 November 1916, were made in the village of Mesnil, just over 1½ miles behind the front lines.

Freyberg described the conditions in the now ruined village just before the battle: 'Battalion headquarters were in a cellar in Mesnil. The house and indeed all the village had been knocked down by shellfire. In this small cave, 12ft. x 14, we lived cooked and slept.'[47] On 10 November Kelly noted that, as he'd just come out of the trenches he was 'very sleepy at dinner', and therefore 'went to bed soon after'. The following day he walked the half hour or so to the village of Martinsart, where he got 'a good hot bath at 10.30am'. Of course, he could not know that his body would eventually be laid to rest in the same town. His afternoon was taken up with a parade and testing the P-bombs – which he thought seemed to make plenty of smoke. Finally, following an officers' meeting at 6pm, he ate dinner and wrote his diary entry. It concluded with his observation that after all the postponements, preparation and months of training, the time for both him and the battalion to prove their mettle had finally arrived. 'It appears to be X day,'[48] he wrote.

Kelly and almost everyone else in Mesnil would have been awake by dawn. That was because the village was in the middle of the division's 'Gun Line'. As Freyberg noted in an addition to Kelly's diary after his friend's death: 'artillery pieces of all calibres were wheel to wheel around us'. In order to confuse the Germans as to the precise date of the attack, these guns had launched a 'hurricane bombardment at dawn every morning for a week before the attack was due to take place'.[49] And Freyberg left no doubt that the deafening sound of the 'shrieking projectiles' meant that 'all those who weren't about already crept from their holes in the ground and stood in the misty darkness witnessing the fury of the scene all around'.

So, from dawn on 12 November, Kelly was fully occupied. Most of his time was taken up with inspecting his company's battle arrangements. Freyberg left no doubt that in the execution of this task, Kelly was especially meticulous. Nevertheless, he tried to grasp a brief opportunity that had seemingly presented itself, to compose an entry in his diary. Unfortunately, even then, events conspired to confound this attempt. He got as far as writing: 'SUNDAY, 12 November, 1916. Hood Battalion.'

It was as well that Kelly was busy because there is evidence to suggest that at the back of his mind may have lurked a sense that he would not survive the battle. Perhaps the activities of that day, where many men wrote home and packed up their personal belongings, may well have prompted thoughts of what might happen. Bentham explained that the men were told to ensure that they had their home address clearly marked on their belongings in case of 'accidents'.[50] There was time for a company lunch at which Kelly made a speech, after which Bentham explained that 'In that context, perhaps Kelly's premonitions were no different to those of others.'[51] But clearly something about his conduct and demeanour that day had stuck with Bentham.

What were Kelly's emotions during that final day? Certainly at least one of his fellow officers – Bentham – thought that Kelly seemed fatalistic and recalled that his company commander 'was insistent that he would not survive'.[52] Others, notably Freyberg and Montagu, detected a sense of enthusiasm, even hope in the Australian.

However, later that night, out in No Man's Land, Montagu spoke with Kelly. The commander of D Company later wrote to Asquith about that conversation and recalled. 'He was so enthusiastic about the whole thing.' And Montagu added that Kelly had also told him then that he was 'really glad to be in it'.[53] That night, Freyberg, too, experienced Kelly's enthusiasm. He wrote: 'At midnight I went across to speak to Kelly … [he] was in very high spirits, certain as he always was, that the war would be over in the spring.'[54] But as dawn and the time for the offensive drew near, Freyberg noted a different quality in the man who had been one of his closest companions for the last two years. The New Zealander wrote (with only a minute or two before the attack was launched):

> I had my last talk with Kelly … he, Asquith, Egerton and I were the sole [officer] survivors of the battalion which had left Avonmouth for Gallipoli … I wanted to wish him 'God speed' but somehow it seemed too theatrical; instead we talked rather awkwardly and synchronised our watches.[55]

With the assault imminent, neither of the two comrades knew how to display the emotions they felt.

Both Kelly and Freyberg's attention to their watches was not surprising. The darkness they and their men experienced that night was so intense that it proved impossible to read a watch unless the dial happened to be luminous. To guard the battalion against a possible German attack, Kelly posted a strong advance patrol, equipped with a Lewis gun. Mercifully, though Kelly's company had been shelled as it marched into position, the battalion suffered only three casualties that night from hostile artillery and the attacking force remained undiscovered.[56]

Though orders had been issued to the effect that only one officer and one man per company were to remain awake, hardly any of the attacking force slept. That much was apparent to Freyberg as he left his command post to speak to Kelly around midnight. The New Zealander's 550 men were then arranged in four distinct waves – with an 8-yard gap between them – over a 300-yard front. Men were strung out along that distance with only 2 yards between them. So, Freyberg had to carefully step over each body lying prone on the damp ground as he made his way towards Kelly's command post.

According to the Hood's war diary, at 4.30am the men were roused and issued with a ration of rum. Freyberg's account recorded that 'a slight stir' happened all along the line at 5.15am. With this movement came

> the ghostlike sound of thousands of invisible men sitting up and taking off their great coats and in spite of all the warnings there came the slight mellow note of the wooden entrenching tool handle against the bayonet scabbard. Then came the unmistakable smell of tea and we knew that for many it would be their last meal.

The Hood's job in the darkness of that November morning, for which the creeping barrage[57] would allow them a 20-minute 'window', was to assault and clear all three German lines. For the first 200–300m of their assault, they would have to attack up a gentle slope. But this flattened out close to the second German line. The plan was that they would clear the first two lines and then ensure that any strong points – which held machine-gun emplacements – in the German third line, which had been missed by the artillery bombardment, would be eliminated. Failure to do this would mean that the assault might fail. It would fall to Kelly and his fellow company commanders to discharge this responsibility. Only when this job was complete would the Hood halt on the third line. This would be the signal for the battalions following behind to launch an assault on positions further towards Beaucourt.

Once the order was given to fix bayonets at 5.40am, Kelly and his company waited for the barrage to begin. As far as we know, Kelly was positioned in the second or third wave of his company. Freyberg's record suggests that his commanders positioned themselves in the second wave. But Montagu later explained that he

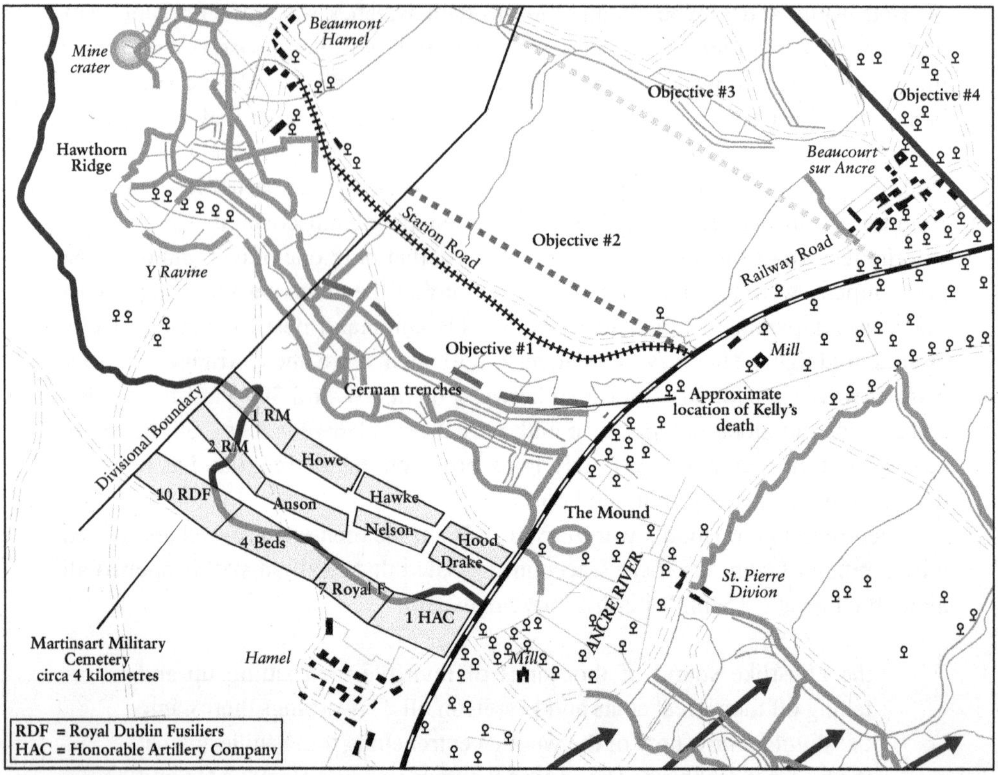

placed himself in the third wave. This was where the lieutenant felt he was most likely to remain in 'control of my company'. Whatever wave Kelly was in though, the darkness and the 'Scotch mist' meant he could not see any of the German lines that he was due assault. So, in his hand, Kelly almost certainly carried a compass – set to the Northeast – to show him the direction in which the German trenches lay.

At 05.45 precisely, the sky behind Kelly and his men turned red with the flashes of hundreds of British artillery pieces. Moments later thousands of shells begun to pass over their heads and 'burst in an impenetrable wall some 150 yards beyond'.[58] With the sound of explosions and gunfire filling their ears and the smell of fumes hanging in the air, Kelly and the Hood rose and started their advance. In one of the most vivid descriptions of what that moment felt like, Richard Tobin, the Chief Petty Officer in Montagu's D Company, described how his initial fear had turned to terror as soon as he started the advance. 'You don't look; you see. You don't hear; you listen. Your nose is filled with fumes and death. You taste the top of your mouth. You're a hunter; you're back to the jungle. The veneer of civilisation has dropped.'[59]

It's impossible to know for certain whether the Australian felt something similar during those first few minutes. It's also not clear if Kelly ran or walked. Surviving members of the Hood all recorded different experiences. Bentham recalled: 'Directly the barrage lifted we in the first wave got up and walked forward, as one had to be careful not to walk into our barrage.'[60] But that contrasted with Freyberg's experience, who remembered: 'Our 12 waves were running hard to get clear of the enemy counter-barrage, which we knew was due to fall on the assembly trenches in 8 minutes.'

Amid the mayhem and confusion that surrounded the initial assault Kelly would soon have become aware that his company were suffering casualties. Some of these were caused by shells of the British barrage, which seemed to be falling short on the very ground over which the B Company was advancing. But the men around Kelly were also being hit by machine gun fire. In the wave or two ahead of Kelly, Bentham noted that 'In spite of the intensity of the barrage, machine guns began taking a toll of those advancing.' Very soon, the sub-lieutenant noticed he was isolated. 'Where there were hundreds on either side of me, I seemed to be alone with my runners and bodyguard; everything was smoke and hell let loose.'[61] Kelly, though, remained unscathed as he forged on to the German lines, revolver in hand.

So battered were the first German trench lines that it's unlikely that, in the confusion and gloom, Kelly even realised he was passing over them. But according to Freyberg, it must have been quickly apparent to Kelly that the Hood's advance was vulnerable from a strongpoint still active in the third line: 'it appears that someone on Kelly's left had missed a dugout entrance from which men were starting to shoot'. And the Hood's commander went on to explain what that would have meant to the assault – which had already suffered significant casualties. 'Unless the strongpoint was captured at once enemy machine guns would pop up everywhere, hesitation would have endangered the success of the whole attack of on our front.'[62] Both the conditions and the extremely heavy casualties suffered by the Hood make it difficult to be certain what Kelly's final movements were. But Jerrold later wrote that Kelly had identified 'a machine-gun post which threatened to enfilade the whole advance on this flank'.[63]

The time would have been around 6am. It was still dark. Having realised he needed to attack this emplacement Kelly must have looked about for whatever men were around him. Though this was a task fraught with mortal danger, Kelly's leadership, and the willingness of the handful of men he found to follow him, remained strong. Probably after issuing the briefest of orders, he began an assault on that position. Freyberg later explained. 'With the few men he had hastily gathered, he rushed the machine gun. A few of the men reached the position, but Kelly with most of them was killed at the moment of victory.'[64]

The accuracy of Freyberg's particular description of Kelly's last moments is unlikely to ever be confirmed. The New Zealander's account is of course entirely consistent with the qualities of duty, courage and leadership that the Freyberg must have known his friend possessed. However, there is other evidence too that points to the veracity of what Freyberg wrote. In his letter to Asquith, Montagu wrote: 'Poor Cleg was killed right at the beginning ... He went to lead an attack on a bombing post ... and they showed fight.'[65] And perhaps the most compelling corroboration was the discovery of Kelly's body by McCracken, as the Hood's doctor later looked for any signs of life among the attacking forces. 'The next I found was Cleg shot through the back of the head just opposite a German dugout in the third line.'[66]

Freyberg was careful not to attribute the later success of the Hood's assault on Beaucourt entirely to Kelly's heroism. The capture of the village and nearly 1,000 prisoners, on the morning of 14 November – by a joint force of the Hood and Drake battalions has been called both 'brilliant and astonishing'.[67] But it would have been impossible without the selfless actions of the other men of the RND to the Hood's left, some of whom struggled on despite appalling losses to secure their positions. If nothing else, this willingness to commit was evidence of both the esprit de corps and the quality of leadership within the RND.[68] But the capture of the villages of Beaucourt, together with St Pierre Divion and Beaumont Hame,l did represent a significant achievement. Edmund Blunden, the British war poet who fought on the Ancre certainly thought so. 'This was a feat of arms vieing [*sic*] with any recorded. The enemy was surprised and beaten.'[69] During the attack, Freyberg was wounded several times and very nearly died. For his efforts he was subsequently awarded the Victoria Cross. His friend Kelly was one of the twenty-two casualties out of the twenty-three officers who had started the attack. To their number must be added some 250 other ranks – nearly half of the battalion's muster.[70] On 15 November, Montagu led the battalion to the rear, back past the village of Mesnil, where Kelly's uncompleted diary lay. Its author's body remained out on the battlefield. The fact this was now territory held by British forces made it much more likely that Kelly would finally be laid to rest in a marked grave. All that remained was for his friends, comrades and family to grieve his loss.

CHAPTER FOURTEEN

EPILOGUE

The Commonwealth War Graves Commission records show that Frederick Septimus Kelly DSC, Lieutenant-Commander, Hood Battalion, Royal Naval Division, Royal Naval Volunteer Reserve, died on Monday, 13 November 1916, and is buried in the Martinsart British Cemetery, Somme, France. Close to the British front line until September 1916, and again from March to August 1918, Martinsart British Cemetery was begun at the end of June 1916. There are now nearly 500 First World War casualties commemorated in this site. Of these, almost a quarter are unidentified. The cemetery covers an area of 2,002 square metres and is enclosed on the north and east by a red brick wall.[1] Kelly is the only Australian buried there. The *Balliol College War Memorial Book* entry, memorialising Kelly as a naval officer, (and probably written by Arthur Asquith) is curiously harsh:

> The standard of discipline and of compliance with its detailed ritual which he imposed upon himself and others was at first too austere to be generally palatable to his subordinates; but service in the field bred in them a healthy respect for his unfailing fearlessness and scrupulous justice. The keenness of his interest in an ever widening field of subjects, the zest which he imported into every argument, his joy in stripping humbug and in critically analysing generalisations – these were the contributions of the highest value to a regimental mess. He was a man of extraordinary vitality and physique, and of great powers which had only begun to mature and to find their unison and harmony. Time alone was wanting.[2]

Leonard Borwick, writing with considerably more warmth of Kelly the musician, concludes the entry:

> In the Diary of 1907 we find Kelly moved to a great resolve, after reading in William James' *Psychology and Ideals of Life,* that *if you*

only care enough for a result you will almost certainly attain it. 'I thereupon decided to be a great player and a great composer', he continues, with engaging acceptance of the idea, – and though the tone sounds playful, his mood is serious, and it may be that here, for the first time, he dared to utter aloud the purpose that has long been forming in his mind.

Of 'caring enough' there could be no question in the case of Septimus Kelly. Music had laid her spell upon him from earliest infancy. Music called up the finest sensibilities of his nature. In music, alone of all the arts, the needs of his spirit were fully answered and satisfied, and to the end [he] served his beloved art as something holy, with a devotion, a faith, a steadfastness that did but grow with the years.

All the same, to aspire to greatness both as a composer and pianist seems to be straining ambition 'beyond a mortal pitch'. Kelly, it is evident, did not stop to consider the extreme rarity in the past and the even less likelihood in our time of such a combination as this of creative genius with the powers of imaginative interpretation and the highly specialised instrumental faculty that are required of the pianist of today. Probably, with his own particular bent and gifts, he would find it more difficult on the spur of the moment to choose one of the two careers than to decide upon both. And indeed, if we reflect upon the shortness of his span of life, and the curtailment of opportunity that he suffered within that span, it strikes one with wonder that he advanced as far as he did to mastery upon either path.

The thought has a deep poignancy in both directions. In composition as in playing, Kelly was freeing himself, finding himself – throwing off in his playing some hampering restrictions that had clung to him through a long routine and habit of practice, and gaining for his composition not only greater vigour and freshness in the ideas but a new judgment and discrimination in the use of all resources, particularly those of form. Certain of the 'Monographs' (a late Opus) and two Organ Preludes may be termed masterpieces of small genre; and since he achieved the masterpiece it would be to do him less than justice and honour were one to discuss here the things he left of a less sure accomplishment … But no record, however slight, of his musical life may leave unnoticed the *Elegy* for String Orchestra written in 1915 and dedicated to the memory of his friend Rupert Brooke. Here he is the poet of deep imagining, finding an utterance in music which, linked by its modal inflections to the Past,

> is no mere expression of personal grief or loss, but, a symbol, rather, of the continuity of life, giving thoughts of Eternity, – and as such, for all who knew and loved 'Cleg' Kelly, his own most fitting and perfect memorial.'[3]

Less formally, Borwick replied to Edward Speyer's note of condolence:

> Thanks for the very kind note … It is all true what you say about dear Clegg.[*sic*] He was like the needle to the hole in his pursuit of what he felt to be the true goal in conduct and life as well as art, and there were very tender impulses too, that were stirring before the War, and which I think ripened much under the influence of Rupert Brooke.
>
> Something is withdrawn from me which I do feel very sadly about at the moments when I realise at all fully.
>
> Thanks again,
>
> Yours ever,
>
> L.B.[4]

Kelly's death was widely reported in Britain, the USA and Australia, in spite of the huge number of such notices after the Somme. All of them gave space to his career as an oarsman. Most published only a line or two about him as a musician.

For a time Kelly's music was kept alive both by family and friends. The *Elegy* had its first public performance in the Rugby School Speech Room on the afternoon of Tuesday 28 March 1919, when Frank Bridge conducted it at a Rupert Brooke memorial concert. On 2 May that year Bridge and the small Queen's Hall Orchestra gave it at Wigmore Hall (the former Bechstein Hall). At this concert Muriel Foster sang *Aghadoe* and what was vaguely reported as 'a group of lyrics by Blake, Byron and Shelley'.[5] Leonard Borwick played his own arrangement of a *Prelude for Organ*, which Kelly had composed in HMT *Grantully Castle* off Rhodes in March 1915, the 'Idyll' and the 'Caprice' from *A Cycle of Lyrics* and *Five Monographs for Piano*. Flautist Louis Fleury gave the *Serenade for Flute.* The *Elegy* was repeated at the end of the concert 'by request'.

Joseph Macleod, the d'Arànyis' biographer, looking back at this event from 1969, wrote:

> The *Elegy* with its inscription from a Callimachus poem […] recaptured something of that wistful, pagan burial on Skyros with a faint breeze beginning to stir the leaves under a beclouded half-moon. If it were revived as a musical counterpart to a Georgian Poem, I think the nightingales would still sing.[6]

Jelly did not take part, but she was there – as were many of Kelly's surviving friends. She had dreamt of him the night before, and found pain in the pleasure of the concert, recalling the times when she found the Bechstein Hall filled because his eager face was in the audience, and so empty when it was not. She was hurt that the organisers of the Wigmore Hall concert had not asked her to play the *Gallipoli Sonata*, and indeed it does seem a strange omission, especially as it was Leonard Borwick who had given its first performance with her in December at a CCS concert. She played it again with Tovey at another Kelly Memorial, in Balliol Hall, when Tovey also played the *Studies and Monographs.* Kelly's sister Maisie sang three of his songs, and Robert Murchie played the *Flute Serenade.* Tom Spring Rice, who by then had succeeded his uncle as Lord Monteagle, accompanied Jelly in three *Hungarian Dances.*[7] Louis Fleury played the *Serenade* for flute, harp, horn and strings again at a later Ridgehurst concert.[8]

According to Macleod, Kelly's name,

> did not slip at once into oblivion. In June 1920, Jelly, Lionel Terris and Arthur Williams played the String Trio which had been first played at Kelly's home at Bisham Hall by T.F. Morris, Frank Bridge and Ivor James in another June, the last before the war. For years Jelly included the Jig, and as late as 1933 at Lausanne her arrangement of the Flute Serenade: in which the same year Lord Monteagle in a concert with a young tenor at Limerick played 'some of the dances in Cleg's Youth Pageant which makes an excellent concert piece'. But alas! by 1933 the world was more concerned with its actual troubles than with past musical losses, and when Jelly played the Serenade at a Halle concert, it was dismissed as 'an amiable but unimportant serenade by F.S. Kelly, a young Australian who was killed in the war'.[9]

At Wigmore Hall on 25 February 1933, Bruce Hylton-Stewart conducted a chamber orchestra with Jelly d'Arànyi as the soloist in the 'first performance in this form' of Kelly's *Serenade for Violin and Small Orchestra.*[10] At one of her last recitals in Britain, Macleod recalls Jelly included 'not only Kelly's *Jig* but also a fantasy of his called *Gallipoli*, which unless it was some special arrangement for violin of the *Elegy,* I take to have been the first performance of a hitherto unknown work.'[11]

Jelly d'Arànyi was not the only one to remember Kelly's music. On Saturday, 19 February 1921, Kelly's *Serenade* and *Elegy* were given in the third concert of the fifth season of the revived Reid Concerts at the Usher Hall, Edinburgh, with Tovey conducting. Fleury was again the soloist in the *Serenade.* Tovey's program notes include this:

> With him [Kelly] there was a time for everything. His duty towards music did not distract him from his duty towards life, nor did life distract him from music. He would abandon nothing until he had mastered it; and so we have in this Serenade an essay in the tiniest of classical forms, each of them different and each of them devoted to expressing its own normal nature clearly and completely. The Prelude, in a small binary form without development, needs no quotations, though it had plenty of material, containing at least three independent themes. The Idyll (also in binary form) is in the key of A flat, a very remote region from E minor, the key of the work. The slow tempo means that the whole movement is really on quite a large scale. Things like the first movement arc by no means as easy to compose as they seem; but it is obvious at a glance that this slow movement is a composition of great distinction and subtlety.[12]

For the *Elegy,* Tovey stepped back from the task of appraisal, quoting instead from Leonard Borwick's notes for a concert at Eton College given in 1916. Borwick claims that Kelly composed this work 'in hospital at Alexandria', and that the manuscript 'bears at the foot of the last page of the score the date 27 June, 1915'.

Borwick then quotes and comments on a letter from Kelly dated 28 October 1916, 'a fortnight before the great advance of the RND along the Ancre Valley'. Kelly enclosed a manuscript fragment, a revision for the *Elegy,* saying: 'The necessity of sweetening the Strings (i.e. by the addition of a Harp) has been giving me no peace, and I have at last found a spare hour or two in which to write out a part.' On leave at home in April 1916, Kelly had begun revisions, raising the question of the harp additive, but 'the idea did not seem to take root, nor was there any hint dropped during the six months following of his intention to incorporate the part until the arrival of the letter of 28 October, with the fragment of MSS enclosed'.[13] The fragment may have been incorporated into this performance. Borwick found the work moving and symbolic:

> The spirit is Greek that breathes from this remarkable work – less perhaps through the direct derivation of its terms from the Dorian mode, than from the lofty and controlled expression throughout, and the skilfully conveyed suggestion of some rhythmic and ceremonial accompaniment for the eye of imagination to grasp. The music moves at a high level of inspiration, and reflects for us faithfully, I think, the composer's state of feeling at this crisis of his life. Suffering indeed under a tragic sense of loss, his mind was yet steeped, as it were, in the afterglow of his friendship and communion with the poet; and the solemn beauty and almost mythical appropriateness of the ceremony

> of the poet's laying-to-earth haunted him through the long hospital days like some beautiful vision or dream.[14]

The letter containing the harp fragment, however, affected Borwick even more than the *Elegy:* 'The letter,' he says,

> gives some account of the conditions under which he [Kelly] was living; but it is not the discomfort of the trenches that bears most hardly upon him, nor the stress and turmoil of life in the ruined village with high explosive and gas shells dropping all around. What 'gave him no peace' was an impulse from within towards the ideal – an overmastering concern that his utterance might lack not one perfecting touch or last fine shade of expression. The incident seems to me to set in a golden light one aspect of his character that I wished particularly to detach and emphasise, namely Loyalty. Loyalty – whether to his friend or his art – to principle, cause, or country – was the chief cornerstone of his character. For those who are left there remains but to cherish with answering loyalty and an abiding affection his memory and example.[15]

The Musical Times simply announced this concert as 'The third Reid concert, on 19 February, introduced two beautiful works – a "Serenade" for flute, with string orchestra, and an Elegy for strings, both by F.S. Kelly.'[16]

In 2007 S.G.S., reviewing a BBC recording that included the *Elegy*, wrote: 'you can mention Frederick Septimus Kelly's *Elegy* in almost the same breath as the Elgar.' ('Spirit of England'.)

> This piece surprises. In evoking Classical Greece, Kelly comes up with an idiom all his own, caught in the no-man's land between late Romanticism and early Modernism, and nothing at all like Tovey. Beautiful, elegiac, it shows a composer who probably (would have) grown into a major voice of English music. He and Butterworth may have counted as England's greatest musical loss of the war.[17]

Balliol gave a memorial concert of Kelly works on 29 May 1927. The *Musical Times* reported that:

> Miss Jelly d'Arànyi played the Violin Sonata which the composer dedicated to her, and Prof D.F. Tovey played the pianoforte pieces, entitled 'Studies and Monographs'. There was a large gathering representative of the Oxford musicians who had known Kelly in the days of his fame and promise.[18]

Sir Henry Wood conducted the Elegy at the Queen's Hall Promenade Concerts, London on 15 September 1927. *The Times* said of it: 'It is a distinguished piece of writing, elevated and strictly austere.'[19]

In Australia the first tribute came not in the form of a revival of Kelly's own work, but as part of an organ recital at Sydney Town Hall given by the city organist Ernest Truman on 6 March 1918. It began with Charles H. Lloyd's *Elegy* no. 2 in C major and was announced as a first performance performed 'by request'.[20]

However, Bertie and Olive Kelly gave a concert at their home, *Caerleon* at Bellevue Hill the following year on 20 April 1919.[21] Henry Staell led the orchestra in the Australian premiere of Kelly's *Elegy.* Bertie played in this orchestra. The *Sunday Times* reported that 'The music bears all the character of the romantic scene, and made a deep impression on the company that was privileged to listen to it.'[22] So deep an impression that there was a move to have it repeated. The Director of the State Conservatorium of New South Wales, Henri Verbrugghen, included the *Elegy* in a concert of exclusively Australian works on 20 December 1919 in the Conservatorium's hall.[23] Verbrugghen conducted. The audience was reported as 'enthusiastic'. Works by W. Arundel Orchard, Alfred Hill, Mirrie Solomon (later Hill's wife), Arnold R. Mote and Arthur L. Benjamin were also performed.[24] Verbrugghen, a Belgian, later became the conductor of the Minneapolis Symphony Orchestra. Sir Henry Wood also gave the *Elegy* on 15 September 1927 in Prom concert 29. This was only revived on 17 August 2014 when it appeared in Prom 42: 'Lest We Forget', a concert commemorating the composers who died in the First World War.[25] Sir Herbert Hamilton Harty conducted the Hallé orchestra in Kelly's *Serenade for violin and orchestra,* a performance broadcast on 9 March 1933.[26] Edgar Bainton conducted the NSW State Conservatorium orchestra in an all-Australian concert which included Kelly's 'most charming suite for flute with chamber orchestra' in March 1938.[27]

In spite of all this Kelly's music eventually fell into silence. Then, with the publication of his 1907–15 diaries, edited by Thérèse Radic as *Race Against Time* (National Library of Australia 1904) and the wartime diaries edited by John Cooksey and Graham McKechnie as *The Lost Olympian of the Somme: The Great War Diary of Frederick Kelly 1914–1916* (London, Blink, 2016) things changed. By then the commemorative events associated with the First World War's beginning and end were in full swing. Performances have proliferated, theses have been written, music has been published and recordings made. Notable among these have been Andrew Manze's conducting of the *Elegy* with the BBC Scottish Symphony at the Proms on 17 August 2014, Edward Antonov's thesis on the *Gallipoli Sonata,*[28] Monash University's free online scores edited by Richard Divall MDAO 22, 23, 24, 25, 26, 42, 43, 44, 46, 47, assisted by the Marshall-Hall Trust, and Chris Latham's 2016 CD (ABC Classics 481 4576) and his limited edition book, 'The Flowers of the Great War' (A Flowers of War Publication, Canberra, 2019).

Bertie wrote of his younger brother in his memoir:

> At this time when he was called upon to fight and die for his country Sep's personality was still trying to assimilate and turn to its own use a mass of knowledge which he had been accumulating. In music he was seeking a path of his own and his works gave indications that he would soon find one of great value. Had he lived I feel sure that the spontaneous buoyancy of his childhood would have reasserted itself to give interest and vitality to any work he might have accomplished.

What he accomplished as a composer consists of a small but important cache of works. Among them the *Elegy* stands out. Australians and the British alike have taken its evocation of the death and burial of Rupert Brooke as symbolising everything that was lost when the 'golden summer' ended. It's shimmering evocation of the Aegean resonates, particularly with devotees of the Anzac myth.

Though possibly one, if not two, symphonies and an opera were contemplated, no such large-scale works seem to have survived. Time ran out. The few Kelly music archives include the British Library holdings of orchestral, piano and vocal music,[29] published music donated by Kelly's niece, Beatrice McPhillamy, to the New South Wales Conservatorium in 1986,[30] and the National Library of Australia's more extensive holdings, MS 3095. These were acquired in 1972.[31]

Although other Kelly works may lie hidden in remote archives and attics, this list comprises his compositional legacy, a small body of intensely felt works, elegantly shaped, every item measured and refined, a legacy only now being realised for what it is.

Larry Sitsky's assessment of all this was that: 'Kelly was essentially a conservative composer, although we know that he was certainly aware of music by composers such as Schoenberg, Oenstein, Ravel, Debussy and Cyril Scott. Yet they do not appear as influences in his output at all.'[32] In the end Sitsky has a bet each way, dismissing Kelly's output as close to that of 'a very talented amateur/ dilettante', but adds the rider that it 'needs nonetheless to be studied, published, and performed'.[33] Pianist Alex Wilson, who made the first recording of Kelly's 24 Monographs and 12 studies in 2020, was far more impressed, finding them:

> wonderful, complex, diverse works […] Harmonically rich and adventurous, melodically lyrical and fiercely virtuosic, [and] quite unlike anything I have performed before.[34][…] This music is full of youthful exuberance, unashamedly unrefined at times and covering a full range of emotions. His music is enigmatic, hard to categorise, but is still very accessible, and has proven to be popular every time I have performed it […] Stylistically the music ranges from romantic

> simplicity to harmonic ambiguity, and the Monographs cover all the major and minor keys, which naturally leads to comparisons with the Chopin Preludes.[35]

Without the prejudices of a previous time, Kelly's music now emerges as intensely felt, austerely expressed, and meticulously constructed within the conservative musical language of his time. He was about to adventure out into the new. It looked as if he was headed towards an important career as a pianist, composer, conductor and patron. It was not to be.

ACKNOWLEDGEMENTS

The authors wish to acknowledge the generous assistance of F.S. Kelly's Sydney family; the National Library of Australia; the Library of New South Wales; the State Library of Victoria; Eton College Archives; Balliol College Archives; the Bodleian Library Oxford; the British Library; the Imperial War Museum; the Leander Club, Henley; the River and Rowing Museum, Henley; the Goethe University, Frankfurt; the Marshall-Hall Trust, Melbourne; the Britten-Pears Arts Archive; Martin Buzzecot; the late Peter Cahn; John Carmody; Jan Coleman; Mimi Colligan; the late Jon Cooksey; the late Richard Divall; Kay Dreyfus; Joan Eaton-Stubbings; Kevin Gordon; Dorothy Graff; Kate Kennedy; Sarah Kirby; Chris Latham; Rosaleen Love; Graham McKechnie; Dale and Michael Mackie; Kerry Murphy; George Newlands; Catherine O'Halloran; Christopher Page; Omega Pott; the late Leonard Radic; the late Steve Radic; Suzanne Robinson; John Rouse; Sandra Shotlander; Tamara Smolyar; the late Ian Templeman; Ivana Tomaskova; Michael Walsh; David Wickham; and Alex Wilson. Professor Gary Sheffield for comments on the Gallipoli and Somme chapters. Wendy Kewley: for commissioning the article that led me to Kelly in 2014. Chris Cross: for driving me round Northern France following the footsteps of Kelly.

Thanks to Harriet Fielding at Pen and Sword whose quiet professionalism has helped make this a better book. And to Karyn Burnham for doing such a great job as copy editor.

ENDNOTES

Preface

1. Leonard Sellers, *The Hood Battalion* (UK: Barnsley, Gloucestershire: Pen and Sword Select, 1993) 168. Able Seaman Joseph Murray in conversation with Sellers.

Chapter One – Sydney 1881–1893

1. *Referee* (Sydney) 31 July 1901, p.6.
2. John Carmody, *Australian Dictionary of Biography* (Melbourne University Press 1983) Vol. 9.
3. http://www.historyaustralia.org.au/twconvic/Captain+Cook+1836. Also: *Sydney Herald* 19 January 1841, p.2.
4. *Queensland Times, Ipswich Herald and General Advertiser* 6 August 1901.
5. Thomas Herbert Kelly, *Memoir of F.S. Kelly* (hereafter *Memoir.*) Unpaginated. This and all letters between F.S. Kelly and his Sydney based family are in the possession of that family.
6. *Sydney Grammar School* at http://www.sydgram.nsw.edu.au/history/
7. Clifford Turney, *Grammar: A History of Sydney Grammar School 1819–1989* (Sydney: Allen & Unwin, 1989), p.82.
8. *Sydneian* Sept., 1891 no. 97.
9. *Prince Alfred College Chronicle* 21 Sept., 1891 vol.4, no. 30.
10. *Dictionary of Sydney* at https://dictionaryofsydney.org/
11. *Sydney Mail and New South Wales Advertiser* 3 June 1893, 1117.

Chapter Two – Eton 1893–1899

1. Guy Nickalls *Life's a Pudding* (London: Faber and Faber, 1939), p.41.
2. John Lewis Heilbron, *H.G.J. Moseley: The Life and Letters of an English Physicist 1887–1915* (University of California Press, 1974), p.20.
3. *Memoir.*

4. Heilbron, *H.G.J. Moseley*, p.16.
5. Valerie Langfield, *Roger Quilter his life and music* (Woodbridge: Boydell Press, 2002), p.8.
6. F.S. Kelly to Mary Australie Kelly enclosed note in a letter to Thomas Hussey Kelly 13 January 1895.
7. F.S. Kelly to Thomas Hussey Kelly 17 Feb.,1899.
8. F.S. Kelly to Thomas Hussey Kelly 24 Apr., 1896.
9. F.S. Kelly to Thomas Hussey Kelly 29 Dec., 1898 (contextually dated).
10. F.S. Kelly to Mary Ann Kelly 13 July 1898 (contextually dated).
11. F.S. Kelly to Thomas Hussey Kelly 24 Feb., 1898.
12. F.S. Kelly to Thomas Hussey Kelly 13 Jan., 1899.
13. F.S. Kelly to Thomas Hussey Kelly 24 Apr., 1896.
14. Thomas Hussey Kelly to F.S. Kelly 16 Apr., 1896.
15. *Memoir.*
16. F.S. Kelly to Carleton Kelly 12, 17 March 1896.
17. F.S. Kelly to Mary Australie Kelly, note in letter to Thomas Hussey Kelly 13 Jan., 1895.
18. *Eton College Chronicle* 11 June 1896.
19. Princess Beatrice, daughter of Queen Victoria. There may have been a previous such event. In F.S. Kelly to Thomas Hussey Kelly 4 November 1897 he wrote that he was to give the Grieg *Wedding March* and the Chopin *Ballade in A flat* at a 'Windsor concert'. He would later appear before the king at Sandringham. See: *Aberdeen Daily Journal*, Dec., 3, 1906, p.4.
20. F.S. Kelly to Thomas Hussey Kelly 24 Apr., 1896.
21. F.S. Kelly to Thomas Hussey Kelly 7 May undated.
22. F.S. Kelly to Carleton Kelly 1 Apr., 1896.
23. F.S. Kelly to Mary Ann Kelly 13 July otherwise undated.
24. *Memoir.*
25. Captain of Boats Record book, Eton College Archives, 1898. Waldorf Astor's reflection following the 1898 Eton crew's victory at Henley.
26. Ibid Guinness 1899.
27. Ibid.
28. Ibid.
29. To bucket up the slide is when an oarsman rushes ahead of the natural rhythm of the boat in an attempt to get on to the next stroke too quickly.
30. Captain of Boats Record book, Eton College Archives, 1899.
31. Ibid.
32. Ibid. Harcourt G. Gold, 1895.
33. Ibid. Guinness 1899.
34. Ibid.
35. Ibid.
36. Ibid.
37. Ibid.
38. The *Times* (London) 3 July 1899, p.9.

39. F.S. Kelly to Mary Ann Kelly, undated.
40. *Illustrated London News*, Henley Regatta, the Finals, 15 July 1899.
41. Ibid.
42. Ibid.
43. F.S. Kelly Diary 15 March 1911. Hereafter these diaries are designated as KD. See: Thérèse Radic, ed., *Race Against Time* (Canberra: National Library of Australia, 2004) at given dates.

Chapter Three – Oxford 1900–1903

1. *Chicago Tribune* 3 June 1900, p.11.
2. John Jones, *Balliol College: A History,* (Oxford University Press, 1988), p.229.
3. Richard Greene, *Edith Sitwell: Avant-garde poet, English Genius* (London: Hatchette Digital, 2011), Ch 7.
4. Edward Speyer, *Edward Speyer: My Life and Friends* (London: Cobden-Sanderson, 1937), p.218.
5. Speyer, *My Life and Friends*, 168–169. Her German father, Traugott Heinrich Weisse, was a language teacher and author. Her mother was Lithuanian pianist Sophie Marquidorff.
6. Grierson, *Donald Francis Tovey*, p.18.
7. Deneke, *Ernest Walker*, p.78.
8. *Jackson's Oxford Journal* (Oxford), 12 May 1900, Issue 7678.
9. Alberto Bachmann, *An Encyclopedia of the Violin* (England: Dover Publications, 2008), p.376.
10. Australia did not have its own currency until 1910 when the Australian pound was pegged to the British gold standard.
11. F.S. Kelly to Balfour Gardiner 22 July 1901, copy in possession of Peter Cahn.
12. Stephen Banfield, *Sensibility and English Song: Critical Studies of the Early Twentieth Century* (Cambridge University Press, 1989), pp.141–143.
13. Lloyd, *H. Balfour Gardiner*, p.33.
14. John Buchan and others, *Balliol College War Memorial Book 1914–19.* (Glasgow: Balliol College, [Oxford] 1924), p.314.
15. Wollenberg, *Music at Oxford*, p.177.
16. OUMC records are scarce and hampered by the ban on public reports in Kelly's day for which only its prospectus, the 'Synopsis of Programmes,' remains. See: Arts and Humanities Research Council. Concert programmes http://admin.concertprogrammes.org.uk and University of Oxford Bodleian Music Section Weston Library http://www.bodleian.ox.ac.uk/weston
17. Kelly's self-belief may have counted against him on occasions when crew selection was being considered. Guy Nickalls – one of Britain's greatest ever rowers and scullers, a man who together with Kelly was part of the British Olympic eight of 1908, had a view on this. In his autobiography: *Life's a Pudding* (Faber and Faber 1939) after calling Kelly: 'the fastest sculler of all time', he added 'Kelly was a poor waterman on the Tideway and a difficult man to train.' Nickalls

perception: that Kelly was not as receptive to coaching as others, may well have kept him out of the Oxford crew of 1902. Perversely, though, the very same quality may also have helped Kelly in the long term.

18. *Manchester Guardian* 9 July 1902. P10
19. To counteract the advantage of the 'Bucks' station at this time the crew on the 'Berks' station was given a slight stagger – of around ½ a length on the start
20. *Times* (London) 10 July 1902. P12
21. Richard Burnell, *Henley Royal Regatta, A celebration of 150 years* (London: Heinemann Kingswood, 1989) 68.
22. *Times* (London) 11 July 1902. P10
23. *Manchester Guardian* 11 July 1902. P7
24. Contained in an account written by George Drinkwater, the Oxford '7' man in G.C. Drinkwater and T.B.R.Sanders *The University Boat Race – Official Centenary History*, (U.K.: Cassall & Co, 1929).
25. C.M. Pitman *Record of the University Boat Race* (London, T. Fisher Unwin 1909). P97
26. *Times* (London) 10 July 1903. P10

Chapter Four – Frankfurt 1904–1908

1. Eight diaries of Frederick Septimus Kelly, dated 1 Oct 1907 – 29 April 1915, NLA MS 6050, (hereafter referred to as KD), 11, 13, 27 Oct, 31 Dec 1907, 20 Aug, 25 Dec 1910, 1 Sept 1911, 27 Oct 1913, 19 March 1916; California San Francisco Passenger Lists 1893–1953 at https://familysearch.org/ark:/61903/3:1:33SQ-G5LD-3CJ?i=487&wc=M6B9-324%3A202082401%3Fcc%3D1916078&cc=1916078; *San Francisco Call* 9 June 1907; *Slough, Eton and Windsor Observer* 29 June 1907; Balliol College Register, NLA MS 3095 score notes for' Burmese Five'. Leonard Borwick in John Buchan (ed) *Balliol College War Memorial Book 1914–1919* Vol. 1 (Oxford, Balliol College, 1924), 317 gives 1 Dec., 1906 as the opening date of the first volume indicating a previous, now missing, diary from this travel period. The NLA also holds a further typescript of a Kelly war diary edited by Arthur Asquith. The original is missing. After ninety-seven years a three-month diary in Kelly's hand tallying with this reappeared. Both are held by the NLA.
2. All in NLA MS 3095.
3. T.H. Kelly, *Memoir of F.S. Kelly.* Unpaginated.
4. Grierson, *Tovey,* p.113.
5. Grierson, *Tovey,* p.114.
6. Grierson, *Tovey,* p.114–115.
7. Grierson, *Tovey*, p.115.
8. Tovey Collection. StEdU : Tov. 2077 University of Edinburgh Library.
9. Larry Sitsky, *Australian Piano Music of the Twentieth Century*, 58–62. Also: http://imslp.org/wiki/Waltz-Pageant,_op. 2_(Kelly,_Frederick_Septimus).
10. Grierson, *Tovey*, p.115.
11. Grierson, *Tovey*, p.116.

12. Theodore Andrea Cook, Henley Races, with Details of Regattas from 1903 to 1914 Inclusive(Oxford University Press, 1919), pp.27–28.
13. Cook, Henley Races. In 1903, together with his partner, Frank Smith, Scholes won both the Canadian and American double sculls titles; in singles he won the Dominion Day regatta in Toronto, the Canadian Henley and then the National Rowing Association of the USA title.
14. Cook, Henley Races, pp.27–28.
15. According to the website of the Don Rowing Club of Mississauga, an estimated 80,000 Torontonians including the famous professional Ned Hanlan greeted Scholes: http://www.donrowingclub.com/oldsite-dan/culture_biographies_scholes.php
16. Vivien Nickalls, *Oars Wars and Horses* (UK: Hurst & Blackett, 1932), p.208.
17. *Manchester Guardian* 8 July 1905 p.12.
18. Guy Nickalls *Life's A Pudding* (London: Faber and Faber, 1939), p.209.
19. Richard Burnell, *Henley Royal Regatta: A celebration of 150 years* (UK: Kingswood Press), p.160.
20. Ibid p.160.
21. Ibid p.160.
22. *The Times* London 6 July 1905. p.10
23. Nickalls, *Life's A Pudding*, p.185.
24. The *London Times* report has the same oarsman catching two consecutive crabs and missing a total of four strokes. 7 July 1905 p.12.
25. Many of the Belgian eight went on to take a silver medal behind France in the 1905 European Championships. By then Traulbaut had been moved to the '4' seat.
26. T.A. Cook, *Henley Races 1903–1914*, p.59.
27. Richard Burnell, *Henley Royal Regatta*, Appendix: 'Of all the Henley records the most remarkable, surely, is F.S. Kelly's time of 8 mn 10 sec in the Diamond Sculls in 1905. No other record fell that year and Kelly…not only sculled over the course four times to win the Diamonds, but also rowed three times in the Leander eight beating Vesper Boat Club of Philadelphia, and Sport Nautique de Gand in the process. Kelly's record stood for thirty-three years before falling to the redoubtable Joe Burk.'
28. Burnell, *Henley Royal Regatta*, p.188.
29. The *Guardian* 6 July 1906 p.6, took the opposite approach. Though the headline spoke of the Belgian victory, the first paragraph explained to the readers that the best fastest rowing and the best technique on show at the Regatta was the contest between the two English fours.
30. KD 16 Feb., 1908.
31. KD 23 Oct., 1907.
32. KD 29 Oct., 1907. Possibly Marie-Adele (Tachard) wife of Peter Karl von Grunelius.
33. KD 15 Nov., 1907. Literally, 'unleash ease' – to play with emotion.
34. KD 4 Dec., 1907. Brother of novelist Henry James. Presumably William James' Talks to teachers on psychology and to students on some of life's ideals (London: Longmans,1899), 108.
35. KD 18 Dec., 1907.

36. KD 17 Jan., 1908.
37. KD 28 Jan., 1908.
38. KD 8, 9, 10 Jan., 1908.
39. KD 25 Jan., 1908.
40. KD 18 Jan., 1908.
41. KD 19 Feb., 1908.
42. KD 3 March 1908.
43. KD 13 March 1908.
44. KD 24 March 1908.
45. KD 7 April 1908.
46. KD 17 Feb., 1908.
47. KD 3 May 1908.
48. Theodor Leschetizky, Polish pianist.
49. KD 19 May 1908.
50. KD 31 May 1908.
51. KD 31 May 1908.
52. Peter Cahn (trans. Professor Marrin Lindsay), 'Percy Grainger's Frankfurt Years', *Studies in Music, no.* 12, (Western Australia: Nedlands, Uni. W.A. Music Department, 1978), p.112.
53. KD 31 May 1908.

Chapter Five – The Olympics 1908

1. *Times* (London) 11 July 1907. P 4
2. R.C. Lehmann, Frederick Septimus Kelly, Raymond Broadly, Etherington-Smith, W.H. Eyre, The Complete Oarsman (London: Methuen & Co, 1908), p.168.
3. Diary 10 May 1908.
4. *Times* London) 9 May 1908, p.19
5. KD 14 May 1908.
6. Ibid.
7. Ibid.
8. KD 19 May 1908.
9. Those three men were: H.A. Steward and A.G. Kirby and H.R. Barker. *London Times* 16 June 1908 p.15.
10. KD18 June 1908.
11. Ibid.
12. KD 4 July 1908.
13. KD 29 July 1908. The final crew, together with their weights and ages on the day of the Olympic final was, from bow: A. C. Gladstone: 11st 6lbs, 21, F. S. Kelly: 12st 1lb, 27, B. C. Johnstone: 12st 11lbs, 25, G. Nickalls: 12st 6lbs, 41, C.D. Burnell: 14st 2 lbs, 32, R. H. Sanderson: 13st 6lbs, 31, R. B. Etherington-Smith: 12st 7lbs, 31, stroke: H. C. Bucknell: 11st 6lbs, 23, Cox, G. S. Maclagan: 8st 4lbs 28.
14. Guy Nickalls, *Life's a Pudding,* (London: Faber and Faber Ltd, 1939), *p.*200.
15. KD 14 July 1908.

16. KD 16 July 1908.
17. The crew eventually decided to use the boat manufactured by Frederick Rough
18. KD 18 July 1908.
19. KD 22 July 1908.
20. Ibid.
21. KD 24 July 1908.
22. KD 27 July 1908.
23. *The Times* (London) 31 July 1908, p.17.
24. KD 30 July 1908.
25. The Cambridge eight, who had won the Boat Race in 1908 had been selected as the 2nd British entry.
26. *The Times* (London) 31 July 1908, p.17.
27. KD 31 July 1908.
28. Ibid.
29. Nickalls, *Life's A Pudding*, pp. 203–4.
30. At 1.5 miles, the Olympic Regatta course was actually 330 yards longer than the normal Henley Regatta distance.
31. KD 31 July 1908.
32. *The Official Report of the 1908 Olympics* (London: British Olympic Association, 1908), p.248.
33. Nickalls, *Life's A Pudding*, p.203.
34. Ibid p.204.
35. KD 31 July 1908.
36. The Official Olympic report has the crew's lead at ¾ of a length after their first 'burst'.
37. *The Times* (London) 1 Aug., p.13.
38. *The Official Report of the 1908 Olympics*, p.249.
39. Ibid.
40. Ibid.
41. KD 31 July 1908.
42. KD 31 July 1908.
43. Ibid.
44. Ian Jobling *The Making of a Nation Through Sport: Australia and the Olympic Games from Athens to Berlin, 1898–1916* (Australian Journal of Politics and History, 1988 Vol. 34; Iss. 2 p.169.
45. Rudolph Chambers Lehmann, *The Complete Oarsman*, (London: Methuen & Co, 1908), p.157 Chapter 16
46. Comment by Andrew Randell Olympic Head Coach GB women email to the author, August 2025.

Chapter Six – Town and Country 1908–1910

1. KD 6 Jan., 1909. Also: Edward Harold Begbie 'Dr. Milne Bramwell and Hypnotism' in *Master Workers* (London: Methuen & Co., 1905), pp.275–288.
2. KD 5 July 1908.

3. Pianist Violet Mary William-Freeman, wife of the banker Arthur Hammersley.
4. KD 5 July 1908.
5. KD 26 July 1909.
6. KD 7 Nov., 1908.
7. KD 21 Aug., 1908.
8. KD 19 Sept., 1908.
9. KD 2 Feb., 1909.
10. KD 22 Nov., 1908.
11. Imperial War Museum online: http://www.iwm.org.uk/memorials/item/memorial/41562.
12. *Musical Times* 1 Dec., 1908, p.780.
13. KD 18 Nov., 1908.
14. KD 22 Nov., 1908. Geoffrey Wycliffe 'Tuppie' Headlam, Eton housemaster with whom Kelly developed a lasting friendship. Maisie Kelly's car was named for the soprano Emma Albani. Cleg's car, 'Clara' was named for Clara Schumann.
15. KD 22 Nov., 1908.
16. The poet was then employed in the Department of Prints and Drawings, soon after this meeting becoming Assistant Keeper there. His interest in oriental art was, however, already apparent.
17. KD 25 Nov., 1908.
18. KD 9 Nov., 1908.
19. KD 7 Dec., 1908.
20. KD 7 Dec., 1908.
21. KD 7 Jan., 1909.
22. J.P. Wearing *The London Stage 1900–1909: A Calendar of Productions, Performers, and Personnel* (U.S.A., Scarecrow Press, 2nd ed. 2013), p.446.
23. KD 14 Jan., 1909.
24. Programme Boston Symphony Orchestra 35th season 1915–1916 p.1183 at http://worldcat.org/digitalarchive/content/server15982.contentdm.oclc.org/BSYMO/PROG/TRUSVolume5/Pub411_1915–1916_BSO_FriSat_Wk19.pdf .
25. Tree was later a playwright and theatre manager. Daughter of actor-manager Sir Herbert Beerbolm Tree, niece of writer, critic and caricaturist Sir Max Beerbohm.
26. KD 24 Jan., 1909.
27. Maurice Leonard Hope and Glory : A Life of Dame Clara Butt (Victorian Secrets Limited, Brighton UK, 2012), p.33.
28. KD 16 Feb., 1909.
29. KD 29 Jan., 1909.
30. KD 26 March 1909.
31. KD 22 Feb., 1909.
32. George Shee, The Briton's first duty: The Case for Conscription (London: Grant Richards, 1901).
33. KD 25 Jan., 1909.
34. KD 3 Feb., 1909.

35. KD 17 Nov., 1908 and KD 17 Jan., 1909.
36. KD 28 June 1909. The former Elizabeth Eberstadt and portraitist John Singer Sargent.
37. John Juxon, *Lewis and Lewis: the Life and Times of a Victorian Solicitor* (Glasgow: William Collins Sons & Co, 1983), 115.
38. KD 28 June 1909.
39. KD 26 Feb., 1909.
40. KD 24 Feb., 1909.
41. Walter Aaron Clark *Isaac Albéniz: Portrait of a Romantic* (Oxford University Press, 2002), 250.
42. KD 12 March 1909.
43. Erik Chisholm 'Men and Music': Lectures given at the University of Cape Town Summer School February 1964' (The Erik Chisholm Trust June 2014) at http://www.erikchisholm.com/menandmusic/tovey.php.
44. KD 15 March 1909.
45. KD 17 March 1909.
46. Joseph MacLeod, *The Sisters d'Arànyi* (London: Allen & Unwin, 1969), passim.
47. Macleod, *The Sisters d'Arànyi,* pp.60–61.
48. Macleod, *The Sisters d'Arànyi,* p.111.
49. Chris Latham, sleeve notes, ABC Classics 481 4576 'Frederick Septimus Kelly': claims composed at Higher Coombe 21 March 1909.
50. Isidor George Henschel also conducted the Royal Scottish National Orchestra and the Boston Symphony Orchestra,
51. KD 21 June 1909.
52. KD 25 June 1909.
53. KD 26 June 1909.
54. He and his wife Lady Helena McDonnell (Lady Nina) leased Bisham Abbey until 1921.
55. KD 27 June 1909.
56. Ibid.
57. KD 28 June 1909.
58. KD 29 June 1909. The English version premier was given on 22 June 1909.
59. KD 11–13 July 1909.
60. KD 13 July 1909. Probably Julian Huxley.
61. Ethel Sands was a member of the Fitzroy Street Group and founder-member of the London Group.
62. KD 28 July 1909.
63. Fire damaged in 1931, Alderley Park was demolished in 1956 after 200 years of occupancy.
64. Russell was a cousin of Bertrand Russell, as well as of the latter's son, his namesake Conrad Russell.
65. Then a quick thinking card game with versions involving drink.
66. KD 29 July 1909.
67. KD 30 July 1909.

68. KD 1 Aug., 1909.
69. Ibid.
70. KD 6 Aug., 1909.
71. Probably the rowing coach.
72. Frederic Spotts *Bayreuth: A History of the Wagner Festival* (Yale University Press, 1994), p.130.
73. Spotts, *Bayreuth,* 131–132.
74. Harold Trevor Baker, MP and later Financial Secretary to the War Office.
75. KD 16 Aug., 1909.
76. Probably known to Kelly from shared years at Eton.
77. She trained as a singer.
78. Thomas Seymour *My Grandfather, A Modern Medievalist: the Life of the 8th Lord Howard de Walden,* (UK, National Trust), 13.
79. KD 16 Aug., 1909.
80. Ibid.
81. KD 19 Aug., 1909.
82. KD 17 Aug., 1909.
83. *Nietzsche contra Wagner* (1888) 'On the Geneology of Morality' at 3.3 on *The Nietzsche Channel* at http://www.thenietzschechannel.com/works-pub/ncw/ncw.htm
84. Oliver Garnett *Brownsea Castle (UK: The National Trust, Swindon, 2005 ed.), 13.*
85. Later Queen Victoria Eugenie. She married King Alfonso XIII of Spain in 1906.
86. KD 10 Sept., 1909.
87. KD 11 Sep., 1909. There were also concerns that his wife could transmit inherited haemophilia.
88. He was also an essayist and biographer.
89. KD 3 Oct., 1909.
90. KD 3 Oct., 1909. 'Mirrors' and 'Harvest' resulted in manuscript scores preserved in the NLA as Item 8.1 and 2, Book one, 1910 in MS 3095.
91. Stephen Banfield *Sensibility and English Song: Critical Studies of the Early Twentieth Century* (Cambridge University Press, 1985) Part 1 Ch.7 'The First World War, its effects and its victims', pp.141;144.
92. NLA MS 3095 Box 2, Vol. 7.
93. KD 11 Oct., 1909.
94. Ibid.
95. *Wigmore Hall Archives* at https://wigmore-hall.org.uk/about-us/history/archive-programmes/1909-10/198-wednesday-20–october-1909-8-15pm/file.
96. Francis Walter Jekyll. Nephew of garden designer Gertrude Jekyll.
97. Daughter of Pierre-Albert Tachard, politician. Wife of the Frankfurt banker Carl von Grunelius. The von Grunelius family was associated with the Rothschilds.
98. KD 17 Oct., 1909.
99. Brief humorous orchestral work dated 1919 and composed in response to Edward Speyer's order not to smoke in the house. Elgar was addicted to cigars.
100. Byron Adams *Edward Elgar and His World* (Princeton University Press, 2007) 231.

101. (Sir) Edward Howard Marsh.
102. Mary S. Lovell The Churchills (London: Little Brown, 2011), 259.
103. KD 24 Oct., 1909.
104. Ibid.
105. KD 27 Oct., 1909.

Chapter Seven – The Matter of Donald Tovey 1910

1. KD 28 Oct., 1909.
2. KD 30 Oct., 1909.
3. KD 1 Nov., 1909.
4. KD 7 Nov., 1909.
5. Percussive instrument devised 1908 by Paderewski to suggest distant thunder.
6. Satirical composition by Charles Villiers Stanford.
7. KD 8 Nov., 1909.
8. KD 15 Nov., 1909.
9. As quoted by Anna Scott in *Romantizing Brahms: early recordings and the reconstruction of Brahmsian identity.* Doctoral thesis, Academy of Creative and Performing Arts, Faculty of the Humanities, Leiden University 2014, 167.
10. Scott *Romantizing Brahms*, p. 167.
11. Ibid. p. 146.
12. Aidan J.Thomson The Cambridge Companion to Vaughan Williams ed Aidan Frogley and Aidan J. Thomson (Cambridge University Press, 2013), pp. 63–64.
13. KD 22 Nov., 1909.
14. Ibid.
15. William Henry Hadow, musicologist and composer.
16. KD 5 Dec., 1909.
17. KD 13 Dec., 1909.
18. Ibid.
19. Ibid.
20. Ibid.
21. KD 20 Dec., 1909.
22. KD 5 Jan., 1910.
23. Felix Walter Warre, son of Edmond Warre, headmaster of Eton College. Both father and son were notable rowers.
24. Thérèse Radic ed. *Race Against Time*, p.53, fn 87.
25. KD 6 Jan., 1910.
26. KD 8 Jan., 1910.
27. KD 19 Jan., 1910.
28. KD 3 Feb., 1910.
29. KD 19 Jan., 1910.
30. Radic ed., Race Against Time. 387. These were: Adila (violin), Jelly (violin), Hortense Emelia (pianist) and their mother Adrienne.
31. KD 5 Feb., 1910.

32. KD 8 and 9 Mar. 1910.
33. KD 4 April. 1910.
34. Marie Soldat-Roeger founded the all-female Soldat-Roeger Quartet.
35. Margaret Deneke later wrote the biography of Kelly's Balliol mentor, Ernest Walker.
36. KD 15 Feb., 1910.
37. KD 19 Feb., 1910.
38. KD 19 March 1910.
39. KD 19 Feb., 1910.
40. KD 3 Mar. 1910.
41. KD 4 April 1910.
42. KD 9 April 1910.
43. KD 2 Mar. 1910.
44. KD 21 Feb., 1910.
45. KD 28 Feb., 1910.
46. KD 10 March 1910.
47. Grierson *Donald Francis Tovey,* p.127.
48. Grierson *Donald Francis Tovey,* p.127.
49. Possibly Joachim Wach, a grandson of Felix Mendelssohn.
50. Email, Rex Lawson Pianola Institute <info@pianola.org> to Thérèse Radic 23 December 2016.
51. KD 11 Feb., 1910.
52. KD 19 April 1910.
53. KD 18 June 1910.
54. KD 23 June 1910.
55. KD 19 April 1910.
56. KD 20 April 1910.
57. Ibid.
58. KD 21 April 1910.

Chapter Eight – Outward Bound 1911

1. KD 2 May 1910.
2. Ibid.
3. Ibid. Also *Web Gallery of Art* at https://www.wga.hu/html_m/m/michelan/1sculptu/pieta/palestri.html
4. KD 3 May 1910.
5. KD 4 May 1910.
6. KD 4 May 1910.
7. KD 6 May 1910.
8. Ibid.
9. KD 7 May 1910.
10. KD 9 May 1910.
11. KD 6 May 1910.
12. Hermione Lee *Edith Wharton* (USA: Vintage Books, 2007), p.295.

13. KD 16 May 1910.
14. *Victoria and Albert Museum* at http://www.vam.ac.uk/content/articles/a/anna-pavlova/
15. KD 16 May 1910.
16. KD 19 May 1910.
17. *Sunday Magazine* (London) 22 May 1910.
18. KD 20 May 1910.
19. KD 12 June 1910.
20. KD 14 July 1910.
21. KD 2 Sept. 1910.
22. KD 7 June 1910.
23. *Los Angeles Herald* 8 June 1910.
24. Theodore Roosevelt 'Biological Analogies in History' *Romanes lecture* delivered at Oxford 7 June 1910 at http://www.theodore-roosevelt.com/images/research/speeches/BiologicalAnalogiesinHistory.pdf
25. KD 6 June 1910.
26. KD 21 June 1910.
27. *Eton College Chronicle* 30 June 1910. Also: *Eton College Chronicle* 9 June 1910.
28. KD 26 June 1910.
29. KD 19 July 1910.
30. KD 2 Aug., 1910.
31. KD 5 Aug., 1910.
32. Ibid.
33. 'Hugh Whitaker Excavator in Egypt' *World Museum* at http://www.liverpoolmuseums.org.uk/wml/collections/antiquities/ancient-egypt/related-person-65828-1.aspx Whitaker's invitation included viewing his excavation of the tomb of Men-kheper-ra-senb, a high priest during the reign of Thutmore III.
34. KD 17 Oct., 1910.
35. KD 18 Oct. 1910.
36. KD 23 Oct., 1910.
37. KD 30 Oct., 1910.
38. KD 27 Oct., 1910.
39. Will Hodgkinson 'Culture quake: the Post Impressionist exhibition 1910', British Library: 'Discovering Literature: 20th century' at https://www.bl.uk/20th-century-literature/articles/culture-quake-the-post-impressionist-exhibition-1910.
40. KD 7 Nov., 1910.
41. Ibid.
42. KD 10 Nov., 1910.
43. KD 27 June 1910.
44. KD 12 Aug., 1910.
45. KD 12 Nov., 1910.
46. KD 14 Nov., 1910.
47. KD 17 Nov., 1910.

48. KD 20 Nov., 1910.
49. KD 22 Nov., 1910.
50. KD 24 Nov., 1910.
51. *New York Times* 21 Feb., 1964.
52. KD 29–30 Nov., 1910.
53. KD 1 Dec., 1910.
54. KD 7 Dec., 1910.
55. KD 10 Dec., 1910.
56. KD 14 Dec., 1910.
57. KD 17 Dec., 1910.
58. KD 25 Dec., 1910.
59. KD 29 Dec., 1910.
60. Ibid.
61. KD 30 Dec., 1910.

Chapter Nine – The Sydney Debut 1911

1. Published in Britain in 1909 as *Europe's Optical Illusion,* republished in 1910 and subsequently as *The Great Illusion.*
2. KD 19 Jan., 1911.
3. Donald Westlake, *Dearest John: The Story of John Lemmone, Flute Virtuoso and Nellie Melba* (New South Wales, Terrey Hills, Bowerbird Press, 1997), 72–73. Lemmone recalled that 'It was practically completed before we reached Sydney. He called it Serenade, consisting of five movements. The first – 'Prelude'-was written in the Indian Ocean; the second – 'Idyll'– off the coast of West Australia; the third – 'Minuet'– in the Great Australian Bight; the fourth –'Air and Variations' – off the coast of Victoria; and the fifth – 'Jig'– off the coast of New South Wales.
4. KD 1 Feb., 1911.
5. Dudley resigned on 31 July 1911.
6. P.F. Leighton, 'Bradley, Joseph', ADB, https://adb.anu.edu.au/biography/bradley-joseph-5332.
7. Head of a local French musical instrument company.
8. *Goulburn Evening Penny Post* (NSW) 16 May 1910, 2. Also: *West Australian* (Perth, WA), 15 May 1911, 5; *Mercury* (Hobart) 15 May 1911, 5.
9. KD 10 Feb., 1911.
10. https://www.northernbeaches.nsw.gov.au/things-to-do/arts-and-culture/manly-art-gallery-museum/collections/collection-stories/duke
11. KD 4 June 1911.
12. KD 7 March 1911.
13. Ethel Kelly, *Frivolous Peeps at India* (Melbourne: George Robertson and Co., 1912).
14. *Truth* (Sydney) 21 Jan., 1912, 'Ethel's Exultation', p.7.
15. *Guerin-Foster History of Australian Rowing* at http://www.rowinghistory-aus.info/club-histories/sydney/05–4.php

16. KD 18 March 1911.
17. KD 18 March 1911. In 1885 Beach defeated Hanlan in a rematch in the same spot. He defeated him again in 1887 but on the Nepean river. Kelly could only have seen Hanlan versus Beach on the Parramatta in 1884 or 1885. See also: http://www.sporty.com.au/shellharbourcityrowing/About-1/Illawarra-Rowing-History.
18. *Daily Telegraph* (Sydney) 25 March 1911, p.6.
19. *Australasian,* 21 Jan., 1911; KD , 2 April 1911. The Duchess of Bedford was a philanthropist interested in women prisoners and women in poverty and isolation. She later chaired the War Fund.
20. Richard Burton Haldane Universities and National Life (London: John Murray, 1911).
21. KD 25 May 1911.
22. KD 9 April 1911.
23. KD 8 May 1911.
24. KD 16 May 1911.
25. KD 26 May 1911.
26. KD 6 June 1911.
27. KD 9 June 1911.
28. Age (Melbourne) 13 June 1911, 8.
29. *Daily Telegraph* (Sydney) 13 June 1911, p. 8
30. Ibid.
31. Therese Radic 'The First Musical Festival of the Empire 1911: tradition as innovative propaganda' keynote address in Proceedings of the XXXth Annual Conference Innovation and Tradition: Music Education Research 3–5 Oct 2008 published by the Australian and New Zealand Association for Research in Music Education Dec 2008, 1–13.
32. KD 16 June 1911. Premiered 1900. First heard by Kelly 1906.
33. KD 16 June 1911.
34. Ibid.
35. *Sydney Morning Herald* 19 June 1911, p. 5.
36. *The Evening News* (Sydney) 19 June 1911.
37. KD 27 June 1911.
38. KD 4 July 1911.
39. *Bulletin* 13 July 1911, 20.
40. *Sydney Morning Herald* 5 July 1911, p. 15.
41. 'Phoebe', Sydney correspondent, in 'Gossip for Women' column *Brisbane Telegraph* 8 July 1911. Also: *Table Talk* (Melbourne) 13 July 1911.
42. KD 5 July 1911.
43. *Sydney Morning Herald* 28 July 1911, p.2.
44. KD 8 July 1911.
45. For example: *Sydney Morning Herald* 9 July 1911, p.4; *Evening News* (Sydney) 10 July 1911, p.3; *Sunday Times* (Sydney) 9 July 1911, p.2.
46. *Sydney Morning Herald* 12 July 1911, p.2.
47. KD 13 July 1911.

48. *Sydney Morning Herald* 14 July 1911, p.7; *Evening News* 15 July 1911, p.14; *Daily Telegraph* (Sydney) p.14 July 1911, p.7; and *Sun* (Sydney) 14 July 1911, p.2.
49. KD 20 July 1911.
50. *Sydney Morning Herald* 6 July 1923, p.10. Brenda Deloitte was the daughter of insurance broker Marmaduke Levitt Deloitte and was well known as a cellist in Sydney.
51. KD 21 July 1911.
52. *Bulletin* (Sydney) 27 July 1911, p.20.
53. KD 29 July 1911. Also *History of Australian Rowing* at http://www.rowinghistory-aus.info/world-pro-sculling/1910–1914.php (accessed 6 December 2018).
54. KD 4 Aug., 1911.
55. KD 5 Aug., 1911.
56. Wouter Vercruysse at https://www.woutervercruysse.com/world-premiere-recording-of-frederick-septimus-kellys-string-trio/
57. KD 8 Aug., 1911.
58. *Truth* (Brisbane) 13 Aug., 1911, p.6.
59. KD 12 Aug., 1911.
60. *Measuring Worth* website.
61. KD 9 Aug., 1911.
62. KD 18 Aug., 1911.
63. KD 19 Aug., 1911.
64. KD 18 Aug., 1911.
65. KD 23 Aug., 1911.
66. KD 26 Aug., 1911.
67. KD 2 Sept., 1911.
68. KD 4, 5 Sept., 1911.
69. KD 12 Sept., 1911.
70. Elizabeth Crawford *The Women's Suffrage Movement: A Reference Guide 1866–1928'*(London: UCL Press, 1999), 313.
71. Beatrice Marion Willmott Dobbie, *A Nest of Suffragettes in Somerset* (UK: Batheaston, Eagle House, 1979), 17.
72. KD 21 Sept., 1911.
73. KD 22 Sept., 1911. Probably gamelan.
74. KD 29 Sept., 1911.
75. KD 26 Oct., 1911.

Chapter Ten – The London Debut 1912

1. KD 31 Oct., 1911.
2. Stephen Lloyd *H. Balfour Gardiner* (UK: CUP, 1984), 26–28, 48, pp.111–112.
3. KD 8 Dec., 1911. Equal to £190,432.57 in 2022.
4. Stephen Banfield *Sensibility and English Song: Critical Studies of the Early Twentieth Century* (UK: CUP, 1985), 131.
5. KD 12 Dec., 1911.

6. KD 31 Dec., 1911.
7. KD 1 Jan., 1912.
8. Grierson *Donald Francis Tovey*, p.149.
9. Grierson *Donald Francis Tovey*, pp.127–128.
10. Grierson *Donald Francis Tovey*, p.150.
11. KD 5 Jan., 1912.
12. KD 29 Jan., 1912.
13. KD 2 Feb., 1912.
14. KD 7 Feb., 1912.
15. KD 13 Feb., 1912.
16. *Daily Herald* (Adelaide) 27 March 1912, p.8, quoting undated *Daily Telegraph* UK
17. *Daily Herald* (Adelaide) 27 March 1912, p.8.
18. Kelly ed. Radic *Race Against Time*, p.24.
19. KD 20 Feb., 1912.
20. KD 21 Feb., 1912.
21. *Times* 21 Feb., 1912, p.11.
22. *Times* 7 April 1933.
23. *Daily Telegraph* 21 Feb., 1912.
24. *Pall Mall Gazette* 21 Feb., 1912.
25. *Scotsman* 21 Feb., 1912.
26. *Globe* 21 Feb., 1912.
27. *Musical Times* 1 March 1912.
28. KD 27 Feb., 1912.
29. *The Times* 6 March 1912.
30. KD 27 Feb., 1912.
31. *The Times* 28 Feb., 1912, p.6.
32. *The Sketch* 28 Feb., 1912, p.240.
33. *The Times* 6 March 1912.
34. Filippo Tommaso Marinetti *The Futurist Manifesto.* First published in *Le Figaro* 20 Feb., 1909.
35. KD 19 March 1912.
36. *Scotsman* 20 March 1912.
37. As reported in the *Daily Telegraph* (Sydney) 27 April 1912.
38. *Pall Mall Gazette* 20 March 1912.
39. *Daily Telegraph* 20 March 1912.
40. *The Times,* 20 March 1912.
41. *Musical Times* 1 April 1912.
42. KD 30 March 1912.
43. KD 31 March 1912.
44. KD 1 April 1912.
45. KD 3 April 1912.
46. KD 4 April 1912.
47. KD 22, 25 April 1912.
48. KD 30 April 1912.

49. KD 1 May 1912.
50. KD 13 May 1912.
51. KD 15 May 1912.
52. *The Times* (London) 16 May 1912.
53. KD 16 May 1912.
54. KD 19 May 1912.
55. KD 21 May 1912.
56. KD 1 June 1912.
57. *Daily Telegraph* 4 June 1912.
58. *The Times* (London) 9 June 1912.
59. KD 18 July 1912.
60. KD 20 June 1912.
61. KD 26 June 1912
62. KD 27 June 1912.
63. KD 6 July 1912.
64. KD 16 July 1912.
65. KD 25 July 1912.
66. KD 1 Aug., 1912.
67. KD 26 July 1912.
68. KD 9 Aug., 1912.
69. KD 13 Aug., 1912.
70. KD 23 Aug., 1912.
71. Francis Robert Eden, 6th Baron Henley of Chardstock who served with Kelly in the Hood Battalion.
72. Philip Southwell Kershaw was in the Royal Naval Volunteer Reserve as a pilot.
73. KD 12 Sept., 1912.
74. KD 21 Sept., 1912.
75. KD 24, 25 Sept., 1912.
76. KD 27 Sept., 1912.
77. *The Times* (London) 28 Sept., 1912.
78. KD 6 Oct., 1912.
79. *The Times* (London) 7 Oct., 1912.
80. KD 21 Oct., 1912.
81. KD 29 Oct., 1912.
82. Anita Mercier *Guilhermina Suggia, Cellist* (UK: Routledge, 2016), pp.115–117.
83. KD 30 Oct., 1912.
84. KD 6 Nov., 1912.
85. KD 12 Nov., 1912.
86. KD 6 Nov., 1912.
87. KD 12 Dec., 1912.
88. KD 16 Dec., 1912.
89. KD 14 Dec., 1912.
90. KD 16 Dec., 1912.

Chapter Eleven – The Classic Concert Society and Ravel 1912–1914

1. Kelly's interim addresses were Flat 6 at no. 87 Wimpole Street., 231A St James Court in Buckingham Gate, and Flat 36 at 11 King Street, St James.
2. KD 23 Feb., 1914.
3. KD 26 April 1913.
4. KD 28 April 1913.
5. Now in the Tate Gallery, London.
6. KD 18 Dec., 1912..
7. In 2018 *Interior with an Easel* was sold to the Getty Museum for over $5 million US dollars.
8. KD 1 April 1913.
9. KD 10 April 1913.
10. KD 29 May 1913.
11. KD 12 April 1913.
12. KD 13 May 1914. Whether this was by Francois Bovin or by his step brother Leon, Kelly fails to record.
13. Peter Davidson *The Last of the Light: About Twilight* (London: Reaktion Books Ltd, 2015), 28. Now in the *Schleswig-Holsteinisches Landesmuseum,* Denmark.
14. KD 10 Nov., 1913.
15. KD 16 March 1913.
16. KD 6 May 1913.
17. KD 7 May 1913.
18. KD 8 Nov., 1913.
19. KD 27 Nov., 1913.
20. KD 19 March 1914.
21. Hugh Montgomery-Massingberd, editor, Burke's Royal Families of the World Vol. 1: 'Europe & Latin America' (UK, Burke's Peerage Ltd, London, 1977), p.71.
22. KD 26 March 1914.
23. *The Times* (London) 27 March 1914, p.13.
24. KD 27 and 31 March 1914.
25. KD 29 Oct., 1913.
26. *Times*(London) 30 Oct., 1913..
27. *Pall Mall Gazette* 30 Oct., 1913. .
28. *Times* (London) 20 March 1914.
29. KD 13 May 1914.
30. KD 14 May 1914.
31. *Times*(London) 15 May 1914.
32. KD 14 May 1914.
33. KD 23 May 1914.
34. KD 26 April 1913.
35. KD 2 Dec., 1913.
36. KD 17 Dec., 1913.
37. Nichols *Ravel*, 392. Written in 1905, premiered Paris 22 Feb., 1907.
38. *The Times* (London) 20 Dec., 1913.

39. KD 17 Dec., 1913.
40. *Sunday Times* 21 Dec., 1913, p.6.
41. KD 18 Dec., 1913.
42. Appendix 3.
43. Wigmore Hall Archives CCS programmes for 1913–14.
44. KD 26 Nov., 1913.
45. KD 2 Feb., 1913.
46. KD 8 March 1913.
47. KD 31 July 1913.
48. KD 29 Sept., 1913.
49. KD 21 Jan., 1914.
50. KD 2 March 1914.
51. KD 4 March 1914.
52. KD 15–18 Sept., 1913.
53. KD 20–23 Sept., 1913.
54. KD 14 April 1914.
55. KD 15–21 April 1914.
56. KD 21 April 2014.
57. 'Zeppelin LZ 13 –Hansa' *Zeppelin History* at http://www.zeppelinhistory.com/list-of-zeppelins/zeppelin-lz-13/
58. KD 28 Jan., 1913.
59. KD 2 June 1914.
60. KD 21 Jan., 1914.
61. 'Carl Hagenbeck' (1844–1913) Encyclopaedia Britannica at https://www.britannica.com/biography/Carl-Hagenbeck
62. KD 8 Dec., 1913.
63. Michael Billington in *The Guardian* 8 May 2007.
64. Michael Hurd 'Somervell, Sir Arthur' *Grove Music Online* 2001 at https://doi-org.ezp.lib.unimelb.edu.au/10.1093/gmo/9781561592630.article.26176.
65. KD 17 Feb., 1913.
66. At 2 Cambridge Gate Regent's Park.
67. KD 5 May 1913.
68. KD 8 May 1913.
69. KD 3 Dec., 1913.
70. KD 2 Sept., 1913.
71. Erik W. Tawaststjerna (trans. Robert Layton): Sibelius Vol. I: 1865–1905. (USA, University of California Press, 1976), 130.
72. KD 11 Jan., 1914.
73. KD 16 Feb., 1914.
74. KD 14 March 1914.
75. KD 20 March 1914.
76. KD 23 March 1914.
77. KD 18 March 1913.
78. KD 20 March 1914.

79. KD 16 Jan., 1914.
80. KD 30 Dec., – 1 Jan., 1913.
81. KD 8 Jan., 1914.
82. KD 18 July 1914.
83. KD 19 July 1914.
84. KD 23 July1913.
85. KD 26 May 1913.
86. KD 5 May 1914.
87. KD 15 Aug., 1913.
88. KD 19 Aug., 1913.
89. KD 1 Dec., 1913.
90. KD 28 March 1914.
91. KD 28 May 1913.
92. KD 12 Jan., 1914.
93. KD 27 May 1914.
94. KD 5 July 1914.
95. KD 10 July 1914.
96. Robert Townsend Warner, barrister. Kelly made his will with him.
97. KD 27 April 1914.
98. KD 15 May 1914.
99. KD 21 July 1914.
100. KD 4 June 1914.
101. KD 10 June 1914.
102. KD 17 June 1914.
103. KD 30 July 1914.
104. KD 2 Aug., 1914.
105. KD 4 Aug., 1914.

Chapter Twelve – Gallipoli 1914–15

1. *The Times* 4 August 1914, p.6.
2. *Ibid.* 16 September 1914, p.9.
3. KD 14 Sept., 1914.
4. KD 18 July 1914.
5. KD 22 October 1914.
6. Quoted in Jon Cooksey and Graham McKechnie *The Lost Olympian of the Somme: The Great War KD of Frederick Kelly 1914–1916* (UK: Blink Publishing, 2015), p.26.
7. Paul Freyberg *Bernard Freyberg, VC: Soldier of Two Nations* (London: Hodder & Stoughton, (1991), p.42.
8. Freyberg was born in Surrey but moved to New Zealand when he was two and a half.
9. Nigel Jones *Rupert Brooke: Life, Death and Myth* (London: Head of Zeus, 2014), p.485.
10. Ibid., p.486.

11. The poem was found written in Shaw-Stewart's handwriting on a blank page in his copy of *The Shropshire Lad.* It concludes with these lines: 'Was it so hard, Achilles, So very hard to die? Thou knowest and I know not…'
12. Jones, *Rupert Brooke*, p.508
13. Christopher Page *Command in the Royal Naval Division: A Military Biography of Brigadier General A.A. Asquith DSO* (UK: Staplehurst , Spellmount, 1999), p.33.
14. Jones *Rupert Brooke*, p.50.
15. Mark Pottle (ed.) *Champion Redoubtable, The Diaries and Letters of Violet Bonham Carter 1914–1915* (London: Weidenfeld & Nicholson, 1998), 28.
16. Jones *Rupert Brooke,* p.501.
17. KD 25 February, 1915.
18. KD 12 April, 1915.
19. Leonard Sellers *The Hood Battalion, Royal Naval Division* (UK: Sword and Pen, 2015), p.53.
20. Geoffrey Keynes ed. *Letters of Rupert Brooke,* (London: Faber and Faber, 1966), p.665.
21. KD 12 March 1915
22. Les Carlyon *Gallipoli* (Macmillan Australia, 2001), p.94.
23. KD 17 April 1915.
24. Carlyon *Gallipoli*, p.94.
25. KD 20 April 1915.
26. KD 22 April 1915.
27. KD 23 April 1915.
28. Ibid.
29. Ashley Ekins ed. *Gallipoli: A Ridge Too Far* (Australia: Exisle Publishing, Woolombie, NSW, Kindle edition, 2013) passim.
30. Carlyon *Gallipoli*, p.279.
31. Sellers *The Hood Battalion*, p.84.
32. Ibid.
33. KD 8 May 1915.
34. KD 6 May 1915.
35. Sellers *The Hood Battalion*, p.132.
36. Edward J. Ericson *Gallipoli: Command under fire* (UK, Osprey Publishing, 2015), p.158.
37. Ibid., p.158.
38. Jon Cooksey, letter to the author May 2017.
39. KD 4 June 1915.
40. Sellers *The Hood Battalion* p.103
41. Ibid., p.133
42. KD 4 June 1915.
43. Ibid.
44. KD 11 July 1915.
45. KD 16 July, 1915.

46. Sellers *The Hood Battalion*, p.148.
47. Ibid. p.148.
48. *Eton Chronicle* 7 December 1916, p.132
49. Sean McMeekin *Ottoman End Game: War, Revolution, and the Making of the Modern Middle East 1908–1923* (UK: Penguin Books, 2015), p.253
50. Alexandra Churchill *Blood and Thunder: The Boys of Eton College and the First World War* (UK: The History Press Ltd, 2014), p.119.
51. KD 12 September 1915.
52. KD 24 August 1915.
53. KD 12 September 1915.
54. KD 19 August, 1915.
55. McMeekin *The Ottoman End Game*, p.261.
56. Quoted in Sellers *The Hood Battalion*, p.133.
57. Ibid. p.66.
58. Asquith typescript 21 May 1915.
59. Kelly was twice on Gallipoli but wounded only once, other claims to the contrary. He was one of the last to leave. He was hospitalised at the Deaconess Hospital then the Majestic Hotel in Alexandria.
60. Asquith typescript 29 June 1915.
61. Kelly would have known the Stanford part-song which uses the William Cory translation.
62. Translation from the Marshall-Hall Trust's Musica Australis Vol.VII edition of the *Elegy for String Orchestra In Memoriam Rupert Brooke* ed. Richard Divall and Bruce Steele 2005.
63. KD 6 March 1916.
64. KD 28, 29 February 1916.
65. KD 6 March 1916.
66. KD 13 March 1916.
67. KD 10 March 1916.
68. Joseph MacLeod, The Sisters d'Arányi (London: George Allen & Unwin Ltd, 1969), pp.120–2. Also: Therese Radic. 'Music Composed during the Gallipoli Campaign in F.S. Kelly's Newly Discovered Wartime Diaries' in Context 40, (University of Melbourne, 2015), pp.1–16.
69. The full MMS is online at <sammlungen.ub.uni-frankfurt.de/musikhs/content/pageview/6802849>.

    The NLA holds a copy as does Therese Radic. One other violin sonata was conceived at this time. On 16 September 1915 in an entry headed 'General Headquarter, Imbros', Kelly wrote, 'I had a new violin sonata in my head in B minor.' On 28 December 1915 at 'Right Sector, facing Kerevez Dare' he wrote on the day his former Command Post Officer Sergeant major R.D. Walker was blown to pieces near him during a shelling of the battalion's trenches: 'I got ideas for third and fourth movements to my B minor Violin Sonata, no. 2.'
70. The original MMS of all but the Gallipoli Sonata are held by the National Library of Australia, though the NLA also holds a copy of this sonata.

Chapter Thirteen – The Somme 1916

1. John Bentham *A Young Officer's Diary* Liddle coll., Edward Boyle Library, Uni.of Leeds, p.25.
2. Bentham *A Young Officer's Diary*, p.25.
3. Ibid.
4. Ibid.
5. *Psychiatry: An evidence-based text*, Bassant Puri and Ian Treasaden eds., (Hodder Arnold-CRC Press, UK, 2009) p.641. See Also: 'From shell shock and war neurosis to post traumatic stress disorder: a history of psychotraumatology, Dialogues in clinical neuroscience', Marc-Antoine and L. Croq, March 2000 in *Dialogues Clin Neurosci* 2000 Mar;2(1):47–55. doi: 10.31887/DCNS.2000.2.1/macrocq. From shell shock and war neurosis to posttraumatic stress disorder: a history of psychotraumatology
6. The following is some recent advice from the National Eczema Association: 'Keep several pairs of cotton gloves around the house to protect your hands while doing chores.' https://nationaleczema.org/protecting-your-hands-at-home
7. *Eton College Chronicle* 7 December 1916 p.132.
8. 'A Linesman in Picardy', unpublished manuscript, Bernard Freyberg, Ref: CAB 45/208, National Archives, Kew, Chapter 1, p.12. Also: Paul Freyberg *Bernard Freyberg, VC: Soldier of Two Nations* (Hodder & Stoughton London, (1991), p.12.
9. Christopher Page Extract, letter, Margot Asquith to Bernard Freyberg 15 January 1917 pp.98–99.
10. KD 29 May 1916.
11. *Eton College Chronicle* 7 December 1916, p.132.
12. Christopher Page, pp.98–99.
13. Commonwealth War Graves Commission, Graves Registration report, Martinsart British Cemetery, Row H, https://www.cwgc.org/find-records/find-war-dead/casualty-details/181674/frederick-septimus-kelly/#&gid=1&pid=1
14. KD 28 August, 1916
15. Bentham's diary, quoted in Leonard Sellers *The Hood Battalion, Royal Naval Division* (Sword and Pen, UK, 2015), 167.
16. Ibid.
17. Part songs were also employed during his English pre-Gallipoli period.
18. KD 22 July 1916.
19. KD 3 September 1916.
20. KD 18 September 1916.
21. KD 6 October 1916.
22. KD 10 October 1916.
23. KD 5 September 1916.
24. KD 22 July, 1916.
25. KD 4 September 1916: 'The CO is wrapped up in the band and is scouring all the neighbouring units for additional players.'
26. KD 16 September, 1916.

27. Both Joseph Murray and Asquith recorded the event in their post-war reminisces. Murray Joseph: Imperial War Museum Department of Sound Record, ref 8209/43 reel 31. Asquith Arthur, footnote in AMA's hand to Kelly's diary entry for 16 September 1916, quoted in Page, *Command in the Royal Naval Division*, p.86.
28. Letter, Maisie Kelly to Arthur Asquith 3 December 1916, quoted in Jon Cooksey and Graham McKechnie eds., *The Lost Olympian of the Somme: The Great War Diary of Frederick Kelly 1914–1916* (Blink Publishing UK 2015), p.306.
29. Freyberg was wrong. *Tchaikovsky's 1812 Overture* premiered in 1882 in a tent, not in St Petersburg, but outside Moscow's unfinished Cathedral of Christ the Saviour during an Arts and Industry Exhibition.
30. Edward Speyer *My Life and Friends* (Cobden Sanderson, London, 1937), pp.218–219
31. KD 16 September, 1916
32. KD 6 October 1916.
33. KD 11 October 1916.
34. KD 4 November 1916.
35. KD 8 September, 1916.
36. KD 16 September, 1916.
37. KD 26 October, 1916.
38. Ibid.
39. Ibid.
40. 'A Linesman in Picardy', unpublished manuscript, Bernard Freyberg, Ref: CAB 45/208, National Archives, Kew, UK, Chapter 1, p.13.
41. William J. Philpott *Bloody Victory* (Abacus, UK 2010), p.414.
42. Ibid.
43. Leonard Borwick, programme notes for the third concert of the fifth season of the revived Reid Concerts at the Usher Hall Edinburgh given on Saturday 19 February 1921, quoted in Therese Radic, Introduction to *Race Against Time: the diaries of F.S. Kelly* (NLA, 2004), p.43.
44. KD 7 November 1916.
45. The army used a system of letters to denote the sequence of days leading up to an offensive, which occurred on 'Z' day. The three days leading up to that were therefore known as 'W', 'X' and 'Y'.
46. Douglas Jerrold *The Great War – I Was There*, pt 22 p.887 quoted in Leonard Sellers *The Hood Battalion, Royal Naval Division* (Sword and Pen, UK, 2015) p.180.
47. 'A Linesman in Picardy', Freyberg, Chapter 2, p.5.
48. KD 11 November, 1916.
49. 'A Linesman in Picardy', Freyberg, Chapter 2, p.5.
50. Bentham *A Young Officer's Diary*, p.34.
51. Ibid.
52. Ibid.
53. Ibid. Also: Letter, Captain Lionel Montague to Arthur Asquith 26 November 1916 quoted in Christopher Page *Command in the Royal Naval Division*, p.97.

54. Freyberg's postscript to the original typescript of Kelly's Diary Quoted in Kelly's War, p.302.
55. 'A Linesman in Picardy', Freyberg, Chapter 2, p.8.
56. National Archives Kew, Hood Battalion War Diary 1–30 November 1916, WO95/3115/1 The National Archives, Kew, UK.
57. A creeping barrage was aimed to land just in front of the advancing troops. It lifted at intervals as the troops moved forward.
58. 'A Linesman in Picardy', Freyberg, Ch.2, p.9.
59. Richard Henry Tobin, 'The Great War Interviews', https://www.bbc.co.uk/programmes/p01tbkqk
60. John Bentham *A Young Officer's Diary*, p.35.
61. Ibid.
62. Freyberg's postscript to Asquith typescript as quoted in Kelly's War, p.304.
63. Douglas Jerrold *The Royal Naval Division,* (Hutchinson and Co, UK, 1923, reprint Naval and Military Press, UK, 2009), p.193
64. Bernard Freyberg's postscript to Asquith typescript as quoted in *Kelly's War*, p.304. (Lost Olympian).
65. Letter, Captain Lionel Montague to Arthur Asquith 26 November 1916, AMA papers, quoted in Christopher Page *Command in the Royal Naval Division*, p.97.
66. Letter, Surgeon W. McCracken to Arthur Asquith 17 November 1916, AMA Papers, quoted in Christopher Page *Command in the Royal Naval Division*, p.97.
67. Douglas Jerrold *The Royal Naval Division,* (originally published in 1923, reprinted by Naval and Military Press, UK 2009) p.205.
68. Gary Sheffield *The Somme,* (Cassell Military Paperbacks, UK, 2007), p.149.
69. Edmund Blunden *Undertones of War* (Penguin Classics, UK, 2000), p.103.
70. Account by Captain Lionel Montagu DSO Hood – 189 Btn, 20.11.1916, (British) National Archives, WO 95/3115/1.

Chapter Fourteen – Epilogue

1. Commonwealth War Graves Commission, Cemetery Details: Martinsart British Cemetery, http://www.cwgc.org/cwgcinternet/cemetery_details.apsx?cemetery~18100
2. Buchan, *Balliol College War Memorial Book 1914–1919*, (Scotland: University Press, Glasgow, 1924), pp.317–319.
3. Buchan, pp.318–319.
4. Speyer, *My Life*, p.220. Leonard Borwick to Edward Speyer 25 November 1916.
5. Macleod *The Sisters d'Arànyi*, p.121.
6. Ibid.
7. Macleod *The Sisters d'Arànyi*, p.120–122.
8. Speyer, *My Life*, pp.199–200.
9. Macleod *The Sisters d'Arànyi* , p.122.
10. Arts and Humanities Research Council Concert programmes d'Arànyi collection. http://admin.concertprogrammes.org.uk/html/search/verb/GetRecord/4234

11. Arts and Humanities as above, p.274.
12. Donald Tovey, Program notes for the third concert of the fifth season of the revived Reid Concerts at the Usher Hall, Edinburgh, given on Saturday 19 February 1921, p.13. at https://www.reidconcerts.music.ed.ac.uk/concert/reid-orchestral-concert-3
13. LeonardBorwick,https://www.reidconcerts.music.ed.ac.uk/concert/reid-orchestral-concert-3
14. Ibid.
15. Ibid.
16. *Musical Times* 1 April 1921. Under 'Provincial.'
17. S.G.S. September 2007 reviewing BBC Symphony Orchestra on Dutton CDLX 7172. www.classicalcdreview.com/7172.html
18. *Musical Times* 1 July 1927.
19. *Times* (London) 1 October 1927.
20. Kelly family Memorial Book. Programme 'Grand Organ Recital by the City Organist Mr Ernest Truman' dated 6 March, 1918.
21. *Sun* (Sydney) 27 April 1919.
22. *Sunday Times* (Sydney) 27 April 1919.
23. *Sun* (Sydney) 21 December 1919.
24. *Sydney Morning Herald* 22 December 1919.
25. *The Proms* at https://www.bbc.co.uk/proms/events/works/ae19b8ab-9054–4bed-a826–d7127e841448
26. *Times* (London) at http://archive.timesonline.co.uk/tol/archives/
27. Curt Prerauer in *Wireless Weekly* 11 March 1938 p.10.
28. Edward Antonov *Formulating an interpretation of* Frederick Septimus Kelly's *Violin Sonata in G major through an assessment of the performance style of the work's dedicatee, Jelly d'Arànyi* (Monash University, M.A. 2015).
29. The British Library's online catalogue at http://blpc.bl.uk/ Indicates that the Library holds thirteen published works by Frederick Septimus Kelly, including *A Cycle of Lyrics* (London: Schott & Co. 1910), the score and parts for *Elegy for String Orchestra* (London: E. Ashdown, 1926), *Two Organ Preludes* (London: E. Ashdown, 1925), and *Six Songs,* op. 6 (London: Schott & Co., 1913).
30. The online catalogue of the Library of the University of Sydney, http://opac.library.usyd.edu.au identifies sixteen published works by Kelly held at the Library of the Sydney Conservatorium of Music.
31. Frederick Septimus Kelly (1881–1916), Music manuscripts 1906–1916, op. cit., descriptive list of the collection.
32. Sitsky *Australian Piano Music of the Twentieth Century*, pp.58–62.
33. Sitsky *Australian Piano Music of the Twentieth Century,* pp.58–62.
34. Alex Wilson at https://www.kickstarter.com/projects/alexwilsonpianist/the-lost-piano-music-of-fskelly
35. Alex Wilson at https://jessicamusic.blogspot.com/2019/03/frederick-septimus-kelly-when-i-was.html

COMPOSITIONAL WORKS BY F.S.KELLY

The National Library's holdings consist of both published works and manuscripts. The published works include: a full score (dated Alexandria, 27 June 1915) and parts for *Elegy for String Orchestra* (published by Edwin Ashdown Ltd, 1926); *Two Organ Preludes* (dated HMT *Grantully Castle/Aegean Sea* off Rhodes 25 March 1915 and also published by Edwin Ashdown), consisting of a Christmas prelude on 'Good King Wenceslas', a second prelude and, like *Elegy,* with copyright given as invested in M. Kelly - his sister Maisie; *Six Songs* op. 6 (published in 1913 by Schott and Co.) consisting of 'March' and 'The Sages' Dance' (both 1910, to words by Logan Pearsall Smith), 'When the Lamp is Shattered' (1910-13, to words by Percy Bysse Shelley) and 'Music, When Soft Voices Die' (1910, to words by Shelley), 'The Cherry Tree' (1913, words by Logan Pearsall Smith), and 'The Daffodils' (1910, words by William Wordsworth); *Two Songs* op. 1 (Schott and Co., 1912) consisting of 'Shall I Compare Thee' (not dated, words by W Shakespeare) and 'Aghadoe' (1903, words by John Todhunter, with the copies inscribed to M.A.K.); *Theme, Variations and Fugue* for Two Pianos op. 5 (published in 1913 by Schott and Co. in a single double score copy showing 11 variations); *A Cycle of Lyrics* for Pianoforte Solo op. 4, titled 'Lament', 'Sea-Piece', 'Idyll', 'Caprice', 'Choler' and 'Reminiscence'. On the covers of these works Schott lists other works by Kelly published by the company in addition to those above. These are: *Waltz Pageant* for piano duet op. 2; *Waltz Pageant* for piano solo op. 2a; and *Allegro de Concert* for piano solo op. 3 (dedicated to Percy Grainger).Fourteen bound volumes of music in manuscript and an unbound collection held by the National Library of Australia enlarge on this list. They include: Introduction and Fugue (dated 4 December 1905, Frankfurt); Orchestral Suite: IV, Introduction and Fugue (dated 4 October 1906, 2nd edition, Frankfurt) which appears to be the conductor's copy; Theme, Variations and Fugue for two pianos op. 5 (dated December 1907, Frankfurt, revised 18 December 1911) with Variation 10 dated 14 October 1907 and dedicated 'To my two masters Professors Iwan Knorr and Ernst Engesser'. All of these are prefigurations of the 1913 Schott publication *Theme, Variations and Fugue for Two Pianos* op. 5. There is a full score and parts for *Elegy;* nos 1 to 11, a page of no. 12, as well as nos 23 and 24 of the 24 Monographs for pianoforte solo op. 11 (dedicated to Dr C.H. Lloyd). Twelve Studies for the pianoforte op. 9 (dedicated to Leonard Borwick) bears the remark 'This copy is very inaccurate. F.S. Kelly' and the date 4 May 1916, and exists in several separated sections in the collection.* Some of the many fragments of vocal and instrumental works date from as early as 1898, with the last written only a few days before his death. The orchestral Scherzo in C Minor is incomplete. The four-movement Orchestral Suite in E flat, with its Intermezzo dated 12 October 1906 at Frankfurt, seems intact. Both Tovey's and Kelly's sets of waltzes, written one in response to the other, are present as *Balliol Dances* (Tovey) and *Bisham Waltzes* (Kelly). The cadenza to the Beethoven Piano Concerto in G op. 58, mentioned in reviews of his concerts, is present. As are *Waltz Pageant* for piano duet op. 2; a Trio in B flat for piano, violin and cello (incomplete) dated 'May 31, 1911 Glenyarrah, Double Bay, Sydney' and dedicated to T.H.K., his brother Bertie; a String Trio in B Minor for the same combination with another copy annotated in pencil, revised and corrected by Tovey as the diary records on 31 May 1911, but dated 4 October 1910, Bisham Grange, as well as two earlier versions (one incomplete). There are manuscripts of *A Cycle of Lyrics* for Pianoforte Solo op. 4, and an incomplete sonata for violin and pianoforte; sketches made during travels in 1906-07, some marked as 'on board ship travelling to China and Japan', one titled 'Burmese Five' written for a 'circular instrument with bells' illustrated with a player seated within the circle and sounding the instrument with a stick; and the *Sèrenade* for flute, harp, horn and strings op. 7, including its Prelude, Idyll, Menuet, Air and Variations, and Jig (an arrangement of this for flute and piano is dated 'April 12 1914, Bisham Grange, Marlow'). An incomplete three movement piano sonata in F minor dates from May 1916. There is a sonata for violin and pianoforte in D minor marked 'Begun circa June 20. Finished Aug. 2, 1901 Glenyarrah, Sydney', Allegro de Concert op. 3 dated 'April 24, 1908, Bisham Grange (written March 28, 1907 revised November 12, 1911)'; and an Irish Air with Variations dated '10-20 August 1898', with interim dates, and places including St Andrews and Woollas Hall. Volume 8 of the bound collections contains fragments and song manuscripts.

Ten are dated 1910. These are 'March', 'Mirrors', 'Fulfilment' and 'Harvest Eve', all to words by Logan Pearsall Smith, and another, 'The Sages Dance', in Pearsall Smith's translation; 'Music, When Soft Voices Die' and 'Away! The Moor is Dark Beneath the Moon' to words by Percy Bysse Shelley; 'The Pride of Youth' to words by Sir Walter Scott; and 'To the Daisy' and 'The Daffodils', words by William Wordsworth. There is a manuscript prepared for the publisher, Schott and Co. of *Six Songs* op. 6 dedicated 'To Gervase Elwes'; and a book of sketches and fragments for songs with texts taken from Palgrave's *Golden Treasury:* 'Away the Moor is Dark Beneath the Moon', dated 'Nov. 5, 1909'; Wordsworth's 'O Nightingale'; 'March' by Logan Pearsall Smith; 'When

* These are in the unbound collection. Twelve piano studies written between 1909-12 in England and Australia are also present in the bound manuscripts. These may be the same set, but there is no indication of this in the Steele lists. Another MMS for Twelve Studies for Pianoforte op. 9, dedicated 'To Leonard Borwick' is dated 'July 23 1913, Bisham Grange', with the keys given tallying with those dated as above between 1902-09 written in England and Australia.

the Lamp is . Shattered'; 'The Daffodils'; 'Song of the Evening Star'; 'Lord Ullin's Daughter'; 'The Soldier's Dream'; 'Prospice', from Palgrave's *Golden Treasury,* second series; 'A Cradle Song'; and 'The Summer is Ended'. World War I produced the sketch 'Green Grow the Rushes Oh', for voice, chorus and brass band, which though undated is probably from his early war service days; *Elegy,* which is dated 27 June 1915 Alexandria; and the three-movement incomplete Sonata in F Minor for piano, dated at Bisham Grange and written on 27 April and 1 and 3 May 1916. What were possibly his last works are also present. These are two fragments: a harp part for *Elegy* 'done from memory 27 Oct. 1916 at Mesnil', and a theme for orchestral variations, preceded by an introduction, and dated 'Mesnil, near Thiepval 28th October 1916'.

The Australian works include: the Trio in B Minor for violin, viola and violoncello dedicated 'To T.H.K.' from 1911 (This has four movements: Allegro appassionato, Romance, Scherzo and Al legro moderato ma con moto) ; some of the series of 12 piano studies dated 1909-12; the *Serenade* for flute, harp, horn and strings, which owes its origins to the shipboard meeting with John Lemmone on the way to Australia in 1911; and the Sonata for violin and pianoforte in D Minor written, like the Trio, at *Glenyarrah.*

SELECTED BIBLIOGRAPHY

Unpublished sources

Antonov, Edward. 'Formulating an Interpretation of Frederick Septimus Kelly's Violin Sonata in G Major through an Assessment of the Performance Style of the Work's Dedicatee, Jelly d'Aranyi'. (MA thesis, Monash University, 2015).

Balliol Sunday Concert Programmes, Balliol College Musical Society. Balliol College Archives, University of Oxford. http://archives.balliol.ox.ac.uk/

Balliol College Boat Club Records at https://www.flickr.com/photos/balliolarchivist/sets/72157625471031867/

Eton College Musical Society Minute Book, Eton College Archives.

Freyberg, Bernard. 'A Linesman in Picardy, Transition Period between Gallipoli and France'. Unpublished manuscript. National Archives (UK). Ref: CAB 45/208.

Hood Battalion. National Archives (UK). WO 95/3115/1.

Kelly, Frederick Septimus: various holdings National Library of Australia including: Diaries 1907-1915 MS 6050, 8 vols; diary three months 1916 MS Acc13.201 also copy of Asquith typescript of lost vol.9 of diaries; music manuscripts, 1893-1926 MS 3095.

Sydney Grammar School Enrolment Records Vol. 01 226 2607; Vol. 01 314 3920; Vol. 01 226 2609; Vol. 01 283 3458.

War Service record of Frederick Septimus Kelly. National Archives (UK). ADM/339/3.

Published sources

Angell, Norman. *Europe's Optical Illusion.* (London: Simpkin, Marshall, Hamilton, Kent & Co., 1909). Republished 1910 as *The Great Illusion.*

Australian Dictionary of Biography, National Centre of Biography, Australian National University, (MUP 1966-2021) : https://adb.anu.edu.au

Australian Music Centre, Sydney, New South Wales: https://www.australianmusiccentre.com.au/

'Australia's Prime Ministers: Andrew Fisher'. National Archives of Australia at https://primeministers.naa.gov.au/primeministers/fisher/index.aspx.

Banfield, Stephen. *Sensibility and English Song: Critical Studies of the Early Twentieth Century.* (Cambridge University Press, 1985).

Bard, Kathryn A., ed. *Encyclopedia of the Archaeology of Ancient Egypt*. (London: Routledge, 1999).

Bean, Charles. *With the Flagship in the South.* (London: Laurie, 1909).

Beckett, Ian. *A Nation in Arms.* Manchester. (Manchester University Press, 1985).

Begbie, Harold. 'Dr. Milne Bramwell and Hypnotism' in *Master Workers.* (London: Methuen & Co., 1905).

Bird, John. *Percy Grainger*. (Sydney: Currency Press, 1998).

***Blevins,* Pamela.** 'William Denis Browne (1888–1915)'. *2000. Musicweb International.* http://www.musicweb-international.com/classrev/2002/may02/WDBrown.htm

Blunden, Edmund. *Undertones of War*. (London: Penguin Classics, 2010).

Bonham Carter, Jane. 'Violet Bonham Carter (Baroness Asquith of Yarnbury), 1887–1969'. *Liberal History*. At https://liberalhistory.org.uk/history/bonham-carter-violet.

Bonham Carter, Mark, ed. *Lantern Slides: The Diaries and Letters of Violet Bonham Carter, 1904–1914*. (London: Weidenfeld & Nicolson Ltd, 1996).

Bridge, Carl. 'Australians in the England and Wales Census of 1901'. *Australians in Britain: The Twentieth-Century Experience*, eds. Carl Bridge, Robert Crawford and David Dunstan, (Melbourne: Monash University ePress, 2009.)

British Olympic Association. *The Official Report of the 1908 Olympics*. (London: British Olympic Association, 1909.)

Brock, Michael, and Eleanor Brock, eds. *Margot Asquith's Great War Diary 1914–1916: The View from Downing Street*. (Oxford University Press, 2014).

Browne,William Charles Denis. *War Composers* at https://www.warcomposers.co.uk/browne

Buchan, John, ed. *Balliol College War Memorial Book 1914–1919*, vol. 1. (Oxford: Balliol College, 1924).

Cahn, Peter. *Das Hoch'sche Konservatorium in Frankfurt am Main: (1879–1978)* (Frankfurt am Main: Kramer, 1979).

———. 'Percy Grainger's Frankfurt Years' Translator: Martin Lindsay, *Studies in Music* 12, (University of Western Australia, 1978).

Carless Davis, Henry William. 'Balliol College'. In *University of Oxford Histories*. (London: F.E. Robinson and Co., 1899).

Carlyon, Les. *Gallipoli*. (Sydney: Pan Macmillan, 2014).

Carroll, Brian. *Australia's Governors-General: From Hopetoun to Jeffery.* (Kenthouse: Rosenberg Publishing, 2004).

Churchill, Alexandra J. *Blood and Thunder: The Boys of Eton College and the First World War.* (New York: The History Press, 2014).

Churchill, Winston S. *The World Crisis, 1911–1918*. (New York: Free Press, 2005).

City of Sydney. 'Thomas Herbert Kelly'. *Sydney's Aldermen.* At http://www.sydneyaldermen.com.au/alderman/thomas-kelly.

Cooksey, Jon, and Graham McKechnie, eds. *Kelly's War: The Great War Diary of Frederick Kelly 1914–1916*. (Chichester: Blink Publishing, Bonnier Books Ltd, 2015).

Corbin, John. *School Boy Life in England: An American View. (New York: Harper, 1897).*

Crawford, Elizabeth. *The Women's Suffrage Movement: A Reference Guide 1866–1928*. (London: UCL Press, 1999).

———. *The Women's Suffrage Movement in Britain and Ireland: A Regional Survey*. (London: Routledge, 2006).

Creasy, Sir Edward. *Eminent Etonians*. (London: Chatto and Windus, 1876).

Crockett, Samuel Rutherford. *Cleg Kelly, Arab of the City: His Progress and Adventures*. (London: Smith, Elder and Co., 1896).

Currency Companion to Music and Dance. eds Aline Scott-Maxwell and John Whiteoak (Sydney: Currency Press 2003).

Deneke, Margaret. *Ernest Walker.* (Oxford University Press, 1951).

Dibble, Jeremy and Horton Julian, eds. *British Musical Criticism and Intellectual Thought, 1850-1950* **Suffolk, UK: Boydell Press 2018).**

Dibble, Jeremy. *Chares Villiers Stanford: Man and Musician*. (Oxford University Press, 2002).

———. *C. Hubert H. Parry: His Life and Music*. (Oxford: Clarendon Press, 1992).

Drage, Geoffrey. *Eton and the Empire.* (Eton: I.R. Drake, 1890).

Eby, Cecil D. *The Road to Armageddon: The Martial Spirit in English Popular Literature, 1870–1914*. (Durham: Duke University Press, 1987).

Elkin, Robert. *Queen's Hall, 1893–1941*. (London: Rider and Co., 1944).

Elliott, Ivo. *The Balliol College Register*. 2nd ed. (Oxford: Oxford University Press, 1934).

Ellsworth, Therese Marie, and Susan Wollenberg, eds. *The Piano in Nineteenth-Century British Culture: Instruments, Performers and Repertoire*. (Aldershot: Ashgate, 2007).

Encyclopaedia Britannica: https://www.britannica.com/

Ericson, Edward J. *Gallipoli: The Ottoman Campaign.* (Oxford: Osprey Publishing, 2015).

Fraser, Nick. *The Importance of Being Eton.*(London: Short Books, 2008).

Freyberg, Paul. *Bernard Freyberg, VC: Soldier of Two Nations*. (London: Hodder & Staughton, 1992).

Foster, Col. Hubert. *Defence of the Empire in Australia.* (Melbourne: Rankine, Dobbie and Co., 1908).

Foreman, Lewis, and Susan Foreman. *London: A Musical Gazetteer. (New Haven and London: Yale University Press, 2005).*

Fuller-Maitland, J.A. *A Door-Keeper of Music*. (London: John Murray, 1929).

Garafola, Lynn. *Diaghilev's Ballets Russes.* (Oxford University Press, 1989).

Golding, Rosemary. *Music and Academia in Victorian Britain.* (London: Routledge, 2016).

Grierson, Mary. *Donald Francis Tovey: A Biography Based on Letters.* (London: Oxford University Press, 1952).

Gregory, Adrian. *The Last Great War: British Society and the First World War.* (Cambridge University Press, 2008).

Greene, Henry Plunket. 'Leonard Borwick: Some Personal Recollections'. In *From Blue Danube to Shannon*. (London: Philip Allan, 1934).

Haldane, Richard Burdon. *Universities and National Life*. (London: John Murray, 1911).

Harvard University Center for Italian Renaissance Studies. 'Bernard Berenson'. *Villa I Tatti*. at https://itatti.harvard.edu/bernard-berenson

———. 'Mary Berenson'. *Villa I Tatti*. At http://itatti.harvard.edu/mary-berenson.

Hassall, Christopher. *A Biography of Edward Marsh. (New York: Harcourt, Brace and Co., 1959).*

Hastings, Michael. *The Handsomest Young Man in England: Rupert Brooke*. (London: Michael Joseph, 1967).

Hattersley, Roy. *The Edwardians*. (London: Abacus 2006).

Hollis, Cristopher. *Eton: A History.* (Hollis & Carter, 1960).

Homans, Jennifer. *Apollo's Angels: A History of Ballet*. (New York: Random House, 2010).

Hornby, Emma, and David Maw, eds. *Essays on the History of English Music*. (Woodbridge: The Boydell Press, 2011).

Horrall, Andrew. *Popular Culture in London c.1890–1918: The Transformation of* Entertainment. (Manchester University Press, 2001).

Hughes, Meirion, and Robert A. Stradling. *English Musical Renaissance 1840–1940.* (Manchester: Manchester University Press, 2001).

James, William. *Talks on Life's Ideals.* (New York: Henry Holt and Co., 1925). First published 1899.

Jebb, Miles. *Patrick Shaw-Stewart: An Edwardian Meteor.*(Wimborne Minster: Dovecote Press, 2010).

Jeffery, David. 'About the Petersfield Musical Festival'. *Petersfield Musical Festival.* At http://www.petersfieldmusicalfestival.org.uk/about-the-festival.

Jenkins, Rebecca. *The First London Olympic 1908*. (London: Hachette Digital, Little Brown Book Group, 2008).

Jerrold, Douglas. *The Royal Naval Division.* (London: Hutchinson & Co., 1923).

Jones, John. *Balliol College: A History,* 2nd ed. (Oxford University Press, 2005).

Jones, Lewis. 'Francis Jekyll (1882–1965): Forgotten Hero of the First Folk Song Revival'. *English Dance and Song* (June 2000).

Jones, Nigel. *Rupert Brooke: Life, Death and Myth*. (London: Head of Zeus Ltd, 2014).

Kelly, Ethel. *Frivolous Peeps at India*. (Melbourne: George Robertson and Co., 1912).

Kennedy, Kate. 'Music and the First World War' at https://www.bl.uk/20th-century-music/articles/music-and-the-first-world-war

Kiel, Hanna. *Looking at Pictures with Berenson*. (New York: Harry N. Adams Inc., 1974).

Leanne Langley , Simon McVeigh , and Cyril Ehrlich. *London Concert Life, 1880–1914: A Social and Cultural History* (Cambridge University Press 2008).

Lehman, Rudolph Chambers. *The Complete Oarsman*. (London: Methuen & Co., 1908).

Levine, Naomi B. *Politics, Religion and Love, The Story of H.H. Asquith, Venetia Stanley and Edwin Montagu Based on the Life and Letters of Edwin Samuel Montagu*. (New York: New York University Press, 1991).

Ling, John. *Debating English Music in the Long Nineteenth Century.* (Woodbridge: The Boydell Press 2021).

Lloyd, Stephen. *H. Balfour Gardiner*. (Cambridge University Press, 2005).

Lundy, Darryl. *The Peerage.* At http://www.thepeerage.com.

McVeigh, Simon. 'Building a Concert Career in Edwardian London' in: Rosemary Golding, ed. *The Music Profession in Britain, 1780-1920: New Perspectives on Status and Identity.* (Routledge, UK, 2020). https://www.routledge.com/The-Music-Profession-in-...

Mangan, James Anthony, ed. *The Cultural Bond: Sport, Empire, Society*. (London: Routledge, 1992).

———. *The Games Ethic and Imperialism: Aspects of the Diffusion of an Ideal.* (Harmondsworth, Middlesex: Viking Penguin Books, 1986).

———. *'Manufactured' Masculinity: Making Imperial Manliness, Morality and Militarism.* (London: Routledge, 2012).

Murphy, Kerry. 'Henri Kowalski (1841–1916): A French Musician in Colonial Australia'. *Australian Historical Studies* 48, no. 3 (2017).

Neue deutsche Biographie / herausgegeben von der Historischen Kommission bei der Bayerische Akademie der Wissenschaften. (Berlin : Duncker & Humblot 1953-2022). As **German Biography** in English at: https://www.deutsche-biographie.de/?language=en

Nicholson, Juliet. *The Perfect Summer: England 1911, Just before the Storm.* (London: John Murray, 2006).

Oxford Companion to Australian Music. ed. Warren Bebbington. (OUP Melbourne 1997).

Oxford Dictionary of National Biography ed.Colin Mathew (OUP 1992-2004): https://www.oxforddnb.com/

Page, Christopher. *Command in the Royal Naval Division: A Military Biography of Brigadier General A.M. Asquith DSO.* (Staplehurst: Spellmount, 1999).

Popplewell, Oliver. *The Prime Minister and his Mistress*. (Morrisville, NC: Lulu Publishing Services, 2014).

Pottle, Mark, ed. *Champion Redoubtable: The Diaries and Letters of Violet Bonham Carter 1914–1915.* (London: Weidenfeld & Nicholson, 1998).

Radic, Therese. 'Editing the Diaries of F.S. Kelly: Unique Insights into an Expatriate's Musical Career'. *Context: Journal of Music Research* 19 (University of Melbourne 2000).

———. 'The First Musical Festival of the Empire 1911: Tradition as Innovative Propaganda'. In *Proceedings of the XXXth Annual Conference: Innovation and Tradition; Music Education Research,* ed. Jane Southcott. (Melbourne: Australian and New Zealand Association for Research and Music Education, 2008).

———. *G.W.L. Marshall-Hall: A Biography and Catalogue.*(Melbourne: Marshall-Hall Trust, 2010).

———. 'Music Composed during the Gallipoli Campaign in F.S. Kelly's Newly Discovered Wartime Diaries'. *Context: Journal of Music Research* 40 (University of Melbourne 2015).

———, ed. *Race Against Time: the diaries of F.S.Kelly.* (Canberra: National Library of Australia, 2004).

———. 'Race Against Time'. *National Library of Australia News* 15, no. 1 (October 2004).

——— with ed. **Suzanne Robinson.** 'Romeo, Juliet and George: The Genesis of the Last Marshall-Hall Opera'. In *Marshall-Hall's Melbourne: Music, Art and Controversy 1891–1915,* (Melbourne: Australian Scholarly Publishing, 2012).

Riley, Matthew, ed. *British Music and Modernism, 1895–1960.* (Farnham: Ashgate, 2010).

Robbins, Keith. *History, Religion and Identity in Modern Britain.* (London: Bloomsbury Academic, 1993).

Rodmell, Paul. *Charles Villiers Stanford.* (Farnham: Ashgate, 2002).

Rosenbaum, S.P.. *The Bloomsbury Group: A Collection of Memoirs and Commentary,* (University of Toronto Press, 2019). https://doi.org/10.3138/9781487573768

Rosenthal, Harold D., and George Henry Hubert Lascelles. *Two Centuries of Opera at Covent Garden.* (London: Putnam, 1958).

Rutter, Frank. Introduction to *Post-Impressionist and Futurist Exhibition. The Doré Galleries.* (London: The Doré Galleries, 1913).

Samson, Jim. ed. *The Cambridge History of Nineteenth-Century Music.* (Cambridge University Press, 2002).

Samuels, Ernest, and Jane Samuels: *Bernard Berenson: The Making of a Legend,* (Harvard University Press, 1987).

Seddon, Laura. *British Women Composers and Instrumental Chamber Music in the Early Twentieth Century.*(Farnham: Ashgate, 2013).

Sellers, Leonard. *The Hood Battalion.* (Barnsley UK: Pen and Sword, 2003.)

Shee, George (Richard Francis). *The Briton's First Duty: The Case for Conscription.* (London: Grant Richards, 1901).

Sitsky, Larry. *Australian Piano Music of the Twentieth Century.* (Westport, Conn.: Praeger, 2005).

Soroka, Marina. *Britain, Russia and the Road to the First World War: The Fateful Embassy of Count Aleksandr Benchendorff (1903–16).* (Farnham: Ashgate, 2011).

Speyer, Edward. *My Life and Friends.*(London: Cobden-Sanderson, 1937).

Spotts, Frederic. *Bayreuth: A History of the Wagner Festival.* New Haven, CT: (Yale University Press, 1994).

Steel, Nigel. *Gallipoli.* (Barnsley: Pen and Sword Books, 1998).

Stempel, John-Lewis. *Where Poppies Blow: The British Soldier, Nature, the Great War.* (London: Weidenfeld &Nicolson, 2017).

Stevens, Mary Anne. '*Hammershøi and England'.* In *Hammershøi and Europe, ed.* Kasper Monrad. (München: Prestel, 2014).

Stowell, Ellery Cory: *The Diplomacy of the War of 1914: The Beginnings of the War. (Boston: Houghton Mifflin Co., 1916).*

The Eton Chronicle, Eton College Archives.

The Eton Register being a Continuation of Stappleton's Eton School Lists 1893–1899. Eton: Spottiswoode and Co. Ltd, 1901.

The New Grove Dictionary of Music and Musicians ed. Stanley Sadie (OUP 2001) and **Grove Music online:** https://www.oxfordmusiconline.com/grovemusic

Tilmouth, Michael, ed. *Donald Francis Tovey. The Classics of Music. (Oxford University Press,* 2001.)

Timbs, John. *Club Life of London: With Anecdotes of the Clubs, Coffee-Houses and Taverns of the Metropolis during the 17th, 18th and 19th Centuries.* 2 Vols. (London: Richard Bentleigh, New Burlington Street, 1866).

Tombs, Robert. *The English and Their History.* (London: Allen Lane, 2014).

Tovey, Donald Francis. ***Essays in Musical Analysis.*** (OUP 1935–39.)

Wearing, John Peter. *The London Stage 1900–1909: A Calendar of Productions, Performers, and Personnel* (Metuchen, N.J.: Scarecrow Press, 2013).

Westlake, Donald. *Dearest John: The Story of John Lemmone, Flute Virtuoso and Nellie Melba.* (Terrey Hills, NSW: Bowerbird Press, 1997).

Weber, Thomas. *Our Friend 'The Enemy': Elite Education in Britain and Germany Before World War I.* (Stanford University Press, 2008).

Who's who and who was who U.K. (OUP annual) **:** https://www.ukwhoswho.com/

Wood, Harry. '"The Play All London is Discussing": The Great Success of Guy du Maurier's *An Englishman's Home*, 1909'. *Theatre Notebook* 70, no. 3 (2016).

Woolf, Virginia. *Roger Fry: A Biography.* (New York: Harcourt, Brace and Co., 1940).

World Museum 'Hugh Whitaker Excavator in Egypt'. At http://www.liverpoolmuseums.org.uk/wml/collections/antiquities/ancient-egypt/related-person-65828-1.aspx.

———. 'Theodore M. Davis'.at http://www.liverpoolmuseums.org.uk/wml/collections/antiquities/ancient-egypt/related-person-63154-1.aspx.

Wotherspoon, Gary. 'Economy' *Dictionary of Sydney* 2008 (State Library of New South Wales) https://dictionaryofsydney.org/entry/economy

Wyndham, H. Saxe, and Geoffrey L'Epine, eds. 'Mackinlay, M. Sterling'. *Who's Who in Music: A Biographical Record of Contemporary Musicians*. (London: Sir Isaac Pitman and Sons Ltd, 1913).

INDEX